KEEP IT IN THE
FAMILY

KEEP IT IN THE
FAMILY

Great Service by Great People

SIR JOHN TIMPSON

ISBN: Paperback: 978-1-80227-145-4

eBook: 978-1-80227-146-1

CONTENTS

CONTENTS

TO THE TIMPSON COLLEAGUES
WHO HAVE SUPPORTED THE FAMILY
FOR OVER 150 YEARS.

INTRODUCTION

I AM PLEASED TO REPORT that some of my grandchildren have already put a toe in our family business; not much more than work experience so far, but that makes the sixth generation to get involved, and over 160 years since it was founded by their great-great-great-grandfather. This thought brings a big smile to my face.

However, we are young upstarts compared with the UK's longest-established family businesses. My friend and regular snooker opponent, John Lea, is Chairman and fifteenth generation of his family business, Morning Foods, a major supplier of breakfast foods to the supermarkets 346 years after his umpteenth grandfather founded the company in 1675 – his sons, Edward and James, are now the 16th generation to run the company. They outrank other famous long-lasting companies, including Berry Brothers and Rudd, founded in 1698, and hatters Lock & Co, 1676 but are preceded by bankers C. Hoare who made their first loan in 1672. Yet all these family companies were youngsters compared with the Whitechapel Bell Foundry that set up shop in 1420 but closed in 2017 after 340 years of bell-making.

The secret of longevity in a family business is to stick to two basic principles – watch the cash and pick the right people, which, in particular, means having talented relatives able to play a key role in the boardroom. The only companies that can truly claim to be family businesses are those with a member, or members, of the family at the helm. Until recently, most families halved their chances of success by ignoring their daughters and making the management team men only.

Most long-term companies, unlike the bell-makers, have to continually reinvent their business model. Despite the comfortable image of a family company, they have to be able to face many crucial strategic choices to survive. The most critical challenge is to pick the right leaders from each generation, and we are no exception. This book describes the abilities and personalities of my ancestors who sat in the boardroom. Finding the wrong brother, cousin, niece or nephew in a position of power can be even more damaging than a hostile market.

Members of the family who own shares but don't work in the business need to be kept onside. A disgruntled relative can cause the management team plenty of bother if poor trading leads to a lower dividend. I was reminded of the problem 25 years ago when Alex and I invited all the surviving descendants of my great grandfather for lunch and 145 people turned up.

Economists don't always give family businesses the credit they deserve. The academics should recognise that nearly every enterprise is started by individuals who provide consistent long-lasting management compared with the revolving doors that exist in large company boardrooms. I will never forget being told by a merchant banker that he was an expert in buying family businesses and putting in professional management – words, I'm delighted to say, he lived to regret. Most big corporations think business is all about marketing, targets, key performance indicators, policy and process. Most family businesses have people (customers and colleagues) at the centre of their thinking.

Luckily, my grandfather, Will Timpson, enjoyed writing and kept plenty of newspaper cuttings, which revealed a lot of the background into how he ran the company. Even better, I got to know him well when I was a teenager and he came into the shop where I was working a month before he died. That contact, together with the annual reports produced since the company floated in 1929, has been invaluable in putting together our early history.

There is a massive contrast between the first Timpson shop in Oldham Street, Manchester and one of the typical Timpson service pods that have popped up in supermarket car parks over the last 20 years. We no longer sell shoes and we repair less every year; our business now relies on key-cutting, watch repairs, dry cleaning and photos. The business has reinvented itself several times and survived two world wars, the continually shifting high street, a takeover bid and the recent pandemic. Yet a common thread runs through our history – the care for our colleagues and the key role they have played for over 160 years.

There were a few light bulb moments that helped the company to reinvent itself and the company has had plenty of pieces of luck along the way. It was very fortunate that Will Timpson, the founder's eldest son, was such a natural entrepreneur with the common touch. His father laid the foundations but Will created the family culture. He thought that a family business should treat every colleague as part of his extended family. After Covid, there has been a lot of talk of kindness in business – something Will was practising 100 years ago. He found personal contact a better way to run the business than command and control from head office. He taught us all to find out about the business by visiting the shops and listening to the people who served our customers – it's a technique that still works today.

Inevitably, this book concentrates on the principal characters, particularly those family members who dictated each chapter of the company history, so, sadly, it doesn't include many of the long-serving colleagues – cutting edge characters who looked after the day-to-day business. Although many magnificent characters don't get a mention, their critical role is still acknowledged as being central to the Timpson story.

The second half of the book was bound to be a bit of an autobiography – the business has occupied so much of my life (Alex thought too much!). Much of the last 20 years is the story of James, a different sort of maverick with amazing energy and a never-ending stream of ideas.

Before I was allowed to start work, I had to attend an interview, something my grandchildren aren't required to do. They are all welcome to join the business but they won't be allowed into the boardroom unless they clearly have the talent to be a future leader. With at least 10 candidates, I'm confident that Timpson will, one day, be led by the sixth generation and help us to 'keep it in the family'. They will learn that as long as your name appears above the shops, your principles are always on show.

PART ONE

CHAPTER ONE

APPRENTICESHIP

ON A SPRING MORNING IN 1860, William Timpson, a 10-year-old boy, walked the 2 miles from his home in Rothwell, Northamptonshire to catch a train from the station at Desborough, a centre for spinning and weaving. He was going to live with, and work for, his elder brother Charles, who had a wholesale boot and shoe business based in Manchester. William was already used to hard work; from the age of 8, he had been making deliveries to outside workers for one of the earliest Kettering bootmakers and also found time to do outwork himself, making bootlaces. He liked saving the money he earned; it made him feel more secure.

William was the youngest of six children, three brothers and three sisters. Their father, a handloom weaver, struggled to get work and find the money to support his family. William's two brothers, who initially followed their father into the weaving trade, soon got disillusioned with wages of 8/- (40p) a week and both went to Manchester, attracted by the booming cotton trade. Charles, William's elder brother, was so keen to find a new life that he walked the 130 miles with a friend. They agreed that if one found a job, the proceeds would be shared until both found employment. Charles, a big man, over six foot tall and weighing 20 stone, had a determined but ruthless personality and quickly found work. However, he failed to stick to the bargain and abandoned his friend. Within a year, Charles had his own business as a boot and shoe wholesaler and William was due to join him for a bit of work and life experience.

William's luggage was sent in advance, so, as he set off from home, waving his schoolmates goodbye, William simply had a couple of sandwiches in his coat pocket and a small bag containing sweets and something to read. The train didn't go straight to Manchester; William had to change trains at Stoke, but somehow, he picked the wrong one and finished up at Sheffield. It was getting dark, the sandwiches and sweets had been eaten a long time ago and the last 'Parliamentary Train' (third class) had gone, so William sat on a platform bench and burst into tears.

Fortunately, William was spotted by a kind man who provided the solution. "I'm going to Manchester; come with me and I will pay the excess fare."

By the time they arrived at London Road Station in Manchester, brother Charles had given up hope and gone home, but the Good Samaritan hired a cab and took William to his brother's house in Bridge Street. William invited the benefactor in so that Charles could refund the fare, but the man departed with a hearty farewell and was never heard of again.

William soon discovered that his brother's tough character was more than matched by his sister-in-law, Mary, who made sure William stuck to her house rules, so it wasn't surprising that his modest amount of spare time was spent out of their home. He joined the Ashley Lane Church Sunday School, and, most evenings, attended night school, which helped to give a surprisingly rounded education for someone who had left school at 10.

For William, Manchester was a sharp contrast to his home village of Rothwell. He had exchanged green fields and hedgerows for an over-crowded, dirty, smelly and noisy city. Manchester only became a city in 1853, but by then, the houses were already overshadowed by factories with furnaces and steam boilers producing thick black smoke which created a perpetual fog. William was living in the fastest-growing city in Europe. The modern railway and canal network gave Manchester the links needed to trade with the rest of the world. Commerce was the priority and local inhabitants had to live with the permanently dingy, half-lit streets and air that was visibly polluted.

Charles treated his younger brother pretty badly. William was the delivery boy, pushing a sack barrow loaded with boots and shoes over Manchester's cobbled streets from warehouse to customer and back again. On those occasions when William was with Charles, he was made to walk several steps behind, carrying his brother's briefcase as well as the usual load.

Despite his menial role, William learnt a lot about business. He was interested in each delivery, taking note of every different type of customer and the margin Charles made on each assignment. Back at Bridge Street, he totted up the 'Day Book' to work out how much his brother was making. It was a good business, so good that Charles retired to London in his 40s, where he slept for much of the day and played cards nearly every night.

William did his best to be the perfect tenant. He lived well within the rules, but gradually developed a social life that included the occasional late night. After one busy evening following a church meeting, William overslept and was late for work. Charles was so beside himself with rage that he picked up a cane and threatened to beat his brother black and blue. The frail now 13-year-old William, facing his 20-stone big brother, picked up a wooden shoe last and coolly told Charles it would be thrown in his face. Within days, William decided to return to Rothwell, where he learnt how to make shoes.

He was employed by an old shoemaker who taught him to make shoes by hand in a workshop that was open to the public. At that time, many shoemakers had well-developed religious and political views and were held in awe. It wasn't unusual for spectators to watch them work and listen to their wisdom. Within a year, the old shoemaker died, but William carried on the business. Although only 15 years old, he had enough confidence to run the workshop. As an added incentive to stay near Kettering, he had met his future wife, Elizabeth Farey, and spent a lot of time with her family. Originally a silk weaver, Elizabeth's father became Kettering's first photographer, with premises in Gold Street which he combined with a bookshop. Talking about the books and meeting the nobility who were photographed, helped broaden Elizabeth's education and, no doubt, William also learnt a lot.

While working long hours in his workshop, William had plenty of time to think. He worked out that it took almost a week to make a pair of boots and only a few minutes to sell them. This thought, at the age of 16, persuaded William to return to Manchester and become a boot and shoe retailer.

CHAPTER TWO

FIRST SHOP

WILLIAM WENT INTO PARTNERSHIP with his sister Eliza's husband, Walter Joyce, who was already based in Manchester. In 1865, they opened a shop over the Easter weekend in premises on the corner of Oldham Road and Butler Street. It was a poor site with little passing trade. William spent a lot of time waiting for the next customer but was remarkably patient. However, he made enough profit to pay his basic living expenses and save a little each month for the project he really had in mind. The longer he worked in the shop, the more he liked retailing, but he wanted a proper shop. In April 1869, he found it half a mile away at 97 Oldham Street, and he agreed a rent of £200 a year, which most people, including his now ex-partner Walter Joyce, thought was so high it would ruin the business. To avoid criticism, William told his friends the rent was £100 but they thought even that was too much. They said he was wrong to open in Oldham Street when the fashionable development was along Deansgate at the other end of town. But William was sure the shop would suit his business, being placed near the market and catering for the popular-priced trade.

William spent all his savings on fitting out the shop so had to buy the stock on the credit provided by his wholesaler, Shaw's of Dantzic Street, whose founder knew William as a Sunday School worker. William wasn't quite 20 and, as a minor, should have been considered an unreasonable risk.

The shop was an instant success. William put his 4 years of dreaming and planning in Butler Street to good use. He was an innovator, especially when it came to windows, using shoes and boots specially made just to be put on display. One ploy was to use a beautiful pair of handmade French calf boots worth 21/- as a decoy, but without a price ticket, amongst a collection of similar but inferior boots priced at about 10/6d. Retailing was very different in 1870; as well as windows packed with specially prepared stock, the boots and shoes inside the dark badly lit shop weren't in shoe boxes; they were hung by strings from the ceiling.

William had help from his sister Maria who was happy to move to Manchester and live above the shop. However, she was so worried that the shop would be a failure, she doubled up as the shop cleaner to save money. She needn't have worried; in the first year, an amazing £1,000 clear profit was made (£117,000 at 2019 prices). But being prudent, as banks in those days were considered insecure, William used part of the profits to buy a property in Withington.

William lived above the shop and worked there all day, serving, in person, as many customers as he could. He learnt about the business by talking to customers; they taught him what shoes and boots to buy, how much to charge and how to lay out the shop. William did his own market research. His reputation grew; the second year was even more successful than the first, but suddenly, the shop's future was under threat.

The tenant of number 99, the shop next door, made an offer for the whole property. William's lease was up for renewal and there seemed no way of stopping his wealthy neighbour from taking over, leaving William to restart his business elsewhere. But, fortunately for William, his next-door neighbour did some interior alterations which caused part of the building to collapse. This displeased the landlords so much that, instead of agreeing the buyout of No 97, the landlord made the way clear for William to take the lease on No 99 and establish a flagship store, which was still trading from the same site 110 years later. Within 10 years, William, always keen to keep his money in the business, managed to buy the freehold, the start of a significant Timpson property portfolio.

When William got married to Elizabeth Farey in 1872, the business was well established, but to save money, the couple lived above the shop where their daughter, Lily, was born. Two years later, they moved to one of his investment properties in Withington, where Elizabeth gave birth to four more daughters – Florence, Nellie, Elizabeth and Mary.

Five years after moving into Oldham Street, William started to open elsewhere, still in Manchester but outside the city centre. Every community had a thriving shopping centre and there were plenty of possible places for William to go on the main roads that connected Central Manchester to the Lancashire and Cheshire towns. But William didn't stray too far, picking sites within walking distance of his first shop. He opened in Stretford Road, Oxford Road and Great Ancoats, all close enough to receive his personal supervision. With little competition, every new shop immediately made money and William either put the profits back into the business or invested in his growing personal property portfolio. He, unlike many fellow entrepreneurs, didn't plan to cash in on his success. He valued his independence, preferring to have cash in hand rather than borrowing from a bank or relying on credit from his suppliers.

The business continued to grow, but, at the age of 31, William became ill and consulted a specialist, who partly blamed the shop's gas lighting for causing him to work in an unhealthy atmosphere and suggested that, to prolong his life, William should leave Manchester and move back to his native Northamptonshire. So, only 10 years after opening his Oldham Street shop, William became semi-retired. He moved with his family to Withington House in Kettering, where his sons, Will, Charles and George, were born.

Although living 120 miles away, claiming to be semi-retired and suffering from ill-health, he still kept in close touch. His loyal employees looked after the day-to-day business and, despite his absence, the company continued to grow.

CHAPTER THREE

EARLY RETIREMENT

WILLIAM FOUND A MAGIC FORMULA that let him live most of his life in Kettering and yet still stay in control of the business. He spent four days every fortnight in Manchester using his season ticket to travel on the old Midland Line train. That gave him 10-day stretches in Kettering to relax, but William never really retired. He always left on a Tuesday on the 1.23 or 3.23 pm train, arriving at Central Station in Manchester at 4.20 or 6.20 pm. He left Manchester at 4.10 pm on the Saturday, getting to Kettering at 7 o'clock. His three-hour trip took almost exactly the same time as it does today!

He had a Manchester manager, Mr Mankin, who was married to Lizzie, the daughter of William's sister Eliza and her husband Walter Joyce, but William still got involved in much of the detail. On average, he opened a new shop every year and would spend much of his time in Manchester walking round the streets to make sure every acquisition fitted with his vision for the Timpson business. He approved every shoe design and specified the detail of every shop fit. Any time left during his four-day visits, when he lived at his house in Withington, south of the city centre, would be spent visiting his shops, talking to shop assistants and making sure they were maintaining his standards.

Each shop had a manager, a senior saleswoman, up to six sales assistants and an errand boy. Compared with today, the shops were dark and dingy, with a strong smell of leather. The manager wore a traditional white shoemaker's apron but the female assistants always wore black. The shops opened until late in the evening, especially on Saturday night when city centre shops hoped to attract theatregoers before they went home. Shop assistants earned commission, but whenever possible, the manager and most experienced assistants served the customers; consequently, junior shop assistants spent a lot of time cleaning with little chance of earning any extra money. The shop managers were in total control – most were strict disciplinarians.

Back in Kettering, William established a small shoemaking team to make footwear for his Manchester shops in a purpose-built shed at the end of his garden at Withington House. Not long after, in 1884, he bought a silk weaving mill in Market Street, Kettering, which he converted into a factory capable of making up to 750 pairs of footwear a week. Part of the building was turned into a boot and shoe shop, the first Timpson shop outside Manchester. That shop was still trading in 1960 when I started working for the company.

To get full value out of the first-class season ticket on the Midland Railway that he had for over 50 years, William made sure that he took a case of boots as passenger luggage on every journey, saving money on the normal carriage. He was so pleased with this economy measure, he insisted that his relatives did the same thing; they were all expected to take some stock whenever going by train from Kettering to Manchester.

As the size of the Timpson chain grew, the warehouse behind the original Oldham Street shop was extended several times and a reserve warehouse was acquired north of the city centre in Great Ducie Street. The transport of goods to shops within 2 miles of the warehouse was mainly done by errand boys pushing a sack barrow. When William opened shops further afield in Rochdale, Farnworth and Radcliffe, delivery was done by a long-established firm of horse carriers. Timpson didn't acquire its own horse and lorry until 1898. The horse, stabled at Pendleton, worked Monday to Friday providing two deliveries a week to every shop in Manchester and Salford.

In 1888, with William looking permanently tired, Elizabeth, fearing he was doing too much, insisted he took on a business partner. An experienced friend, Davis Gotch, was asked to do the job. The partnership didn't stop William's fortnightly routine, but Davis Gotch gave support for 8 years until he, too, had health problems and resigned.

William had some simple business principles. He was wary of over-trading, so always made sure he had enough money in the bank to pay his bills. The business made a profit from day one but William always watched the cash, only taking out a modest personal income compared with many other successful entrepreneurs. Much of the surplus cash was invested in property, including a large house, Sunnylands, on the Headlands in Kettering, which he proudly built for his wife Elizabeth. Sadly, Elizabeth never lived there. She died at the age of 41, leaving William with 8 children. Two years later, he married Katherine Mursell, the daughter of a local clergyman, so it was Katherine who got to live at Sunnylands, where she had two boys and two girls – Noel, Alan, Joan and Hope. For a man who was semi-retired due to ill health at the age of 31 and was considered to be very frail at 48, William managed to fulfil a varied and active life which, outside business, included a leading role at the Fuller Baptist Church in Kettering, a spell on the Kettering Council and being a founder member and future President of Kettering Golf Club.

William expected all employees to follow his strict guidelines, but also showed plenty of kindness in the way he did business. Walter Joyce, his brother-in-law, who worked with William when they opened the shop in Butler Street, went on to build up a thriving group of over 10 boot and shoe shops before he died and his widow, William's sister Eliza married Fred Cartwright – a handsome bearded man, dapper and sleek, but a bad character. Fred took over the management of Walter Joyce's shops and they soon ran into trouble. He, like Joyce, bought a lot of boots from Eliza and William's brother-in-law, Tom Butlin. Tom had several outstanding accounts and needed the money to pay his wages. Fred Cartwright couldn't pay so William bought one of Cartwright's shops and paid the £600 involved straight into Tom Butlin's bank account. Inevitably, the Cartwright business collapsed and Fred fled the country. William, who never approved of her second marriage, became estranged from his sister Eliza, but on her death bed, they were reconciled and William promised to care for her seven daughters who all became assistants in Timpson shops before they were married.

By 1896, when his eldest son Will entered the business, William had built a chain of 20 shops.

CHAPTER FOUR

SECOND GENERATION

WILLIAM'S SIXTH CHILD and eldest son, also called William, known in the business as 'Mr Will', started working in the business when he was sixteen. The school he was attending closed down and his father saw little point in sending him to another one. He started work in his father's office, a gentle introduction before going to Manchester. Initially, he was offered 5/- (25p) a week, but his father had second thoughts. He wasn't sure his partner, Davis Gotch, would be happy with such a large sum, so Will's starting pay was reduced to 2/6d (12.5p).

Once Will moved to Manchester, his pay shot up to 10/- (50p), from which he had to pay travel to Kettering every Saturday (despite taking a case of boots on every journey). His father considered the city to be too wicked for a young boy, especially on Saturday nights.

For two years, Will worked in the warehouse behind the Oldham Street shop. By then, the business had 24 shops run by Mr Mankin, 'Chief of the Shop Managers', who was also responsible for a reserve warehouse in Great Ducie Street, which Will went to manage at the age of 18.

Will saw his father, then aged 47, as a really old man, although he later wrote, 'Men were older for their years in those days; they lived the life of older men and few of them played games or kept in touch with the sporting side of life. They may not have been old but they looked or acted as such. Since then, men in middle life look a lot younger. If today, men over 40 were to wear beards, dress in thick and clumsy clothes, take little exercise and eat a lot of food, they would look as old as my father's generation'.

There were early signs that Will wanted to show his father what he could do, but the teenager had to be patient. In 1897, William had a renewed ambition to grow his business, while still keeping some cash in the bank. With the help of Mr Mankin, he opened eleven more shops in six years. The shops were outside the city centre but William stuck within what we now know as Greater Manchester.

Will's work in the warehouse didn't just involve moving shoes in boxes; he also got first-hand experience in buying and merchandising. At Great Ducie Street, he concentrated on ladies' shoes, but a move back to Oldham Street gave Will the chance to take over the Men's Department from a man who had to retire following a railway accident. This gave Will a four-year apprenticeship in men's footwear design and buying – it became his speciality.

In 1904, Mr Mankin, finding the workload of the bigger business too taxing, resigned leaving nobody in Manchester to look after the shops. William made a bold move and put 23-year-old Will in charge. Will took this new role just before he married his first cousin, Florence Butlin, and made his permanent home in Lapwing Lane, Didsbury.

Will not only ran the 37 shops, he also started to look for new ones. His father no longer had the energy to walk the streets hunting for the perfect site so he put his trust in Will. At the end of 1904, Will took on a new shop in London Road, Liverpool, virtually off his own bat. His father was desperately disappointed and gave Will a hard time, especially when takings for the first few weeks were way below Will's expectations.

Will made matters even worse by advertising the shop as 'William Timpson – the Liverpool Bootmaker'. This was the only Timpson shop in Liverpool and father William was far from happy. "Kindly note," he wrote to Will, "I'm not The Liverpool Bootmaker and have no wish to be called The Liverpool Bootmaker". He went on to give a lecture on how one bad shop can eat up all the profits made by the rest of the business. The young Will's brave move ultimately paid off, however. His shop on London Road was one of the company's most profitable and the Elliot Street branch had the highest turnover. At one time, Timpson had 25 shoe shops within the Liverpool City boundaries.

It took time for William and Will to iron out their working relationship. Will was in his mid-twenties, full of ideas and enthusiasm, needing the freedom to learn by making a few mistakes. William was struggling to let go, having ruled the business for over 30 years. But the relationship was never going to break down as Will had enormous respect for his father.

For years, William watched his son very carefully. Will was offered a shop on Pinstone Street in Sheffield and went over the Pennines several times to walk round the city and study shoppers on different days, at various times during the day. The annual rent of £250 a year was higher than he expected. In fear and trepidation, Will put the proposal before his father, who claimed he was too ill to travel to Manchester. So, Will went to Kettering to discover his father had been to Sheffield, liked the shop and was going to London to agree a new lease.

There were regular battles between father and son. Will found a site in Blackburn, a town he thought perfect for Timpson, and couldn't understand why his father hadn't opened a shop before. But William was wary of paying over £150 a year for fear that he would simply be working for the landlord. Will got the rent down to £70, but discovered the landlord wanted a £150 premium, which his father regarded as robbery – he never paid premiums on principle. But Will won the day by getting the premium down to £120 payable in two instalments. Authority to run the business was rapidly passing over from father to son.

CHAPTER FIVE

YOUNG WILL GETS STUCK IN

FROM ABOUT 1906, Will was the driving force behind the business. In 1912, with William wanting to protect the business for future generations, Timpson became a limited company. Will was the Managing Director, with his father taking the title of Governing Director. Also on the Board were Tom Mursell, William's brother-in-law, who ran the factory in Kettering, his nephew, Will Chappell, a close friend of Will's who was responsible for the buying of women and children's shoes, and Will's younger brother, Charles.

By this time, William seemed happy to leave day-to-day details to Will, who got involved in every part of the business, visiting shops, knowing his people, understanding shoe fashion and following the latest shopfitting trends.

In the 1900s, the shops sold many more boots than shoes, for women as well as men. Two factors increased the demand for women's shoes. First, the comic opera 'The Gibson Girl', in which the star, Camille Clifford, walked down a long flight of stairs wearing a glacé derby shoe with three big eyelets – it made such an impression that shoes suddenly became fashionable. When short skirts were the rage in the 1920s, boots for women all but disappeared. As more women wore shoes rather than boots, men followed the trend and boot and shoe shops simply became shoe shops.

Although Timpson shoes weren't the very cheapest on offer, they were thought to offer great value. Will wouldn't sell inferior quality made from the cheapest leather; his vision was to provide working families with boots and shoes that they were proud to wear at prices they could afford. It was the perfect pitch to build strong customer loyalty and make Timpson the market leader around Manchester.

Will was fascinated with the men's fashion trends coming from America, and, despite his father's cautious advice, was keen to introduce the latest styles. In 1911, the Americans introduced a new leather colour called 'Ox Blood' which Will copied but quickly found it was too brash for English tastes. To sell off the slow-moving stock, the leather was dyed black and the price reduced. Sadly, when worn on a wet day, all the dye disappeared.

This didn't deter Will from stocking American tan willow boots with bright brass eyelets and big square block toes, that most buyers viewed with horror. At heart, Will loved trying new ideas; he was a risk-taker who wanted to be the first to get the latest styles onto the market. This fashion flair added to the appeal of the window displays, but Timpson's reputation relied on the classic styles on well-fitting lasts created by William in his early days and reproduced in his Kettering factory.

Will studied feet wherever he went, his eyes looking downwards to see the footwear, only glancing at faces to check what character was wearing them. He loved stealing a march on the opposition by stocking winning styles that couldn't be bought elsewhere. His many successes included Block Toe boots, Patent caps, Freak toes, something he called a Camp Boot and styles known as Freaks. But there were a few failures, including a range of green leather boots that Will admitted was the shortest vogue he could ever remember – "It lived but a day and we were landed with a considerable stock at giveaway prices." With such an appetite for fashion, he needed to know when to stop buying more stock before customers moved on to the next trend.

Fashion also affected the look of his shops. As lighting improved, shop interiors looked much brighter, the solemn black worn by the lady assistants was replaced with more cheerful uniforms and, instead of stock hanging by a string threaded through the heel, every pair was in a shoe-box. The interiors were improving but Will's passion was window display. He aimed to match the drawing power of the big tailoring shops' window displays and the dramatic promotions put on by Kendal Milne, the modern department store in Deansgate, Manchester.

In 1904, Will was in charge of ordering and distribution of tickets, giving him the chance to flex his flair for publicity by filling windows with slogans and descriptive tickets alongside the price. Victorian bulk window displays were replaced by more delicate designs using shoe holders of various heights balanced on a complicated tower of glass shelves. Window dressing became a real skill, beyond the ability of most shop managers, who became frustrated if two days' work was ruined when the display collapsed like a house of cards. Eventually, a specialist team travelled from shop to shop to dress every window.

This attention to retail detail helped Will develop a better business, but despite inheriting a portfolio of nearly 40 shops, he was jealous of some of the sites occupied by competitors. His father never had much of a geographical ambition. He felt comfortable trading near Manchester with the addition of two shops near his Northamptonshire home, in Kettering and Wellingborough. Will had other ideas, first spreading to Liverpool, Lancashire and Yorkshire, then expanding nationwide. He felt his father's shops, although profitable, were in second-rate locations. He wanted to be in the busiest part of town. With this in mind, he found a shop on Market Street, the busiest pitch in Manchester. Agents offered the premises for £425 a year but his father wouldn't accept this. Over lunch, the agent announced he had been offered £450 from another shoe retailer but wondered whether it was wise to accept their covenant. William, unselfishly, told him to accept their deal and the rival made the shop a great success.

Despite only being a 'Governing Director', William still kept his finger firmly in the property pie. He bravely broke away from his Manchester heartland by taking a shop in Nottingham without discussing the deal with his son. Will was aghast; he knew Nottingham well enough to realise that, although the shop was in a central position, it had limited potential. He must have been a little bit smug when the shop started really badly. In the second week, the total turnover of ladies' shoes was 6/11d (35p).

Despite his poor health, William still enjoyed looking for new sites. One day, they went together to Hull, but as soon as they got off the train, William decided, "This place is like the dead-end of the world; let's go home". Will ignored his father's advice and acquired a shop that became very successful and continued trading until the 1970s.

Once, Will took him to Bradford to view a shop he considered to be all but perfect, but his father disagreed. Disappointed but determined to get something out of their trip, Will took his father to Leeds to see another good site, which was also rejected. Before going home, they were walking up Briggate, the best shopping street in Leeds, when William spotted an old friend called Wallis who had a men's outfitter in the prime spot. They went inside and, over a cup of tea, agreed to take over Mr Wallis's liabilities and acquired a stunning Elizabethan building which was turned tastefully into a great shoe shop. Sadly, in the 1960s, an architect called Paulson was commissioned to modernise the building and ruined the prettiest shoe shop in Britain. The rebuild wasn't a great success and the shop struggled to meet expectations.

Will managed to find time for his main hobby – long-distance cycling, day trips or even weekends to North Wales, The Lake District, Derbyshire and Shropshire. He also started to play golf and enjoyed regular Saturday night dinner parties, when he often entertained members of his large extended family. However, most of his time was spent with the business.

By the outbreak of war in 1914, the business was starting to spread well beyond Manchester and had grown to 56 shops.

In a personal tribute following Will's death, Billy MacKenzie, who started in 1910 as a young shop boy in Oxford Road, Manchester, remembered his first meeting with Will 50 years later. "I will never forget the kind way in which he interviewed me. He had a wonderful knack for putting people at their ease, irrespective of age or station in life. I was to learn that his kindness at our first meeting wasn't to be short-lived; whenever he called at my shop, sometimes with his father, he never failed to talk to me about my progress. But I wasn't singled out for attention; he knew every employee by name, in warehouse and shop alike, and took a real interest in their lives outside work."

"During the First World War, most of the men joined the armed forces and Will ran the business without much of his usual support, but, despite his heavy workload, he found time to follow the fortunes of his people during their enforced absence, and, on many occasions, had the sad task of consoling the relatives of those who had died.

The business survived remarkably well in wartime. All new shops were put on hold and costs were cut in line with the national drive for austerity, but there was still a steady demand for footwear and the company remained financially robust.

When the War ended, he set about placing the returning men in suitable jobs, interviewing each one as they returned. One loyal ex-serviceman commented, "I vividly remember my interview at the beginning of 1919 and was impressed by his patience and understanding, especially during the next few months when I inevitably made mistakes after being away from the business for four years".

By then, William, although still checking the sales every week, keeping an eagle eye on the bank balance and vetting any proposed new shop, was almost fully retired. Will was multi-tasking as Buyer, Staff Manager, Area Manager and Property Controller, stealing days from his regular routine to visit cities and towns, often on a Saturday. Sometimes, the week's warehouse wages were made up by Florence at their home in Lapwing Lane, Didsbury. Will wrote "Establishing a circle of shops is a hard task; it involves weeks, months and years of travelling by night as well as by day; you need knowledge of trading centres, shopfitting and building alterations. Above all, you must be quick-witted in dealing with landlords or their agents to negotiate suitable leases or buy premises on terms that give you a chance to make money. One has to be a 'Jack of all trades' and, at least, master of some."

CHAPTER SIX

THE BIG NEW SHOE FACTORY

IN 1880, WHEN WILLIAM started making boots and shoes in a shed at the end of his garden at Withington House, Kettering, it was not much more than a hobby, but the footwear proved popular with his Manchester customers. In 1881, with the hobby turning into a serious business, a proper factory was established in an old silk weaving plant in a yard off Market Street, Kettering. The narrow five-storey building was so top-heavy that one storey was removed for safety reasons.

The new factory specialised in men's and boy's boots and shoes. The leather uppers were cut in what the shoemakers call a Clicking Room, and then stitched by 'closing rooms' elsewhere in Kettering or Wellingborough. The completed uppers came back to Market Street where the footwear was manufactured and finished. In 1896, the factory management was taken over by William's brother-in-law, Tom Mursell, who, being a young man, was closely supervised by William and his partner, David Gotch.

Some additions were made to the original building and a further factory in Newman Street, Kettering was leased in 1912 to keep pace with growing demand. When Tom took over, the factory was making 750 pairs a week, which quickly rose to 1,250. By 1914, weekly production was 5,000 pairs and in 1919 it was 7,000. This success was achieved by making sure the factory in Kettering was making styles customers wanted to buy in Manchester. Design was decided at meetings between Will, his men's buying assistant, Allen Booth, and Harry Bunker, the factory's shoe designer.

During the War, the factory started to make ladies' boots and shoes, first for women munition workers and tramway conductors, but eventually, on the suggestion of a shop manageress, they were sold in Timpson shops.

The idea of a purpose-built factory was mooted before 1914, but, apart from Tom Mursell, everyone, including Will, and especially William, considered the project was too ambitious. However, with Will's plans to create a national chain and Tom Mursell's vision for a state-of-the-art factory, opinions changed and when the war was over, the Board approved the creation of a factory at North Park, Kettering. The decision was finally made when the Newman Street landlord sold the lease to another tenant who required rapid possession – the new factory was more than a dream; it became a necessity.

The biggest problem was how to find the money. In the early 1920s, Will was creating enough cash to open two or three new shops a year, but a factory costing £75,000 (£3.3m today) was tricky to finance without breaking William's strict guideline of always keeping money in the bank. Will found the answer by making a special range of shoes for a one-off sale at fantastic prices – the extra turnover almost paid for the total cost of the factory.

It was a new landmark in Kettering, a prominent four-storey building, making men's and women's footwear, slippers and even football boots. (The first goal in a Wembley Cup Final was scored by David Jack for Bolton Wanderers wearing a pair of Timpson boots).

In addition to the factory, there was an office building, to be home for the finance section (William always kept control of the figures in

Kettering) and a bowling green, but no canteen – everyone was expected to go home for lunch.

Sadly, Tom Mursell died before the factory opened but he left a legacy that gave Timpson a strong competitive advantage by providing a regular and exclusive supply of shoes to Timpson customers.

Following the completion of North Park, Will went into overdrive in his ambition to build a national chain, wanting enough outlets to take advantage of a factory producing 17,000 pairs a week. He added more shops in Lancashire and Yorkshire, but his big gamble was in the North East where there was industrial unrest in the coal industry and a slump in shipbuilding. Despite increased unemployment, the shops in Sunderland, West Hartlepool, Middlesbrough, South Shields and Darlington were all a success.

Will also went into Scotland, first to Edinburgh, then Glasgow. He liked the Scots, making numerous trips to walk every high street and understand the taste of Scottish customers. He didn't offer the same style selection on sale in Lancashire; Timpson shops in Scotland stocked a range that appealed to local demand. From the outset, Will recognised the need to have Scottish shops run by someone from Scotland. This was an early form of 'upside-down management', trusting local managers with the freedom to do what they knew best.

Will didn't just build the business one shop at a time; sometimes he acquired a group of properties, like in Edinburgh where three shops, all on Leith Street, were offered in a single deal. His first London shops came from buying a company with sites in Hammersmith, Clapham and Peckham. Another small business provided his first three shops in Birmingham. His best deal was nearer to home – a site in Elliot Street, Liverpool, which for many years was the company's highest turnover branch.

On January 23rd 1929, the founder, William, died aged 79 and the death duties and provisions within his will (William had 12 children and over 30 grandchildren) brought the tightly owned control of the business to an end. Later that year, on October 9th, William Timpson became a public company with 136 outlets, 80 having been added in only 10 years. The first accounts showed that the business had a profit of £121k.

CHAPTER SEVEN

LIFE WITHOUT
THE FOUNDER

FEW WHO ATTENDED THE FUNERAL would have guessed, if he hadn't told them, that the Rev Thomas Phillips was asked by William's widow, Katherine, not to be over laudatory in his remarks. He said, "William Timpson had a wonderful combination of individualism and socialism in the widest sense. His belief in initiative, push and self-reliance were signs of that individualism. Yet, his helpfulness made him one of the greatest socialists in Kettering."

He went on to praise William's generosity and pointed out that his personality was charged with a dynamo of energy, yet he was wonder-fully patient.

This praise was repeated by a comment page in the local paper, The Kettering Leader, which read; 'It falls to our lot to chronicle the passing of one who, though not actually a native of Kettering, stands worthy to be ranked alongside its most illustrious sons. Like that of many another captain of industry, the career of William Timpson was a romantic one. Denied the advantages which boys of today take as a matter of course, he rose from humble beginnings to be the head of a great manufacturing and retail concern, known throughout the length and breadth of the country. A capacity for hard work, a genius for organisation, and the ability to recognise and make the most of every opportunity contributed to his success, and, in achieving it, he benefitted hundreds of fellow townspeople. Not only did he provide employment on a large scale, he also realised that the duty of the employer does not end with paying wages for work done, and he saw to it that his workpeople worked under good conditions.

The erection of the great factory near the North Park, Kettering, was the crowning achievement of his life, embodying as it did his conception of all that a factory should be. Not only was William Timpson a model employer, he was also a citizen of the finest type, interesting himself in all movements that had the welfare of the town for their object, and lending his talents to every good cause. Nonconformity and the local Baptist following, in particular, have reason to remember his generous support, and his enforced retirement from public affairs some years ago was widely felt. He has gone, but the influence for good that he wielded remains, and the memory of his gracious personality will ever be enshrined in the hearts of all who had the privilege of knowing him."

Four of William Timpson's sons were directors of the company when it was floated in 1929 – Will, who was Chairman and Managing Director, his brother Charles and his half-brothers Alan and Noel, the Deputy Managing Director. Alongside Will, Noel was the other driving force who inspired the growth of Timpson between the First and Second World Wars.

Noel, the eldest son of William's second family, born on Christmas Day 1895 at Sunnylands, the family home, left Mill Hill School at 17 to start work in the Kettering office, moving to the warehouse in Manchester a year later, where he much preferred managing stock to the paperwork his father made him do at Kettering. At the start of the First World War, he joined the 19th Royal Fusiliers going to France in 1915. In March 1916, he was commissioned in the Lincolnshire Regiment and was posted to Newcastle upon Tyne before returning to France, but returned home with typhoid fever. Back in France in July 1917, his unit was captured and Noel was taken prisoner of war and sent to Germany, being released after the Armistice in December 1918. While he was a Prisoner of War, still thinking of the business back home, he met fellow prisoner Gordon Akester, who was persuaded to join Timpson and was the Company Secretary when the Company went public 10 years later.

When Noel returned to the Company, in 1919, he became the assistant buyer of ladies' and children's footwear, a job combined with being a Shop Inspector. By 1923, he was working closely with his brother Will and had clearly become the second in command, with a special interest in developing the shoe repair business. Noel represented the company in a range of trade associations helping to found the Multiple Shoe Retailers' Association, The Footwear Distributors' Joint Council and The National Association of Shoe Repair Factories. He was an enthusiastic committee man particularly supporting the Manchester and District Federation of Boys' Clubs and was President of the Royal Oak Centre in Wythenshawe, which received support from the company as recently as 2017.

Although today's Timpson shops claim, on the fascia, that Timpson established the shoe repair business in 1903, it offered a shoe repair service well before that. From the 1880s, journeymen boot repairers called at William Timpson's shops two or three times a week, taking shoes away for repair at their own workshop, or a shed behind their house, then bringing them back between three days to a fortnight later. It was a haphazard business, depending partly on the keenness of the branch manager, but mainly on the quality and speed of the local cobbler. An enthusiastic manager could provide enough repairs to keep two or three local cobblers busy.

In 1905, William Timpson opened his own shoe repair factory, using an old building he owned in Clopton Street near Alexandra Road in Hulme, an area of South Manchester now known as Moss Side. Boys on bicycles took the repairs between the factory and shops around Manchester and Salford; branches beyond Manchester sent the shoe repairs by rail. The repair trade flourished because Clopton Street provided a 24-hour service; this speed of service is still important today. Footwear received at Clopton Street was repaired and returned on the same day. Within 15 years, the original factory couldn't cope with demand so a second shoe repair centre was opened in Adlington Street off Rochdale Road, Manchester. Eventually, these two factories were replaced by a special extension to the main shoe warehouse on Great Ducie Street.

The growth of shoe repairs was driven by an enthusiastic factory manager, Mr W E Davies, whose vision went well beyond his Manchester workshop. It was Davies who suggested to Will that the company should develop a ring of small factories providing a quick service to the local shoe shops together with a counter to offer customers a while-you-wait service. Noel was given the task of developing this new business. The first of these factories, in Liverpool, was an immediate success and was followed by more factories with their own counters, in Sheffield, Birmingham, Stockport, Longsight, Oldham and Middlesbrough.

By 1939, there were 11 shoe repair branches, but with the market at a record level, there was a good case for opening many more. Before 1914, the demand for repairs was limited to wealthy customers who wore expensive new shoes. In those days, the public could buy a new pair of ladies' shoes for as little as 2/11d (15p) but a pair of ladies' shoes couldn't be repaired for less than 2/6d (12.5p). Many poorer customers only had one pair so they couldn't leave them overnight to be repaired. After the First World War, lighter shoe construction, higher prices and more consumer spending power produced an increase in demand for shoe repairs, which was to continue until the mid-1960s. However, it wasn't until after the Second World War that Noel Timpson fully realised the potential of shoe repairing and opened a comprehensive chain of factories to serve the Timpson shoe shops.

When William Timpson Limited was floated in 1929 and, for the next 34 years, the Company's registered office was at North Park, Kettering, evidence of a strange geographical split appeared in the management of the business. While the day-to-day running of the shoe and shoe repair shops was organized in Manchester, the finance department was based in an office next to the factory in Kettering.

In 1928, a large building, Empiric House, on the opposite side of the road to the Timpson Shoe warehouse in Great Ducie Street, was acquired to accommodate more warehousing and offices for those involved in buying, distribution, staff management and administration for the retail branches.

This office and warehouse complex was half a mile from the posh shops on Deansgate. To get there you had to go beyond Manchester Cathedral and under some railway bridges. It was a ragbag collection of buildings, next to Boddington's Brewery, backing on to a Salvation Army Hostel and within 250 yards of Strangeways Prison. It provided, without any glamour, all the office and storage space needed to build a 250-shop chain.

The 110 miles between North Park in Kettering and Empiric House in Manchester created a cultural divide that caused considerable conflict between the two centres. Any shortage of factory production was blamed on the retail team's inability to place enough orders and the company secretary's office in Kettering did what most finance departments do, they criticised any shortfall in sales or profit on the day-to-day management. The team in Manchester didn't take kindly to criticism and would come back with comments about the quality of shoe production and the accuracy of the management accounts. While Will and Noel dominated the business, these spats between Kettering and Manchester were a minor irritant, but in the 1950s, this culture gap became more of a liability.

CHAPTER EIGHT

TOUGH TRADING
IN THE 1930s

WILLIAM TIMPSON DIED within days of Will and Florence's silver wedding anniversary, so the splendid party they planned had to be cancelled. They had married in the year Will took charge of the family business. Florence played a supporting role from her home in Lapwing Lane, Didsbury, where their four children, Ruth, Hester, Anthony and David, were born. Florence Butlin was Will's first cousin, being the daughter of Tom Butlin and Maria, the youngest of William Timpson's sisters. The Butlins were well-established shoe manufacturers near Kettering, so they had both a family and business connection with the Timpsons. Butlins were regularly supplying men's' shoes to Timpson shops for over 75 years. Ruth, Hester and particularly David suffered from severe deafness. Some people suggested this was the result of their parents being close relatives, but Will himself was quite deaf suggesting that the disability was a Timpson family problem; indeed, his uncle Charles's daughter Kathleen was almost totally deaf from the age of 8. Kathleen didn't allow the disability to hamper her progress through life. She became a celebrated mathematician, an international skater and hockey player, a leading expert on education, a politician who became Lord Mayor of Manchester and was made Dame Kathleen in 1971. At the age of 80, she took up astronomy, which became a major hobby until she passed her hundredth birthday. Her uncle Will showed the same determination and commitment.

Will was deceptive. Leaving school at 16, he wasn't an intellectual but had charm. Everybody liked Will. It isn't easy for the boss's son to gain the respect of long-serving employees in a family business, but Will was so quick to be accepted that he was in charge of a warehouse before his nineteenth birthday and running the whole business when he was 23. Less than five foot five and bald by his mid-twenties, he was always immaculately dressed and best described as 'dapper'. With his small circular spectacles, Will didn't look like a dynamic entrepreneur but he packed more into his life than most friends and relations realised.

In 1923, Will and Florence moved the family home from Didsbury to Hale, where Will bought an imposing house, The Gables, which he changed so extensively that the family moved to a big furnished house on Ashley Road, Hale, until the alterations were complete. The Gables had a grass tennis court below the long terrace and a three-acre garden manicured by Head Gardener, Phillips, who grew prize-winning chrysanthemums. Hale was Manchester's new stockbroker belt but Will wasn't one for the social scene, preferring to spend his leisure time with family and close friends. There were regular tennis and tea parties on summer Saturday afternoons and most months he would invite about 10 people for dinner followed by snooker in a big games room at the end of the house with an alcove where non-snooker players had two tables of bridge. In his teens and twenties, Will played football and went on long bike rides. He was a regular spectator at Maine Road to watch Manchester City, and both Old Trafford grounds to see Manchester United and either Lancashire or England play cricket. In his 40s, he took up golf, becoming captain of Hale Golf Club in 1935.

Will had neither the time nor the aspiration to become part of the Cheshire set; he was simply too busy growing the business and visiting all his shops. Will loved cars, buying the latest models including a Sunbeam, Austin12, Humber, Rolls Royce and Bentley. Before he employed Fred Booth, his first chauffeur, when Will arrived at a branch, he immediately asked a young shop boy to guard his car – many suburban Manchester shops were in areas where a Bentley was a rare and tempting sight.

Will spent several weeks a year on the move, searching for new sites, negotiating with landlords or freeholders, visiting his shops, going round factories (both North Park and other suppliers) and most years crossing the Atlantic, initially to research men's' footwear fashions and latterly to develop an export business for the Kettering factory. His biggest strength was his character; a cheeky charm captured the respect of employees all over the country and he created a strong company culture through his attractive personality. Apart from being the perfect people person, Will was an expert men's' shoe buyer, helping Timpson to sell a higher proportion of men's' shoes than any multiple competitor.

Somehow, Will fitted in several holidays every year. In February, while all his children were away at school, he took Florence to the Caribbean. February was always a bad month for business so Will left strict instructions: "Don't send me any figures – I know they will be awful". At Easter, the family stayed in Norfolk, where Will played golf at West Runton. Every summer they went on a cruise to the Mediterranean or the Northern Capitals, seeing Stockholm Town Hall and the midnight sun. But it is difficult to imagine that Will ever stopped thinking about the business.

Despite being released from his father's inhibitions, Will wasn't able to grow the business quite as quickly. 80 branches had been added between 1919 and 1929, but he only opened 56 in the next 10 years. Business was tougher in the 1930s with the depression making life difficult for a company firmly entrenched in the north of England and Scotland's industrial centres. Will still opened plenty of shops in high unemployment areas, particularly the north-east, but, before the threat of another war made all businesses wary of capital investment, another event sapped Will's appetite for growth. In 1935, following 9 months of heart problems, his wife, Florence, died. During 31 years of marriage, Florence had been Will's mentor and frequent travelling companion. In grief, he threw himself back into the business and fulfilled his commitment as Captain of Hale Golf Club, but the loss of Florence sapped his zest for new ideas and was a major blow to their eldest son, Anthony (my father) who was, at 23, setting out on his career with the business and was engaged to be married the following year to my mother, Hilda, who was working as a secretary at the North Park factory.

Although Will was the architect and inspiration behind the company's development, he relied heavily on his half-brother Noel. Noel was the eldest child of William Timpson's marriage to Katherine Mursell, whose brother Tom developed the Timpson factory in Kettering. Noel was 16 years younger than Will, but they made a perfect partnership. Will was a true entrepreneur, loving new ideas and focused on building a big business. Noel was the safe pair of hands, more serious than Will, with less flair, but passionate about the detail. Employees were in awe of his somewhat cold personality but Noel had a kind heart, shown by the way he helped to develop Lads' Recreation Clubs around Manchester and wider afield.

Noel picked up the bits that Will didn't do. Will was the men's' shoe expert, whereas Noel looked after women's and children's footwear and when the shoe repair trade started to grow, Noel handled that as well. Will ran the warehouse while Noel looked after office administration. Everything to do with finance was handled by the Secretary's Office in Kettering, run by Gordon Akester, who was appointed by Noel after they met as prisoners of war. Noel also took on most of the trade appointments, being Chairman and President of both the Multiple Shoe Repairer's Association and the Footwear Distributors' Federation.

Noel and his wife, Milly, had four children – Ann, Elizabeth, Pamela and Margaret. Like Will, he moved to Hale, where he bought a large and outwardly ugly house in fashionable Broad Lane. Surprisingly, the house is still there – one of the few properties in the road not to be knocked down to build something even bigger and less attractive. The two top Timpson directors were established in the smart part of Greater Manchester but they weren't interested in becoming part of the establishment.

Will and Noel were in charge of strategy and kept a tight rein on capital expenditure but they built a talented team to run the day-to-day business and most key employees started as shop boys or were other members of the family.

Allen Booth was such a key player; he was a director of the original public company. Allen started as a shop boy in Altrincham. Within three years, he was a branch manager and William Timpson singled Allen out to help out in Kettering and buy the women's and children's shoes. In the 1920s, Allen moved back to Manchester to work with Will on the men's shoe buying and was described as the greatest shoe buyer of his generation, his expertise helped by regularly visiting the shops. Allen identified the specialist needs of Scottish customers, through regular trips north of the border, which taught him about the Scottish property world and helped Will develop shops in Edinburgh, Glasgow, Stirling, Falkirk, Aberdeen and Perth, where Will got to know his next-door neighbour, a tobacconist called Rattray. For forty years, Will ordered regular supplies of Rattray's specialist pipe tobacco – Rattray's Red Rapperee.

Billy McKenzie started as a shop boy in the third shop William Timpson opened, 'C' shop, Oxford Road, Manchester – near the theatres so it stayed open until at least 11.00 pm every Saturday night. Billy's career went all the way – first sales, shop manager, area manager and what was called Staff Manager. For sixteen years from 1948 to his retirement in 1964, he appointed every shop manager at a face-to-face meeting. The same protocol applied to dismissals. Following a summons by letter, with a travel warrant, candidates came to Manchester to meet Billy, who, without any sign of a sense of humour gave them the good or bad news. I have an inkling of their experience – my father insisted that I had to be interviewed by Billy McKenzie and was relieved when he said I could have a three-month trial. In those days, we were a command and control business and Billy was in command.

Ewart Hawthorne, who managed the North Park factory for its first 25 years, was another raw recruit. He was the office junior under Tom Mursell and was given the chance of looking after the original factory when Tom Mursell went to America to study the latest shoe factory techniques, while designing North Park. Ewart did so well that he was the natural choice to run the new factory after Tom's sudden death.

Charlie Stafford started as the most junior boy in Hightown outside Manchester before becoming another Altrincham shop assistant who rose through the ranks. Charlie became a highly competent warehouse manager with a wicked sense of humour. His sister, Lillian, followed him into the business and became Will's personal secretary. In 1938, when Will remarried, she became Lillian Timpson. Lillian was 24 years younger than Will, but with Will being so young at heart, the age difference was of little consequence. Having been his personal secretary, Lillian knew how to support Will in the business and she became his faithful friend and partner for the rest of his life.

I have mentioned some of the highest flyers, but the real heroes (sadly in those days no heroines) were the branch managers, who all started as shop boys, cleaning the back stockroom and polishing shoes for at least six months before they were allowed to serve a customer.

CHAPTER NINE

SHOE SHOPS
BETWEEN THE WARS

WILL WAS KEEN TO TAKE the Timpson name well beyond Manchester. Apart from the two shops in Kettering and Wellingborough, William, the founder, had concentrated on the centre and suburbs of Manchester. Clearly not expecting to have more than 26 shops, he identified each shop with a letter. His second shop on Stretford Road in Hulme became B Shop, Oxford Road near the Palace Theatre was 'C' and Regent Road Salford was 'D'. The original Oldham Street branch was the 'A' shop. He got right through to 'Z' (Lower Broughton Rd, Salford) without leaving Greater Manchester. The branches were in community shopping areas within walking distance of cotton mills and terraced, back-to-back housing – including Pendleton, Miles Platting, Ardwick, Collyhurst and Openshaw. The first shops with numbers were still in Manchester; Levenshulme was No 1 and Chorlton-cum-Hardy No 2. It isn't surprising that William was shocked when his son wanted to open in Liverpool.

Will took some time to fulfil his wish to become a national chain. In 1914, when the business reached a total of 56 shops, 33 were in

Manchester with 16 in Lancashire. The only signs of geographical expansion were the shops in Sheffield, Nottingham and Leeds.

(Some other family shoe chains, including Stead & Simpson, George Oliver and Hiltons, already had over 100 shops, but most were based in Leicestershire, the centre of the ladies' shoemaking industry. Timpson's Manchester base and the expertise in men's shoemaking gave the shops a unique place on the high street.)

Once the First World War ended, Will went on the expansion trail and totally transformed the business, but he didn't go much further than Birmingham. Manchester already had a Timpson shop on every busy street, but there was plenty of scope in the rest of Lancashire. With textile mills booming, the company did well in all the major towns, including Bolton, Bury, Preston, Burnley and 10 shops in Liverpool. Even when the company reached 150 branches, half of them were in Lancashire.

When picking sites, Will looked for industrial chimneys; near woollen mills and steelworks in Yorkshire, mining in the north-east and ship-building in Glasgow. Within a decade, Will opened 18 shops in Scotland, starting with a business of three shops on Leith Walk in Edinburgh and another with branches in Greenock, Stirling and three in Glasgow. Will liked his visits to Scotland, not only finding shops in the industrial low-lands but also opening in Hawick, Galashiels and Inverness. He didn't get to Birmingham until the late 1920s, but by 1937, had 17 shops in Birmingham and Coventry with a further 11 across the Midlands which included Leicester, Derby and Rugby.

His shops appealed to value-conscious families, so Will's strategy of creating a major presence in the industrial centres made perfect sense, but other acquisitions seemed, in retrospect, somewhat haphazard. Some were discovered while a workaholic Will slipped away during family holidays – Bournemouth, Spalding, Brighton, Lowestoft, Norwich and Great Yarmouth come into this category. In the 1930s, seaside towns benefitted from a population that used the train to go on holiday in the UK.

Timpson development around London lacked conviction. The first London branches, Hammersmith, Clapham and Peckham, came from a business acquisition, but when the shops were given the Timpson fascia, few customers knew what to expect. The company opened in High Wycombe, St. Albans, Barking, Wembley and Hounslow but instead of exporting the northern magic, they simply became another shoe shop on a south-eastern high street. (Other chains such as Trueform, Freeman, Hardy & Willis, Saxone, Dolcis and Clerkenwell Footwear were more in step with the fashions demanded by customers living around London).

Despite failing to create a solid base in the South, Will used his property flair to pay £40,000 for the freehold of a big building, 33/37 Queen Street Oxford, which he converted into a new Timpson unit while renting the double unit next door and a restaurant upstairs. Nearly 50 years later, it proved to be Will's most inspired property deal and is the one that insured that Timpson would remain a family business.

Before the First World War, goods were still delivered by horse and cart to the Manchester shops while three lorries took deliveries to Victoria Railway Station to be sent by rail to the 28 shops outside Manchester. The first petrol lorry was bought in 1920 and, by 1929, there was a fleet of five. The drivers were a loyal bunch; George Hill and Walter Tomlinson were still delivering to Timpson shops forty years later in 1965. Timpson lorries starting delivering to Scotland in 1930. By 1932, a fleet of 9 Timpson vehicles were calling on every shop, with the big turnover branches getting two deliveries a week.

As well as opening 8 shops a year, Will and Noel updated existing branches. The original Timpson shops were very dark. Smelly gas lighting and the dark decor made them claustrophobic for colleagues and customers. To emphasize value for money, the founder used a 'pile it high and sell them cheap' approach with shoes and boots hanging on poles.

The 1920s called for a higher standard of shopfitting, display and lighting. Bulk displays of boots outside every shop were banished and replaced by elaborate window dressing. Balancing boots, shoes, slippers and sandals on the new glass shelves and metal stands was a work of art. Few branch managers were up to the task so most windows were dressed by a team of specialists who covered about 7 shops each. Despite their expertise, it took at least three days to complete all the displays in a single shop. The better presentation helped, but the biggest difference was the window lighting. The shops shone out like beacons on the high street.

The new fascia had an Art Deco feel – it was hard to miss the Timpson name which, as well as being above the door, was all around the window and written in tiles on the arcade floor. It wasn't subtle but the Timpson image appealed to honest northern families.

The windows were packed with merchandise but no footwear was displayed inside. The shopfloor was full of chairs, with 'fitting stools' to help staff sit down, measure feet and help customers try on shoes. The walls were lined with shoe boxes in wooden fixtures. The quality wooden interiors were so important, the company employed a team of French polishers to keep standards up to date.

In the 1920s and 30s, you could only buy footwear at a shoe shop or a shoe stall at the local market. Shoe shops sold everything from slippers to wellingtons and Timpson did just that for men, women and children. The range included boots for policemen, warm-lined winter boots for women, school shoes and baby bootees, a vast range of Christmas slippers, football boots for men and boys, overshoes for wet weather, sandals for the seaside, formal shoes for the office, dancing shoes and hobnailed working boots. When it came to footwear, Timpson was a one-stop shop, with personal service, but the star of the show was always the range of men's shoes and boots, which took a bigger percentage of business than any competitor.

With so many shops in Lancashire, sales of children's shoes shot up every spring for the Whit Walks when new white shoes were needed for the religious processions. Sandal sales were triggered as each town had its Wakes Week when the mills shut down for their annual holiday. In the winter, with little central heating and most people walking to work, slippers and boots were big business.

The busiest branches, Elliot Street in Liverpool, Grange Road in Birkenhead and Grainger Street in Newcastle-upon-Tyne, had up to 40 shop assistants on a Saturday. A few were part-time – mostly Saturday girls and boys, hoping, often successfully, to become full time as soon as they left school. Men served men and women looked after all the women and children; it was a formal atmosphere with the manager having total authority. He (they were all men) had his own office, and a shop boy to do his errands. The shop managers ordered their own stock and some gave their staff a tough time, but the real power was held by the area inspectors who ran about 20 shops. With up to 300 staff under their control, they were some of the most powerful people in the business.

By the 1930s, nearly every shop operated a five-and-a-half-day week, closing at lunchtime on the specified half-day closing day. The half-day differed from one town to another. Edinburgh, Burnley and Keighley closed at 1.00 pm on a Tuesday, Stirling, Accrington and Keighley closed on Wednesdays and Thursday was the day for Kettering, Peckham and Spalding, hence a tour round the shops required careful planning. No one, apart from the odd rogue trader, ever considered opening on a Sunday.

CHAPTER 10

NORTH PARK FACTORY

THE NEW FACTORY AT NORTH PARK gave Timpson a major advantage over the competition by helping to create a flourishing men's shoe business. Although the factory made ladies' footwear, some shoes for children and a few football boots, its strength was the traditional shoes and boots for men. It was fortunate that Will expanded the chain so quickly, with production at North Park increasing to nearly 20,000 pairs a week, as the factory needed big orders to keep it at full capacity.

It was an imposing building on four floors, and visitors were greeted with a strong smell of leather. The hides were stored and selected on the ground floor, shelves filled with rolls of upper leather in different colours and various grades, French calf for top-quality footwear and lower grades for the popular-priced products. The stout leather 'bends' for soles were stored on pallets along with synthetic sole materials that were gradually introduced to keep prices down.

On the first floor, the leather was cut by 'clickers', sometimes by hand but usually on lethal-looking hydraulic presses. Clicking was the most skilled job in the factory. The clicker arranged metal or cardboard patterns to make maximum use of the hide. But it wasn't a simple jigsaw puzzle; the leather had to be cut with sinews in the right direction, to avoid disaster when stretched over the last in the making room.

The cut pieces of leather were sent upstairs by lift to the closing room where the uppers were stitched together. This room was full of women sat at sewing machines – stitching was seen as women's work with the only men to be seen being the chargehands and the supervisor. The closing room had a busy buzzy sound, unlike the making room where the noise was almost deafening. This was where the upper was stretched over the last (another highly skilled job) and the sole attached, either with cement or, for traditional welted shoes, by a stitcher. The welting section was the noisiest part of the whole factory. The making room was a male preserve. Unlike the closing room, where girls sat in front of their sewing machines, the men were standing all day. They each had their individual way to cope with the monotony; some moved from one foot to the other as if in a dance, others whistled or hummed to themselves and one constantly moved his head and shoulders from side to side.

Production started at 8.00 am with everyone clocked in and at their work station, ready to go. A loud hooter signalled lunch at noon and, within 2 minutes, the factory was empty, as most employees could get home for lunch and back within an hour. Amazingly, the guy who led the charge for the exit never heard the hooter. He was totally deaf, but an expert clock-watcher. The minute hand on the factory clock went half a degree backwards five seconds before moving on to show midday. As soon as the hand flicked back, the deaf guy set off and was the first to get on his bike to go home for lunch. Nearly all the factory workers lived in terraced houses within a mile of the factory.

The factory relied almost totally on selling the products through Timpson. In the 1930s, it struggled to keep pace with demand. The traditionally welted 'Empiric' branded shoes were steady sellers in every Timpson shop, providing quality and value that beat the competition. The secret was the shape of the last (the 'mould' on which the shoes were made). Timpson customers found North Park footwear stylish and comfortable while also fitting their pocket.

To boost production, the factory made shoes from surplus leather for the January Sale. The shops had a July Sale but the main event started on January 1st (most shops were open on New Year's Day). These extra lines were distributed at an inflated retail price during November, then marked down after Christmas. Some managers sold these special lines at full price to create a surplus ahead of their next stocktaking.

From the day it opened in 1923, the Kettering factory was managed by Ewart Hawthorne, while the other factory-based director, Alan Timpson, looked after external relations and represented the company in trade associations. Alan started working for his father at the Market Street factory. After the First World War, in which Alan was a victim of mustard gas, he returned to Market Street, before becoming shop inspector for the 8 shops in Northamptonshire and East Anglia. He became a director when he joined the team at the newly opened North Park and was a prime mover in a joint venture, Kettering Cartons, that supplied packaging to Northamptonshire shoe manufacturers and was on the Council of SATRA, the shoe research association based in Kettering. In 1933, Alan was the Captain of Kettering Golf Club, which had become an important parent of the local social scene.

Among the long-serving employees was leather buyer, Jack Taylor, whose father had been William Timpson's chauffeur, Percy Thomas, the Assistant Factory Manager, who had the vital role of interviewing and appointing new colleagues, and Arthur Fifield, who bought all the supplies other than leather. Both Will's sons worked at North Park. His younger son David, who suffered from severe deafness, spent his working life in the leather department, while Anthony, my father, had a three-year apprenticeship working in every part of the factory. During that time, he met my mother, Hilda, who was a secretary in the factory office.

When she met my father, my mother was living with her parents, Bert and Mercy Smith, on Beatrice Road half a mile up the hill from North

Park. It was a comfortable house with a garage that Bert had added, but despite having a lavatory on the first floor, the old outside loo was still in use when I stayed there in the 1950s. Bert was in the leather trade, a director of local tanners and leather merchants, Stimpson Perkins (Hilda's younger brother Alan joined his father's business). Bert's parents, Joe and Annie, both lived into their 90s; she died when she was 93, at which time Joe was still playing bowls for a local team, a sport he played until a year before he died at the age of 97.

It must have been a precarious courtship for both my mother and my father – the boss's son taking out a girl from the office – but they were a good match; two modest and fairly shy people, who had no ambition to be pillars of the establishment, but who shared an altruistic streak. They were a devoted and conventional couple who led a very private life together. They married in 1936, the year after my father's mother died. He was devoted to her and her death must have cast a big cloud over the wedding, but Will could not have done more to give them a great start to their married life – his wedding present was 'Cranoe', their family home which my father lived in until he died in 1997.

There was another Kettering-based director, Gordon Akester, who ran his department in a separate building next to the factory. It was called 'The Office of the Secretary'. The office was home to rows of 60 uniformed women adding up the figures that Gordon used to produce management reports and company accounts. Then, as now, accountants liked to be in charge and seemed to take a sinister delight in delivering bad news; Gordon Akester was no exception. The distance between Kettering and Manchester, both geographically and culturally, didn't help to create harmony. The Office of the Secretary made regular demands to cut capital expenditure, reduce markdowns and improve margins. Team Manchester thought the Kettering bean counters were acting like party poopers. But, despite this underlying tension, the system seemed to work.

A bowling green in the factory grounds was used every summer evening and hosted matches against local clubs and other footwear factories. North Park also fielded a cricket team with an extensive fixture list, Assistant Factory Manager, Percy Thomas, being a founder member. Timpson was the biggest employer in Kettering; a critical part of the community. The position brought added responsibility in a similar way that Clarks dominated Street in Somerset and K Shoes were the key employer in Kendal. North Park provided Timpson shops with a competitive advantage but it came with a big weight.

CHAPTER ELEVEN

THE WAR YEARS

IN 1939, AT THE START OF THE WAR, all parts of the business were busy. North Park was on full production, mainly making boots for the armed forces. The repair factories experienced greater demand with extra repairs from both the Army and the Air Force. Shop sales also rose as the public bought in anticipation of future shortages. This mild attack of panic buying was repeated in 1940 after the government proposed the introduction of purchase tax (a tax, like VAT, paid by wholesalers and distributors, ultimately passed onto the consumer by retailers). Attention was centred on the luxury goods tax of 33.3% (which was increased, first to 66.6%, then to 100% before the end of the war). Fortunately, footwear attracted the lowest rate (16%) and all children's shoes were exempt.

Despite many government restrictions, Timpson continued to be busy throughout the war. The drop in consumer demand caused by rationing and clothing coupons, introduced in 1941, was compensated by the armed forces wanting massive supplies of footwear from North Park and demanding more shoe repairs, particularly new rubber soles on Wellington boots. To streamline footwear production, the government required factories to work together. As a result, we became a coordinat-ing 'Nucleus' firm working with our designated associate company, Tite and Garfirth, a smaller manufacturer in Morley Street, Kettering, making similar footwear to North Park.

Three new shops were opened during 1939 bringing the total number to 194, with an additional 11 shoe repair factories. As soon as war broke out, the development of new branches ceased and wartime restrictions on shopfitting materials meant that, apart from work in progress, no development took place. These barriers were a blessing in disguise. In a wartime budget, the company's profit tax almost doubled to over £100,000 and all the cash left was needed to patch up branches damaged in the Blitz.

One government restriction brought an unexpected benefit. The Paper Controller issued strict instructions that printed material should be kept to an absolute minimum. The Timpson Board took the regulation to heart by producing their 1943 annual report to shareholders on both sides on one sheet of A4. The Chairman's report was somewhat brief but the figures told shareholders just about all they needed to know. With 21st-century shareholders wading through as many as 200 pages to find true facts, perhaps it is time for the Paper Controller to make a comeback.

Cardboard rationing put a temporary block on new shoeboxes. Shops improvised with reusable boxes and although some stock was damaged, the lack of packaging was only a minor irritation. At the beginning of the war, three of the company lorries were requisitioned (and lost at Dunkirk). Journeys beyond 50 miles needed a special permit, which was often refused, particularly for trips to London and North East England. The drivers often took a chance and drove without a permit. Without fail, every shop received its weekly delivery throughout the war.

At the outbreak of war, Timpson employed just over 3,000 colleagues. During the next five years, half either joined up or worked in one of the essential services. Four hundred retail staff signed up by 1942; a year later, that had increased to 1,040, joined by 300 recruits from North Park and 80 shoe repairers. The company kept in contact with their employees wherever they were and regular allowance payments were made to them or their dependents. Will Timpson recorded in his 1941 Annual Report – 'the Directors consider the case of every employee serving his country and we make suitable allowances to support his home.'

The vacancies created by employees on military service were, wherever possible, filled by their wives or ex-employees who came out of retirement. Somehow, the company was never short of the help needed at Kettering, in the shops, in shoe repair factories, the warehouse or the office.

My father very seldom mentioned his wartime experience. When war was declared, he was disappointed to be drafted in as a fire service auxiliary in Manchester, but he was delighted to join the RAF in 1941. After training in Montreal and Prestwick, he flew several missions as a navigator during the last two years of the war.

Sensibly, the Chairman's statements never mentioned the substantial damage suffered by the warehouse and several city-centre branches. Shops were destroyed by the major bombing attacks on Bristol, Hull, Coventry and Norwich. Perhaps the biggest potential loss was during a Manchester raid on 22nd/23rd December 1940 when the original Strangeways warehouse was severely damaged by an exploding mine. Long-time colleague Walter Dixon was on duty as a fire watcher and summoned Noel to the scene. He found the Men's Warehouse was a wreck, Empiric House, across the road was severely battered and the flames shooting up from the nearby Victoria Goods Yard were, according to Noel, "Terrific – a wonderful, if appalling sight". Early attendance of the Fire Brigade saved part of the building, but, for the rest of the war, Empiric House became both a men's and ladies' shoe warehouse – a role that continued well after the war.

Although the company came out of six years of conflict and disruption in pretty good financial shape, more than 100 Timpsonian lives were lost. The majority of company employees who survived returned to take up their jobs and found the company was probably more prosperous than when they left.

North Park was busier than ever making demob footwear including ankle boots and traditional black Oxford shoes for the officers who were returning to Civvy Street. There was still rationing and clothing coupons lingered on until 1949, but, as soldiers, sailors and airmen went back to the mills, mines and shipyards, families wanted to go shopping. The relief that came with peacetime led to a mini consumer boom and Timpson was a big beneficiary.

Despite the declaration of war, in 1939, Timpson produced a profit of £189k, an all-time record. That figure was maintained throughout the war, but, allowing for inflation, over the six years, profit fell by nearly 20%. However, in 1945, the company was still making a profit of £232k (over £9m at 2019 prices). For the next three years, the business beat all expectations. The North of England and Scotland got back to work and families went shopping. In three years, the Timpson profit grew by 250% to £587k (over £20m in 2019 money). This proved to be the company's peak performance, which, in real terms, was only equalled once (in 1961) during the next 65 years. The halcyon days were nearly over.

Charles Timpson – William Timpson's eldest brother, who gave him his first job

Elizabeth Farey – William Timpson's first wife

Florence Butlin – Will Timpson's first wife

Katherine Mursell – William Timpson's second wife

William Timpson – Founder of the Company

A shop Oldham Street Manchester

Miss Kinsey and sales team, Oldham Street Ladies' Department 1895

First retail shoe repair shop

Early Manchester delivery service

Original Repair factory

Briggate Leeds – 1910   *Briggate Leeds – 1914*

Briggate Leeds—1959

Kettering Shoe factory opened in 1923

Shoe production line

Factory shed in William Timpson's garden at Kettering

Timpson Directors in the 1920s

William Timpson (Founder)

William Henry Farey Timpson

Noel Mursell Timpson

Charles Timpson

Alan Geoffrey Timpson

Gordon Akester (Finance Director)

Ewart Hawthorne (Factory Manager)

Francis John Noakes
(Ladies Shoe Buyer)

Graham Kennedy
(Ladies Shoe Buyer)

Tom Howell
(Children's Shoe Buyer)

Tom Hardman
(Ladies Shoe Buyer)

Fred Potts
(Warehouse and Transport Manager)

Shoe Repairing in the 1930s

TIMPSON
Boot & Shoe REPAIR SERVICE

Let the ACTUAL MAKERS repair your Shoes—
ALWAYS—
for complete satisfaction

SUPER QUALITY REPAIRS

	Sole & Heel	Soled only	Heeled
MEN'S	5/3	4/3	1/4
LADIES'	3/9	3/-	10d.

LONG SOLE REPAIRS

THE BEST OF ALL REPAIRS. The sole is carried right through from toe to heel, in fact your shoes are practically re-made and turned out equal to new. Prices (sole and heel):

MEN'S **7/6** LADIES' **5/3**
(Breasted Heels 6/-)

Never dry your shoes in front of the fire. The heat will cause the soles to crack and wear away quickly.

Note our Standard Prices!

		Sole & Heel	Soled	Soled only	Heeled
MEN'S		4/9	4/6	4/-	1/3
LADIES'		3/3	3/-	2/9	9d.
YOUTHS'	Sizes 2 to 5	4/-	3/9	3/3	1/-
BOYS'	11 to 1	3/-	2/9	2/4	11d.
BOYS'	7 to 10	2/9	2/6	2/2	10d.
GIRLS'	11 to 1	2/9	2/6	2/3	8d.
GIRLS'	7 to 10	2/6	2/3	2/-	7d.
CHILDREN'S	4 to 6	2/3	2/-	1/9	6d. to 8d.

RUBBER TIPS fitted at no extra charge of ... Men's 4d. ... Ladies' 3d.

NEW HEELS

New heels can be easily fitted in place of old and worn ones thus giving the shoes a new lease of life at a modest cost. Prices

Leather Built Heels	2/- per pair fitted complete
Celluloid Covered Heels	2/3
Kid Covered Heels	2/9

NEW DOUBLE WEAR STUDDED SOLE REPAIRS

	Half Sole & Heel	Through Sole & Heel	Heel only
Men's	4/6	5/6	1/-
Ladies'	3/6	4/6	9d.
Youths' (Sizes 2 to 5)	4/-	5/-	1/-
Boys' 11 to 1	3/-	4/-	9d.
Boys' 7 to 10	2/9	3/9	8d.
Girls' 11 to 1	2/9	3/9	9d.
Girls' 7 to 10	2/6	3/6	8d.

USKIDE REPAIRS

	Men's	Ladies'
Through Sole and Heel	4/6	5/-
Half Sole and Heel	3/6	4/6
Heel only	1/6	1/-

TIMPSON "EMPIRATA" SOLES

Let us sole and heel your footwear with this wonderful long-wearing leather. A Timpson speciality, which cannot be obtained elsewhere. Prices

	Men's	Ladies'
Soles and Heels	5/9	4/3

BRING YOUR REPAIRS TO TIMPSONS, NO MATTER WHERE YOU BOUGHT THE SHOES

The radioactive pedoscope

Personal service for every customer

The building in Oxford that paid for nearly 10% of the Management Buyout

Empric House, Great Ducie Street, Manchester

Mens Warehouse 101-115 Great Ducie Street 1941

Typical Timpson Shoe Shops in the 1930s

63 High St. Cheadle   Oxford Rd, Manchester 1938

Stockport

Altrincham

Timpson Directors September 1972

Geoffrey Noakes

Norman Redfern

Alan Simmons

Bill Simmons

Bert Brownhill

Professor Roland Smith

Bob Kirkman

William Anthony Timpson

John Timpson

The first Long Service Lunch

CHAPTER TWELVE

WILL TAKES A
BACK SEAT

IN 1949, AFTER 55 YEARS as Managing Director, Will decided to
hand over day-to-day management to his half-brother Noel, who had
been the Deputy Managing Director since the company went public in
1929. Will, who remained as Chairman, was nearly 70 and starting to feel
his age. From a health viewpoint, it was a wise decision. Although Will
had several periods of illness over the next decade, he enjoyed plenty of
holidays and kept a close but more detached interest in the business. His
mood can be detected in extracts from a letter he wrote to every branch
manager in May 1955.

'To the Manager

Dear Sir

*I have been thinking of you for some time and feel I should like to write to
you. As you are aware, I have been ill and unable to communicate with
you. However, I am pleased to say that I am a great deal better and can
now enjoy life and attend to a limited amount of important business.*

During my illness, I often wondered why I had done so much for so long a time and the answer came very clearly – because I loved doing it; I liked working with you all and it would have been a great sorrow to me not to be able to do so.

I have to tell you that as far as my visits to shops are concerned, that day has passed. I can hear you say, "Well, he has never been to my shop for years" and you may be right; indeed, if you are at one of our latest branches, I may have never seen your shop. However, it may surprise you to know that I have, even very recently, visited more than a hundred shops each year.

What I will miss more than anything else is personal contact with managers and staff; nothing gave me more pleasure – I enjoyed it immensely and felt the goodwill was mutual.

I have had a full life. We only had 37 shops when, at the age of 24, I took over the management of our retail business. In the next 50 years, I established 163 shops and 17 repairing factories, in addition to arranging the details of every lease and freehold that we acquired.

I still hope to give some service to the company and I shall always welcome any opportunity of seeing our people because there was a time when they were my people, just as there was a time when they were my father's people.

Yours Sincerely

W.H.F. Timpson
Chairman'

That letter told the branches that 'Mr Will' had almost totally retired, but it may also have been written to give a strong message to his half-brother, Noel, who was 16 years younger than Will and a very different character. Noel didn't have the same cheeky charm that made Will such a hit with all his colleagues. At Great Ducie Street, Will would spend part of his day wandering around the offices and warehouse chatting to anyone and everybody. He knew about their families and their hobbies, equally happy talking to the stocky and jovial Frank Wells who loaded the lorries or Cyril Snape, the men's shoe warehouse manager.

Noel was a highly competent manager but didn't have Will's personal touch – he didn't walk around the office; employees were expected to come to him, summoned by a distinctive continuous ring on their internal telephone. Noel was just as dedicated as his elder brother but followed process rather than intuition, more comfortable spending time in meetings than visiting branches.

A new generation was running the buying departments, a critical part of most multiple retailers. In March 1949, Allen Booth retired after 46 years with the company. Allen, who understood every part of the market – footwear for men, women and children, was one of the outstanding buyers in the trade. It was Allen, more than anyone else, who helped to make Will's life worry-free.

John Noakes, one of Will's nephews (the son of Will's sister Elizabeth), took charge of ladies' and children's shoe-buying from Allen Booth. John spent two years at North Park before going to a girls' shoemaker, E. A. Johnson & Co, in Leicester, where he trained to be a salesman. In 1929, the senior ladies' shoe buyer, Tom Eggleton was poached by a competitor, the Benefit Shoe Company, and became their General Manager, so Noel persuaded John Noakes to join the business.

John became a director in 1937, but his Territorial Army experience inevitable led him to join a Battalion and gain rapid promotion. His distinguished army career included a spell on General Eisenhower's general staff and the award of an OBE. When John returned to Timpson in 1945, he was already suffering from ill health, which he bore with courage for over a decade. Graham Kennedy, who had been given a great fashion grounding at Saxone under the legendary ladies' shoe buyer, Bill Abbott, was appointed as the new Timpson buyer in 1957, shortly before John died.

Graham Kennedy was a whirlwind, dashing off on fashion trips to Italy and Paris, buying bold quantities of some adventurous styles and promoting his new approach to branch managers at fashion parades around the country. Graham was a culture shock for Timpson but he injected new life into what had been a humdrum range of basic ladies' shoes. Graham arrived at a perfect point in the fashion cycle. Within three years, winklepickers and high stiletto heels became the must-have fashion item and Graham had the courage to put a big range into Timpson shops. By 1959, he had persuaded the Board to back his plan to advertise in colour through women's weekly magazines, using the slogan 'Mad about Milan'.

The Board were reluctant to spend on advertising, having been embarrassed in 1952 when the company promoted the 'Ranger Slipper' – a child's bootee, with a toy gun in its side pocket. Advertising helped the slippers to sell amazingly well, then a trial started at the Old Bailey involving 16-year-old Christopher Craig who shot a policeman during a burglary after his 19-year-old accomplice, Derek Bentley, said, "Let him have it!" Bentley was hanged but Craig was too young to face the death sentence. One letter in the Daily Express, complaining that Timpson were inciting children to copy Craig, was enough to turn the country against the company and Ranger slipper sales came to a grinding halt. Fortunately, there was a manufacturing fault, the boot fell apart and the unsaleable stock was returned to the manufacturer and full compensation was claimed from them. A lucky escape.

My father, Anthony, bought the men's and boys' shoes. Following his three years at Kettering, he was well placed to develop men's shoes, and, by the time he left to be a navigator in the RAF, he had experience of warehousing, distributing and buying. Being a natural handyman (he built several radios and two televisions), he had an expert understanding of shoemaking techniques. Encouraged by his father, Will, he visited lots of shops to discover what customers and branch managers wanted.

When Anthony returned to the business in 1946, he joined the Board and, for the next 14 years, had the support of two talented buyers who both started as shop assistants. Leslie Hearn, who relied on blunt common sense and a dry sense of humour, bought men's footwear. Jack Milligan, a somewhat shy and tentative guy, had the magic touch. His low-key character was deceptive; he bought the boys' range and made very few mistakes.

CHAPTER THIRTEEN

A COMPETITIVE MARKETPLACE

SUDDENLY, THE COMPANY FOUND it more difficult to make money. The annual reports didn't look too bad, but, throughout the 1950s, once profits were adjusted for inflation, they didn't match the record year in 1949. Will's Annual Report to shareholders covered a range of obstacles that got in the way. Supply shortage, the increased price of leather, higher rents and rates, increased taxation and unseasonal weather were all to blame. But Timpson's biggest problem was industrial unrest and increasing concern for the future of mining, textile manufacturing, steelworks and shipbuilding. The industrial North was still doing ok, but the future didn't look bright. With most of the shops located in declining areas, it was hard to grow the business.

Noel showed a close interest in the footwear repairs division (which was being called FRD) – acronyms had already shown their ugly face in the 1950s. However, when he became Managing Director, Noel gave more responsibility to John Noakes's brother Geoffrey who joined the company in 1933 and, after his apprenticeship, helped to build the shoe repair chain. Like his brother, Geoffrey was a keen soldier, taking the rank of Colonel and getting his OBE for work with the T.A. When Geoffrey became a Timpson director in 1953, FRD became his baby.

Geoffrey's character was much more like Noel's and was in stark contrast to the light-touch, caring management style developed by Will. Geoffrey was ambitious. Although he lived with his wife, Ann, and four children in Hale, down the road from Will, Noel (who downsized from his ugly house on Broad Lane to a new build in nearby Carrwood), his brother John and my father, Geoffrey also bought a house in Malpas so he could go hunting and mix with Cheshire's aristocracy.

FRD was run like a military operation, with everyone expected to follow the 'Standing Orders for Shoe Repair Factories'. Although they both carried the Timpson name, the shoe shops and the shoe repair factories had dramatically different cultures. Rivalry between the two sometimes became confrontational, especially when FRD operated a shoe repair counter inside a shoe shop.

Although Noel was happy to delegate management of the shoe repair business, he kept close control of the property – both shopfitting and acquisitions. With the development of new shopping precincts around the country and a shift from local shops to town and city centres, Noel played a critical role in setting the future direction for Timpson.

The number of shoe shops increased as quickly in the 1950s as it had in the 1930s. In addition to opening in new towns, the company had to replace shops destroyed in the Blitz or knocked down by slum clearance and redevelopment. During the 50s, many of the original Greater Manchester shops disappeared. With mills closing and 1,000s of back-to-back terraced houses demolished, shops like Miles Platting, Openshaw and Hulme lost most of their customers. Other shopping areas, including Droylsden, Middleton, Salford and Stretford, were replaced by new precincts and many of the traditional independent shops were replaced by multiple retailers – that is when all our shopping areas started to look alike. Between 1950 and 1960, the number of shoe shops increased from 217 to 260, including 'men only' branches in Bolton, Norris Green and Edinburgh.

With profits falling behind inflation, Noel had to invest carefully. In the 1930s, Will could travel round the UK, look at high streets and know exactly what he was getting, whereas Noel had to go on plans of unbuilt shopping precincts offering units at much higher rents than the shops being replaced. Taking on new shops became a chancy business and Noel didn't take many risks.

Most new shops were leased on modest rents, in traditional Timpson territory from Birmingham north. That meant new shops in Middleton, Ellesmere Port, Ilkeston, Beeston, Wallsend, Scunthorpe and Newall Green, a row of shops in the Wythenshawe Estate. To keep rents down, the company opted for single 18-foot fronted property, although a double unit was more suitable for selling shoes. It was the wrong strategy; by opting for secondary shops with cheap rents, Timpson lost the opportunity to dominate the high street and allowed the more aggressive competitors, particularly Charles Clore's British Shoe Corporation, to take the initiative.

A few big shops were opened in prime city-centre pitches, including replacements for the bombed branches in Coventry and Norwich. A successful big unit was acquired in Market Street, Manchester, in conjunction with Prices Tailors, who traded as John Collier, and bigger prime site units were found in Dundee, Barnsley, Bury and Ashton-under-Lyne. All these bigger shops were highly profitable.

As well as the new shops, Noel spent a substantial amount of capital keeping existing shops up to date. This produced some magnificent shops in Grainger Street in Newcastle, Sunderland and Birkenhead where a commanding pitch on Grange Road was rebuilt. In retrospect, the business should have been ashamed of rebuilding the shops in Darlington and Leeds, where magnificent buildings (Briggate, Leeds was a black and white Elizabethan oak building dating back to 1613) were replaced with characterless 1950s concrete monstrosities.

The company claimed to be in 'All the principal towns and cities in the UK.' but it wasn't. There were no shops in Cambridge, Canterbury,

Guildford, Bath or Basingstoke and there wasn't a Timpson shop in Central London. This was due to the company's northern roots and a cautious approach, expressed by Noel in 1959 – 'Great shops in large cities can be very attractive. They have advertising value and bring big turnover, but can equally produce big profit or heavy loss. The rents asked for such sites and the cost of providing the setup are great, and progress in that direction must be slow. Shops in new and suburban areas or in smaller towns present a better chance of advancement, although their turnover may be limited.'

For most of the decade, North Park was on full capacity, helped by a new production line that made vulcanised men's shoes retailing at 39/11d (£1.99) with a six-month guarantee. Priced just below the well-advertised 'Tuf' brand, the new range was soon selling over 6,000 pairs a week.

In the early 1950s, the factory started exporting to the USA and Canada. From a modest start of the odd 1,000-pair order, this built rapidly to a business approaching 4,500 pairs a week, but the factory had to make completely different shoes for the transatlantic market. They wanted welted shoes with a hint of bling – lots of brogues, in eccentric cordovan leather and traditional Oxfords, with patent leather toe caps – shoes that looked clumsy to the British eye, but the buyers in Chicago thought they were very British. The designers not only produced special styles; they also made them on different lasts. Americans liked tight-fitting shoes and had, on average, bigger feet than British customers. North Park made shoes up to size 13 and 14 with very narrow width fittings.

Unlike their American counterparts, UK customers prefer shoes to be wide and comfortable, with an average width fitting of '5' compared with the '3' fittings that sold over the Atlantic. Timpson even stocked an '8' fitting which could accommodate just about anyone's foot with loads of room to spare.

Timpson shop assistants got wise to their customers' liking for comfort. When a shoe fitted but the customer said it was too tight, if a wider shoe wasn't available, the assistant would get the customer to try on a narrower shoe before bringing back the original pair that then felt more comfortable and the sale was made.

With sales going so well both at home and abroad, Tony Dutoy, who was appointed as factory manager following the retirement of Ewart Hawthorne, inherited an upbeat and profitable business.

North Park had an active social calendar. In addition to the cricket and bowling clubs, they held an annual flower show and a 'Great Summer Outing'. In Manchester, picnics were organised for warehouse employees and a series of dances were held around the country, giving every manager and his wife the chance to attend one of these formal occasions. Timpson family members, even those who didn't work for the company, were expected to attend. Every year, there would be dances in Manchester, London, Liverpool, Glasgow or Edinburgh, Newcastle, Leeds and Birmingham. Black tie was the dress code, which was strictly followed by the directors, members of the family and many employees. The dances were phased out in the mid-50s in favour of less stuffy company dinners.

The company acquired a Sports Ground in partnership with Kendal Milne, the department store in Deansgate, then a subsidiary of Harrods, now part of the House of Fraser. These facilities, as well as providing a place for employees to play tennis, cricket and football, also hosted an annual garden party and sports day.

In 1951, the Board decided to give long-serving employees more recognition. Previously, those completing 25 years were presented with a photograph, before the picture was handed back and displayed in the canteen. The upgrade was a long service certificate, signed by the Chairman and a badge or brooch. Happily, in 1956, when 'Mr Will' completed 60 years of service, his diamond jubilee was celebrated by presenting a gold watch to every employee who had completed 25 years. Four hundred and fifty employees were presented with their gold watches at lunches held at Belle Vue, Manchester and Wickstead Park, Kettering. We have continued with this tradition, but today, the presentation lunch takes place at my house in Cheshire.

Noel's contact with competitors at the Multiple Shoe Retailers' Association convinced him that Timpson needed to be at the forefront of new ideas and best practice.

The introduction of a National Retail Distribution Certificate, in 1950, encouraged Noel to take a formal approach to training, which had previously been left to the initiative of branch managers and area inspectors. A hostel in Altrincham provided accommodation to managers and sales assistants who attended courses in a newly opened training centre, above the small shop on Gt. Ducie Street, across the road from Empiric House.

In the mid-50s, the company started to experiment with a form of self-service, using shoe racks on the sales floor. This was particularly successful at Christmas when the shops built temporary slipper stalls. A very popular addition was the X-ray devices used to fit children's shoes – big machines that allowed both parents and shop assistants to see whether the child's bones were being restricted inside their shoes. They were great for finding the perfect fit, but in doing so, gave children a dangerous dose of radiation and the devices were abandoned in 1965.

Noel wanted tighter control on cash security and to get more accurate information on stock and sales. In 1949, the company introduced impressive National Cash Registers which, in the big city centre shops, were operated by central cashiers, linked to the sales floor by a Lamson tube system which transported the cash and sales docket round the shop by magic.

In the mid-50s, stock distribution went through a major change. Before then, branch managers ordered their own stock, but the new scheme transferred decision-making to Manchester. Branches simply listed the sizes in stock and the distribution department decided what to send. In 1958, a computer was ordered, which was expected to streamline merchandising, reduce stock and increase sales.

Timpson was going to catch up and then overtake competitors in the race to introduce retail engineering. Noel declared, "We are no longer going to be treading in the footsteps of other multiples."

CHAPTER FOURTEEN

DEVELOPING
SHOE REPAIRS

NOEL SAW SHOE REPAIRING as a big opportunity and Geoffrey Noakes grew the business in as many directions as he could find. At the end of the war, there were just 11 factories all set up to serve local Timpson shops. Most factories had a retail counter to look after passing customers. The second major factory was opened in Liverpool, RF3 was in Sheffield and RF4 in Birmingham. By the mid-1930s, Greater Manchester branches were served by the factories at Stockport, Longsight, Oldham and Pendleton. The big factory in Manchester, next to the warehouse, serviced shops around the country by rail, but it became clear that better business was done when customers got a 24-hour service. For every shoe shop to be within driving distance of a factory, new premises were needed as quickly as possible.

Noel and Geoffrey looked for small retail shops at a modest rent attached to sizeable workshops, which could be out the back, above the shop or in a basement. They found a few properties that filled their brief in Altrincham, Bolton, Bangor, Edinburgh, Inverness and Oldham. They also converted old Timpson units in Ellesmere Port and Patricroft where the shoe shops had moved to new premises. In some places, the company opened both shoe and shoe repair shops next door, as at Northenden and Hawick, or in the same shopping precinct. This is why the company acquired two shops in Billingham and two in a tiny shopping area in Wythenshawe called Newall Green.

Three of the most successful shoe repair units were part of a Timpson shop property, with separate public access. Sale, Rotherham and Leigh were all corner shoe shops with a repair unit down the side road. Before long, factories appeared inside some of the shoe shops. Little workshops were put in the basement of the shops at Hyde and Accrington, with a small counter to serve repair customers on the shop floor. In the big city centre shops, Elliot Street, Manchester and Market Street, Manchester, Footwear Repairs Division (FRD) put their own staff behind the counter.

Suddenly, FRD had the answer to their property problem; they became corporate cuckoos, invading the shoe shop portfolio, hunting for space to do their shoe repairing.

They needed at least 200 square feet with easy access to accommodate the team of benchers, repairers and finishers with their range of scouring machines, trimmers, Blake Stitchers, sewing machines, cement presses and benches. Although many shops had space upstairs (that used to be used as a manager's flat), few could accommodate a fully equipped factory.

Undeterred, the FRD team found a compromise – small workshops that concentrated on the simple jobs. They couldn't repair welted soles but heeling wasn't a problem. Factories based in a shop were identified by putting a '6' before the shoe shop number so the factory inside 191 Knutsford was 6191 and the one in 40 Sunderland was 640. The smaller workshops used the prefix '4' – the first, in 26 Bolton, was 426, hence the business started talking about '400' and '600' units.

Factory workers got a basic wage plus a piece rate for every job. In bigger factories, there could be 20 benchmen and finishers wearing white aprons, standing for eight hours a day in what was often a hot and sweaty workroom. The managers had more fun, usually getting an office of their own. They were the top craftsmen who were invited to Manchester for conferences and training courses, where they discovered whether they had won the latest shoe repair quality competition. Producing exhibition shoe repairs is still a highly specialised skill.

The counter assistants (always women!) were on a separate bonus scheme based on total sales, which included shoe care products and, in a few shops, hosiery and handbags. With ladies' heels costing 2/6d (12p) and a sole and heel 8/11d (45p), they had to serve lots of customers to earn a decent bonus. Everyone was keen to sell a top-grade men's leather through sole and heel costing 21/9d (£1.09p).

Between 1946 and 1959, the number of Timpson repair factories grew from 11 to 152. 'FRD' became a significant business with a team of area inspectors led by chief inspector Reuben Guest who combined his field role with designing all the technical layouts – a particularly skilled task with the small '400' units. Reuben was a workaholic, exhausting his travelling companions on trips to distant branches by leaving home at 5.00 am and not expecting to return home before 9.00 pm.

Today, it is difficult to imagine the volume of shoe repairs that came into our shops during the 1950s and 1960s. Busy shops could be handling over 1,000 pairs a week with many requiring a full sole and heel repair. At least 10 shoe repairers and 4 'counter girls' were employed in the bigger turnover shoe repair shops.

There were plenty of competitors; a reasonably sized shopping area like Sunderland or Stafford had at least 10 independent cobblers, all making a decent living. Timpson wasn't the only multiple shoe repairer. Malones in Scotland, Paynes in Birmingham, Shoecraft and Coombes, which were nationwide, in a series of acquisitions, all became part of Allied Leather Industries and became known as Allied Shoe Repairs – the market leader with over 500 shops. Automagic, which was founded in London, spread to 110 city-centre sites. Broughall's, founded in Luton, opened 40 shops from Norwich to Cheltenham and Essex Shoe Repairs built a chain of 25 branches. Many more independent shoe repairers expanded to create chains of over 10 shops.

The relationship between the retail business and FRD had some tricky moments and caused political tiffs between the respective area teams. There was a constant argument about commission and rent – how much FRD should pay for their space and what commission the retail side should pay on repair turnover. The politics went up to another level when FRD put their employees behind a repair counter in every shop with a '600' unit.

The repair counter had its own stock of shoe polish and hosiery and only served shoe repair customers. On Saturdays, few customers wanted repairs, so, while the shoe shop assistants were serving three customers at once, the repair counter girls just stood and watched. This rivalry in the field was matched back in Empiric House.

In truth, both parts of the business needed each other. FRD were able to find and afford the premises to grow quickly and the shoe shops got some extra turnover at a difficult time. A turning point came when one of the shoe shop managers, Neville Gilbert, who ran a small shop in Coventry, fell in love with shoe repairs and quickly built a business of over 350 pairs a week. When he was promoted to run the shop in Hanley, where there was a repair factory above the shop, Neville took full advantage and shoe repairs became over 25% of his business.

By growing inside the shoe shops, in the 1950s, FRD had become the UK's second-biggest shoe repair chain.

CHAPTER FIFTEEN

NOEL PULLS THE SHORT STRAW

ON MAY 20TH 1960, his 80th birthday, Will announced he would be stepping down as Chairman and handing over to Noel. The changeover took place in the last week of September when Will became the company's first President. Noel was keen to make his mark and had a full agenda. The company computer was due to be delivered, he had signed an agreement to build a new office and warehouse complex in Wythenshawe, a new closing factory had opened in nearby Corby and the company opened its first shop in the centre of London, on Oxford Street to the east of Oxford Circus.

On top of an active Timpson agenda, Noel was being recognised for his work outside the business. He continued to be involved in the shoe retail and repair trade associations and received an Honorary Degree from Manchester University for his charitable support for Boys' Clubs and Playing Fields. Five days after his 64th birthday, he was appointed OBE in the New Year's Honours list.

Tragically, Noel never got the chance to develop the role of Chairman. On the first Sunday in October, while gardening at his home in Carrwood,

Hale Barns, he had a heart attack and died before getting to hospital. Three months later, on January 12th, his brother Will died, so, within the course of three months, the company lost the two people who had guided the business for over 50 years.

The last article Noel wrote for the company magazine, The Timpsonian (a quarterly publication originally edited by Noel's daughter Anne), was a tribute to 'our Mr Will' on his retirement as Chairman. In the article, he pointed out how Will made the major decisions that transformed the business from 24 shops to 260 shops, 155 repair factories and a factory making over 20,000 pairs a week.

'It was Will who moved the business out of working-class cobbled streets in Manchester suburbs to Liverpool, Sheffield, Nottingham and the North East', reported Noel. 'With a skeleton staff, Will ran the business throughout the First World War, whilst being on duty as a special constable in the evenings.

'After 1917, he had little guidance from his father William, whose active working life had come to an end, and his right-hand man and best friend, W F Chappell's health broke down in 1920, then, three years later, his only remaining senior executive, Tom Mursell, died so he was left to run the business with a band of men in their twenties. Will steered the company through deflation and unemployment in the early 1920s, while providing the capital to build the North Park factory and open an average of seven new shops a year.

'Without doubt, Will has been the most skilled judge of men's footwear fashions in this country over the last 50 years, able, without hesitation, to pick out the bestseller in any manufacturer's range.

'Most of all, Will has had a kindliness of heart that gave him an unerring judgement to do the right thing for people at the right time. His understanding of the other person's view made everybody love him.'

Noel concluded by saying, 'Today, William Timpson Limited is strong, respected and even envied because it is prosperous and as sound as a bell. This tribute to our President, W H F Timpson, is meant to assure him that the business, in whose service he has spent his whole working life, will continue to forge ahead and hold the priceless goodwill which has been built up over nearly a century of progress.'

Will was pretty much on his own until the company went public in 1929, with profits of £121k (the equivalent of £7m today). In the 1930s, Noel became an important part of the brothers' double act that increased profits to £207k (£12.8m at 2017 prices). After holding the profit level during the Second World War, profits surged to £598k (£20m today) in 1949, the year Noel stepped up to become Managing Director at the age of 53.

In retrospect, it is easy to see that Noel was taking on a difficult task. The substantial Timpson presence in Northern England and Scotland, which created such a strong and profitable business, now appeared to be a weakness, as the industrial north faced tough times. Property development changed too. Whereas Will grew the business by spotting suitable sites and buying businesses as he travelled around the country, most of Noel's new shops arrived in the post – new developments' plans with every retailer invited to take a punt by sticking a pin in the unit they preferred. High street retailers were starting to play a different game.

Timpson wasn't the only family building a chain of shoe shops. In the 20th century, there were over 75 shoe chains of 20 shops or more with familiar names like Stylo, Barratt, Shoefayre, Ravel, Tylers, Turners, Wyles and Bata. Some of these family businesses were older and bigger than Timpson. George Oliver opened his first shop in Willenhall in 1860, and, by 1889, had 100 branches, rising to 140 in 1914 when the family claimed to be the biggest shoe retailer in the world.

Stead and Simpson started as manufacturers. In 1875, when claiming to be the world's biggest shoemaker with 3,000 workers, they also had 45 retail shops, a figure that grew to 100 by 1889. In 1934, Stead & Simpson traded through 250 shops, which included 115 freeholds.

In addition to the value retailers (direct Timpson competitors), a number of branded manufacturers opened their own shops including

K Shoes, Lotus and Norvic. By the 1950s, Clarks owned Peter Lord and Bayne and Duckett, while there were a number of independent chains that specialised in selling branded footwear – John Farmer, Millwards, Clinkards and Clifford Turner.

The high street became very competitive. Lots of footwear multiples were looking for similar sites, with the right size and affordable rent. As a consequence, some towns had as many as six shoe shops trading next door to each other in a continuous row. There was some small but increasing competition from chain stores – Littlewoods, British Home Stores, Woolworths and, most important of all, Marks & Spencer. Off the high street, a significant 7% of the shoe market was claimed by mail order catalogues.

There were plenty of competitors but I have yet to mention the biggest threat of all. In 1953, Charles Clore bought Sears, a shoe company that started trading as Trueform in 1891 and purchased Freeman Hardy & Willis in 1929. Two years later, Clore bought the Fortress Shoe Company, owned by Harry Levison who ran a chain called Clerkenwell Footwear. Levison was the genius Clore needed to build his shoe business. Clerkenwell was changed to Curtess, catering for the value market, and Levison was also given control of Trueform and Freeman Hardy & Willis. In 1956, after Clore purchased Dolcis and Manfield, Sears' shoe subsidiary was renamed the British Shoe Corporation and got even stronger in 1962 when they bought Saxone and Lilley & Skinner.

While putting together a commanding group of shoe shops, Clore made an amazing series of property deals. He bought companies, which had valuable portfolios of freehold property on their balance sheets, at a substantial discount. While Timpson and other multiples grew by paying market rent in new precincts, Clore was grabbing lots of prime sites at a discount. Harry Levison targeted each chain at a different part of the market and assembled a strong team that used its buying power to provide better styling at keener prices. In 10 years, British Shoe Corporation went from zero to become the dominant market leader.

A few years ago, along with long-time shoe trade friend, Thomas Black, I played a game we called 'Shoe Shops'. The rules were simple; in turn, we had to name a UK shoe shop chain of more than 10 shops, which has been in business during the last 65 years – the game goes on for some time because there are over 70 on the list. No wonder Noel found it so difficult to increase Timpson profits in the 1950s.

CHAPTER SIXTEEN

NEW BOARD ACHIEVES RECORD PROFIT

NOEL'S SUDDEN DEATH CREATED an immediate problem. There was no succession plan. I was at home in the drawing room when my father received a phone call telling him the sad news. He sat for several minutes, his head in his hands, saying nothing. I imagine similar thoughts going through the mind of King George VI when he heard of his brother's abdication. My father would have been the bookies' favourite to succeed. He was the obvious choice as Chairman, being Will's eldest son, with nearly thirty years of experience in the business, the last fourteen of which as a director. However, he didn't expect the overall responsibility to fall on him so soon. He was never an ambitious man, but loved the business and felt it was his duty to follow in his father's footsteps and care for the employees. In many ways, his elder sister Ruth was better suited to the role – a tough character with a sharp brain who was guided through life by blunt common sense – but daughters seldom went into their family business, so Ruth never got the chance to play a part.

The other member of the family on the Board probably hoped to be seen as a better candidate; Geoffrey Noakes, my father's cousin. Geoffrey, who liked to be called Colonel Noakes, was full of self-confidence. His military training produced a belief in process in preference to flair and initiative. He had forged a strong political platform, based on his position as head of the fast-growing shoe repair business. In private, and occasionally in public, he questioned the value of a family business, suggesting it could be a barrier to developing more professional management.

Geoffrey and my father, Anthony, were complete opposites. My father understood the retail business and cared about both the company's history and long-serving colleagues who had created success. He didn't have a burning vision for the future, preferring to pursue more of the same. Some said he was too nice for his own good and would have benefitted by being a bit more ruthless and less sensitive.

The directors came to a compromise. Gordon Akester, the Company Secretary, was appointed Chairman, with my father as Deputy Chairman and Joint Managing Director with Geoffrey Noakes. It is difficult to see what else they could have done; it was a good short-term fix but didn't point to any long-term solution.

At seventeen, I wasn't aware that a significant power game had just begun. I had just left Oundle School, a year earlier than planned, because my father was keen for me to get experience as an accountant. I hated the job, and, after six weeks of sorting crumpled receipts and ticking off figures, I walked out of the mill that I was helping to audit in Miles Platting and turned up in my father's office to ask for a proper job.

I became an assistant at the Timpson shoe shop in Altrincham where I got three valuable training sessions every day. The basic training was delivered by my customers – each was a new challenge and the measure of success was my commission (we called them spiffs). I earned 6d for selling a pair of shoes at 59/11d, 1/- for top-grade Empiric leather Oxfords, 2/6d for a slow-moving clearing line and 6d for every pair of Indestructible Socks that retailed at an extravagant 6/9d – I said they were the perfect Christmas present – it worked pretty well! On every break,

I had an invaluable conversation with branch manager Bill Branson, while we drank tea in the musty shop cellar, only yards from trains on the Chester to Manchester railway line which shook the shop and interrupted our conversation. Bill made a big impression, so much so that I sought him out 42 years later when Alex and I went to the Sydney Olympics. Bill retired to Australia, where his daughter lived. We met for lunch; Bill was 97 and just as sharp as he had been 42 years earlier and survived long enough to celebrate his 100th birthday.

My third training session took place at home, nearly every evening when my father and I did the washing up. He washed and I dried (the dishwasher didn't arrive until 1965!) Every night, we talked business, a shop assistant talking to the Managing Director. I talked about lost sales due to stock shortages and my father tried to teach me about cash flow, profit and stock control. Fifty-eight years later, I had a similar discussion with my 20-year-old grandson, Bede.

On Christmas Eve, when I realised we were about to break the shop record, I telephoned my father to ask him to call at closing time and make a presentation to Bill Branston. Meanwhile, my proudest moment was when my grandfather came into the shop and, seeing that I was serving a customer, simply said, "I won't interrupt; you are making a sale and I'm sure you need the commission." It was only a month before he died; he is still my role model.

Will's death, following a heart attack in January 1961, caused the family a severe cash flow problem. He still owned over 25% of the equity, worth about £3m (£65m at 2019 prices) and this led to death duties of over £1m. The only way to raise the money was to sell shares and dilute the family shareholding to less than 55%. My father did what he could to place the shares in friendly hands, including a number of helpful buyers who were members of Hale Golf Club, but the company, with its valuable freehold portfolio, was certain to attract the attention of takeover specialists. For the next eleven years, my father received several approaches from Sir Isaac Wolfson of Great Universal Stores and Sir Charles Clore of Sears

Holdings who was rapidly building the British Shoe Corporation into the UK's dominant shoe retailer.

Gordon Akester provided stability at a tricky time. Tony Dutoy, the factory manager, joined the Board, as did non-executive director David Roberts, a property expert, who had been a fellow pupil with my father at Shrewsbury – giving him a welcome source of support. Due to ill health, Alan Timpson, who was already taking a back seat in his supporting role at Kettering, retired from the Board leaving my father and Geoffrey Noakes as the only family directors.

The newly formed Board seemed to be too busy to be bothered about company politics. My father continued to control the buying of men's and boys' shoes, with an increased programme of shop visits. As Deputy Chairman, he took on Will's ambassadorial role – employees saw him as the new family figurehead.

Graham Kennedy, the women's shoe-buying director, enjoyed a purple patch. Fashion was going through a dramatic change as toes became more pointed and heels got slimmer and much higher. Graham had the confidence to give Timpson more ladies' fashion than the company had ever seen before. His bold buying brought in loads of new, younger customers and shop managers were delighted to see the innovation which Graham proudly presented with panache at a series of fashion parades. With Tom Howell, an expert safe pair of hands, buying the children's shoes, what had been the weakest merchandise department became a growing strength.

Tony Dutoy was running the factory on full production, helped by a new closing factory at Corby and the successful Enduric, moulded men's shoes at 39/11d. North Park was the first shoe factory in Northamptonshire to introduce Work Study and invested in new machinery, including the recently designed Formulast Shoemaking System, a massive, powered conveyor belt (enclosed in a moisturising tube) imported from America. No one could claim North Park was being ignored.

Geoffrey Noakes also had plenty to keep him busy. FRD, his shoe repair business, was in overdrive. Forty-six new factories opened within two years, and, by 1963, there were 175 factories plus a further 60 repair units in retail shops. The new heel bars, introduced in Bolton, Aberdeen, Inverness and Hull, were particularly successful. This renewed the emphasis on a While-You-Wait service and the fashion for stiletto heels, more than compensating for a drop in men's shoe repairs due to the wide availability of low-priced men's shoes with a six-month guarantee.

FRD also benefitted from a new service – shoe-dyeing, using a spray method from the USA. To comply with Government fire precautions, the spraying took place in a specially constructed booth built near the back door or in a back yard. This new service was very popular, with sales rising to 10,000 pairs a week, which, at 12/9d (64p) a pair, made a big difference to the total turnover.

With every part of the business performing so well, Gordon Akester, in his first year as Chairman, reported a record profit of £967k – over £20m at 2017 prices – matching the profit in 1949.

CHAPTER SEVENTEEN

MOVE TO WYTHENSHAWE

1962 DIDN'T GO SO WELL. Like many retail chairmen, Gordon Akester blamed the weather in his annual report. 'The extremely cold weather that started in the spring continued to the end of May, then wet weather in July curtailed the sale of summer shoes. October, when we needed autumn rain, was too dry to encourage the sale of winter footwear and December fog delayed Christmas buying'. Profits fell by £134,166 to £833,021. Unsurprisingly, Timpson shares dropped well below the price friends had paid to support the family following Will's death – my father met some glum faces at the golf club.

However, despite their difficulties, the new Board continued to be busy. They opened 18 more shoe repair factories and 8 heel bars. Twenty existing factories were updated with more modern machinery, including Nu-Shade kit and the much-admired 'Autosoler', the latest machine to streamline a cobblers', imported from the USA.

Shoe shop development continued to concentrate on small shops in modest shopping centres in northern towns, but the team took a risk on two sites that became the company's most profitable shops over the next 25 years. Haymarket, Sheffield, was a prime corner site next to Woolworths and by the busiest market in the city. There were four other Timpson shops in the city – one close by which was due to close, the original Timpson shop on the corner of Pinstone Street and two other shops that Will Timpson never loved. He was particularly embarrassed about the shop on The Moor. I'm embarrassed too, because, 35 years later, I ignored his advice; "Never open a shop on the Moor" – I opened one and discovered how wise he was.

The other successful opening was in the newly built Merseyway Shopping Centre in Stockport. Despite having two shops in Princess Street (which both stayed open), the company showed unusual boldness by taking a unit on two floors in the prime position. Sales were so strong that the unit next door was added to create the company's top turnover branch.

This brave investment was a rare example of the Board being bold; they were normally nervous of paying big rents, particularly south of Birmingham. My father commented in the 1963 Annual Report: "The ever-rising costs of rents, rates and freehold premises in top trading positions make it increasingly difficult to sell enough pairs of shoes in the serving space to achieve the turnover to obtain a satisfactory profit". A year earlier, Sir Charles Clore had grabbed some of the best shoe shops in Britain when he acquired Saxone, Lilley & Skinner, with prime sites from Glasgow to Guildford and the biggest shoe shop in the world, Lilley & Skinner on Oxford Street, London, a few doors away from Selfridges.

During 1962 and 1963, life at Timpson was dominated by the move to a purpose-built office and distribution centre on Southmoor Road, Wythenshawe, in South Manchester, near to Manchester Airport and the proposed motorway network. (The M6 wasn't completed until 1971).

The move was overdue. From the 1890s, when a reserve warehouse was opened behind the Oldham Street shop to support the distribution centre, the company expanded its warehousing and administration into a number of buildings on Great Ducie Street, a mile north of Manchester's city centre. As the business grew, more space was acquired to provide separate storage for shoe repair materials, hosiery, shoe polish and other accessories. The patchwork of buildings housed the Architects' and Property Department, a Training Centre, Display design, the production of display materials, the Shoe Repair team and the transport fleet. The staff canteen was in the shadows of Strangeways prison.

None of these buildings was purpose built and, although the company spent a lot of money adapting them, they were not ideal. Empiric House, which was home to the retail shop offices and main shoe warehouse, was acquired in 1928. It had been built 60 years before as the Manchester and Salford Boys' and Girls' Refuge, for poor and destitute children, but was requisitioned as a hospital during the First World War. It was empty for eight years before becoming the Timpson HQ.

It made sense to put everything on one site, including the 'Office of the Secretary' that was still in Kettering. The preferred 9-acre site was owned by Manchester Corporation, which offered a 99-year lease and a lot of encouragement. Wythenshawe was a suburban development, started before the Second World War, housing 80,000 people, regarded as a showpiece and forerunner to the 'new towns' developed in the 1950s.

Timpson wasn't the only retail shoe chain building a new warehouse; British Shoe built a monster at Braunstone on the outskirts of Leicester close to the M1 – so big that supervisors used bicycles to travel inside the building. The Wythenshawe warehouse was nowhere near as big but was a trailblazer in the use of an automatic overhead runway, programmed to pick up and carry crates of footwear from the storage area to the loading bay and straight into the back of a lorry.

The office building, not fully occupied until mid-1963, had plenty of modern features but kept many old-fashioned values, with a uniformed Commandant, Sergeant Boles, guarding the reception and a masterclass of inequality between management and staff. There were four dining rooms – the general canteen, junior executives' room, senior executives' dining with waitress service and finally the directors' dining room where a free glass of sherry was available every day. There were separate senior executive lavatories and parking was strictly according to seniority. Most employees had to park near the garage which was a 500-yard walk from the office. On their way, employees would pass the 40 numbered executive parking bays, with numbers 1 and 2 occupied by my father and Geoffrey. The higher you climbed up the management chart, the nearer you parked to the office door. I never got into the top 40 until I was made a director and went straight into the charts at number 8.

Every detail had been sorted, but the new HQ didn't have a name. A 'name the warehouse' competition in the quarterly house magazine produced two winners who shared the £10 prize for proposing "Walkright House" (Walkright being the company's children's brand). When the office opened in 1964, Walkright was ignored and the building was called Timpson House.

The warehouse moved from Empiric House to Wythenshawe in December 1963 and the shops received no goods for 5 weeks. When I came home from University for Christmas (after a year working with the business, I went to Nottingham to study Industrial Economics), my father sent me to Kettering to help organise shop deliveries of the footwear leaving the production line. Helped by fellow trainees Jim Taylor and John Driver, I had great fun and learned a lot about the business. On Christmas Eve, with it starting to snow, I loaded my car with warm-lined boots and delivered them to shops on the way back home. My Great-grandfather would have approved.

The new warehouse was controlled by the Univac computer and some of the traditional parts of the business had to change, but this modernisation was all in a good cause. According to a Board report —

'It will be possible to entirely abolish writing out reports, sales receipts won't be necessary and it will be easy to search for stock in the warehouse because the computer will already know what is there. Above all, we will relieve our people of dull tasks, giving managers and shop staff more time for selling shoes and helping our team at Head Office to send the right goods to the right shops'.

Newly arrived computer manager, Bert Brownhill, and his programmers, Keith Hayes and Roy Normanton, explained they could perform lots of new tricks, but only worked with numbers. Shoe labelling had to change, the bestselling shoe could no longer be 9119B in black and 9119D in brown, nor could the policeman's boot be labelled 15E (as it had been for 50 years) – it became 111-111. To explain, 1 = men's department, 1 = boot, the third 1 = black with 111 being the style number).

A period of dual numbering caused confusion. It took two years to convert every box end label and longer to convince long-serving employees that things had improved.

Another problem was the shop numbers. The company still used the letters used by William Timpson for his first 26 shops, many of which were still trading. But the computer couldn't recognise 'A' shop, the original Oldham Street branch, or 'C' shop in Oxford Road and 'H' in Kettering. To keep up tradition, 'A' shop became 250, 'B' turned into 251, 'C' was 252. The old shops got a new identity, but everyone knew things would never be the same again.

CHAPTER EIGHTEEN

JOINT MANAGING DIRECTORS

GORDON AKESTER STAYED FOR two years before handing over to my father who, in 1963, became Chairman and Joint Managing Director, with Geoffrey Noakes as Vice Chairman and Joint Managing Director. Gordon Akester and Billy Mackenzie retired from the Board and were replaced by Arthur Fasham and Will Simmons. For many years, Arthur was responsible Stationery, Display, Advertising and Budget Control, which gave him the perfect opportunity to be involved in almost every part of the business. Arthur was an administrative Mr Fixit. He was with the business for 41 years and for the last 20, was the first person to ask if you needed to know facts about Timpson. An intense man who spoke quickly and was still biting his fingernails at the age of 65, Arthur was a supreme organiser, making sure every shop opening and the move to Wythenshawe ran smoothly. He was a man for detail, knowing the timings of every mainline railway journey – when travelling by train, there was no need to consult a timetable; just ask Arthur.

Bill Simmons replaced Billy Mackenzie, who started as a shop boy in Oxford Road 'C' shop and retired 53 years later as the Staff Director. It wasn't just the equivalent of what most organisations call HR, Billy also managed the area managers. Billy was only 5 foot 2 inches tall but everyone was terrified of him. Whenever a branch manager was promoted or fired, he (all the managers were men) had to be at Manchester at 10.00 am to get the news, face to face, from Billy. One unfortunate manager, who travelled from Birmingham, arrived very early and parked his car in Bay number 2. His interview with Billy went well; he was promoted to a bigger shop, but as he left to go home and celebrate, he found Geoffrey Noakes's big car was blocking him in. He had to wait at Timpson House until after 5 pm when Geoffrey went home.

Bill Simmons, a tough Scotsman with a wry sense of humour, started as a shop boy in Inverness, and, after various shop management roles in Scotland, was promoted to Area Manager. His son, Alan, joined the business in 1950 as a sales assistant in Princes Street, Edinburgh. After National Service, when Alan was a pilot, and two more years working in shops, he joined the Ladies' Buying Office, responsible for ladies' gloves. In 1959, after two years working in shoe factories, he joined my father's men's merchandise team buying slippers and sandals. When the reliable Leslie Hearn retired, Alan became responsible for buying men's shoes.

Despite all the new shops, the total number stayed at 260. Fifty outlets were knocked down by urban development schemes or relocated to a new precinct down the road. Several branches got a makeover, with elements of self-service. Most family shoe multiples were struggling to grow, apart from Stylo, who, against the odds, beat British Shoe in a takeover battle to buy Barratts and obtain a useful property portfolio.

Fairly abruptly, FRD, the 50's Cinderella, found sales starting to fall. The new heel bar business and the lucrative Nu-Shade service were still doing well but something was happening to traditional shoe repairs. The shoe repair industry relied on a simple formula; as long as you could produce a quality repair for no more than one-third of the price of a new shoe, you were in business. For years, everyone's day shoes had been made of leather and made in the UK. But shoemaking and buying habits were changing. The moulded sole shoes were bad news for cobblers, as was the increase in imports with prices well below British competition.

After a decade of enthusiastic investment, the FRD team needed a new way to stay profitable; their answer was to sell merchandise – shoe care products and hosiery had already proved successful. FRD started to sell slippers and cheap footwear, but with prices well below the cost of shoe repairs, the move probably did more harm than good.

Despite a poor start, with temperatures never above freezing point for the whole of January, February and March, 1963 was a good year for the shoe shops. The fashion for Winklepickers and Beatle boots attracted more young customers, and, with plenty of the right styles in stock, sales were buoyant. Graham Kennedy's aggressive approach to buying brought some spectacular successes. If he thought a style was a winner, he didn't bother with modest trial quantities; he bought big – sometimes ordering 20,000 pairs of a brand-new design – 6,000 black, 5,000 blue, 4,000 white, 4,000 beige and 1,000 pink for a bit of fun. It was like playing roulette and putting all your savings on a single number. Graham had a great fashion sense but attracted criticism from the Board for his high stock levels and big markdowns.

North Park hit problems in 1964 when, despite a full order book, they hardly made any money. Poor quality control was blamed for a high percentage of faulty footwear that was unsaleable at full price. The production problems were fixed but the factory faced another major problem. It was getting more difficult for the factory to match the foreign competition and the Timpson buyers found it tough to place enough orders to fill the factory.

Despite niggling worries about the future of shoe repairing, production problems at North Park and high stock levels, the company increased profits in 1963 and 1964, reaching a record £1,045k (in real terms, close to the record years in 1949 and 1961). The company celebrated success with confidence.

In 1964, the Lord Mayor and Lady Mayoress of Manchester were present at the opening of Timpson House. Later that year, Timpson had its first Royal visit when Prince Philip was escorted around the office and warehouse by my father and Geoffrey Noakes.

1965 was designated as the company centenary, being 100 years since William set up shop with his brother-in-law in Butler Street. To mark the Centenary, a special ashtray, with a cobbler centrepiece, was commissioned from Beswick Pottery (Gilbert Beswick was a family friend). Some snide shareholders suggested a higher dividend would have been more welcome, but surviving cobbler ashtrays now fetch £50 or more on e-Bay. It was rumoured that over 30 ashtrays had been received at Braunstone, the British Shoe Head Office, indicating that Sears were building up a stake in Timpson with a view, one day, to making a takeover bid.

Some said the Centenary should have been celebrated 5 years later, to mark the day William opened his own shop in Oldham Street, but perhaps it was a wise decision; things were going to be more difficult in 1969.

In the mid-60s, the Board decided to introduce a five-day week, with shoe shops closed on Sunday and Monday. At the time, most shops, other than in city centres, closed half a day during the week, either on Tuesday, Wednesday or Thursday. It made sense to shut on Mondays, cut costs and give staff a 'long weekend'. Several other retailers agreed, so, encouraged by their support, Timpson shops adopted a five-day week, with shoe repair units closed on Saturday and Sunday (few customers wanted repairs on a Saturday). Apart from the John Lewis Partnership whose provincial stores, including Jessops in Nottingham, Robert Sayle in Cambridge and Bainbridge in Newcastle, closed every Monday, very few other retailers followed suit and, after losing business in the bigger towns and cities, Timpson scrapped the idea and moved to a six-day week, with some shops keeping the half-day closing.

Unsurprisingly, the Timpson computer took time to fulfil its promise. It needed a room at a constant temperature – a line of cabinets with ever-moving discs that took all night to update the warehouse stock. Before long, Univac, the supplier, said we needed an update.

The computer was expected to do much more than controlling the warehouse. The dream was that, by magic, the shops would be better supplied and buyers could base orders on perfect sales' statistics. Automatic allocation of stock to shops became a reality in 1966, when two managers, in Urmston and Stockport, agreed to be guinea pigs and put the control of their stock in the hands of a machine. It went better than expected; the shops survived, although there was no evidence that the computer did a better job than real people.

Encouraged by the experiment, more shops were 'computerised' without a hiccup until it was discovered the computer could only cope with 50 shops. Once more, the computer was upgraded at a considerable cost.

People who know me may be surprised to hear that I got closely involved in developing our computer distribution system. With an interest in mathematics, I enjoyed using numbers to help the business. I had returned to the business in 1965 after completing my degree at Nottingham and spending six months on a graduate training scheme with Clarks in Street. After a few months, I joined the team that bought our ladies' shoes and I loved the job.

The Men's' Buying Department, developed by my father and grandfather, had plenty of talent, so I got involved in Ladies' Shoes, initially as little more than a clerk. It was a lucky move; I worked with Graham Kennedy, who generously taught me how to pick a range of fashion shoes. Graham, like many of his contemporaries, lived life in the fast lane. On my first nervous trip to an Italian Shoe Fair, he took me to a nightclub in Florence. At 1.30 am, I was dropped back at the Grand Hotel, so Graham could have a proper night out.

Graham taught me how to recognise the winning styles in Rome, Florence, Verona and Paris, so we could forecast what would sell at home next year. His genius was to copy these shoes for one fifth the price from factories in Lancashire.

Graham wasn't going to be at Timpson much longer, but he was around long enough to turn me into a half-decent ladies' shoe buyer.

CHAPTER NINETEEN

A COMPANY IN CRISIS

IN THE 1950S, 'MR WILL' wrote a half-yearly 'Chairman's Report' to the Board, a practice continued by my father. Both used the opportunity to highlight their concerns. In 1965 and 1966, my father was worried about the high level of ladies' stock and markdowns. In July 1967, he wrote, "During thirty years, I have never known our stock to be so much in excess of requirements, a real puzzle because we are dealing with simple arithmetic; we have an expensive computer, which, apparently, is quite useless. When we worked out the figures with pen and pencil, we never got into such difficulties." A month later, Graham Kennedy was dismissed for failing to keep to the buying budgets. My father's next Chairman's report said, "Mr Kennedy had a good fashion flair that brought many successful styles, but he didn't have good judgement on the pairage to buy, incurring losses on large purchases of doubtful sellers and poor-fitting footwear."

Graham Kennedy wasn't replaced; the existing ladies' shoe-buying assistants, including myself, worked together to fulfil the role – suddenly, I became a fashion buyer and was paid more than £1,000 a year (about

£20,000 in today's money). At the same time, a new Sales and Marketing Department was established under Geoffrey Noakes, giving him the chance to get directly involved in the retail shoe shops.

Kit Green, a 30-year-old with experience in the John Lewis Partnership, joined Timpson in the new role of Marketing Manager and started redesigning the corporate image. Geoffrey Noakes introduced a new sales incentive for shop assistants, giving them the chance to earn S&H (Sperry and Hutchison) Pink Stamps which could be exchanged for items from their catalogue. The new incentive was very popular – too popular. Pink stamps were offered so generously that some sales assistants acquired televisions, furniture and dishwashers. Timpson Head Office was losing touch with the shop floor.

Fortunately, Graham Kennedy (who quickly got a new buying job at Norvic) taught me enough about buying to keep our ladies' footwear business going, in partnership with talented long-serving colleague, Tom Hardman, my friend and mentor for the next 5 years. We developed successful teenage ranges and a value section called Penny Wise that sold the sort of volume Graham Kennedy had taught me to buy. However, I made an expensive mistake. I spotted the opportunity of selling shoes alongside matching clothing. After a successful trial in Market Street, Manchester, we developed a retail format called Shoetique. The concept was slightly ahead of its time and well beyond our skillset.

In 1967 and 1968, I was so wrapped up in getting married to Alex and getting to grips with the buying job that I didn't realise the rest of Timpson was going through turmoil. If I'd seen my father's 'Chairman's Report', I would have seen that there were plenty of problems.

The report, in February 1969, stated, "Kettering factory order book has been strong throughout the year with exports at 342,000 pairs, double last year, and we expected the profit would be satisfactory. It was, therefore, a staggering blow to learn, at a very late hour, that the Cost Accountant had falsified the figures and we produced a huge loss of £80,656." Six months later, things were even worse; "It was depressing enough to see such bad results last year, but to find that this loss was not only repeated but increased was an even bigger blow".

The loss at North Park came at a tricky time. Shoe repair profits were also well down, partly due to a long cold winter, but mainly because, with cheaper shoes in the shops, repair demand was falling.

Retail sales finished just ahead of last year, but profits were hit by high markdowns, a substantial cost of the Pink Points and Selective Employment Tax – a new tax on workers in the service sector (an extra £160,000 a year).

The costs of installing a new computer, introducing a marketing department and extra expenditure on training put up overheads and higher stock levels led to a bank interest increase from £109k to £142k. The half-year profit after tax fell from £322k to a meagre £7,917. The company got a bad press. 'W. Timpson shock – cuts interim 1%' said the Financial Times and the share price fell to 7 shillings (35p), well below the asset value of 12s 4d (62p).

The press release revealing these results also announced the resignation of Tony Dutoy (who stepped down as factory Manager to take on a marketing role) and the appointment of four new directors – Norman Redfern (Property), Bert Brownhill (Computer Manager), Alan Simmons (Men's Shoe Buyer) and myself. It was only at our first Board Meeting that we discovered the company was in crisis.

At the tender age of 26, I didn't realise how quickly I needed to grow into the job.

CHAPTER TWENTY

MANAGEMENT BY OBJECTIVES

IN THE SEARCH FOR A route to recovery, Geoffrey Noakes met Professor Roland Smith, Professor of Marketing at the Manchester Business School, a Manchester United supporter and non-executive director of several companies. Roland Smith ran a management course for 22 Timpson executives, who spent two days in the Grosvenor Hotel, Chester, learning about Management by Objectives. A few weeks later, Roland Smith spread the message to middle management over a weekend at Timpson House.

He preached the importance of setting financial targets that went right down to store level – total top-down management – if everyone believed in the plan and was committed to their individual target, the whole business would succeed.

Geoffrey was winning the political battle by undermining my father. The new approach, using Professor Smith's Management by Objectives, was painted as the modern approach to professional management, compared with the old fashioned and quaint caring family company style that was being pursued by my father.

A few months later, my father, without consulting me, gave in to the pressure for change and Geoffrey got the job he wanted. In early 1970, Roland Smith became a member of the Board, replacing David Roberts, and Geoffrey Noakes moved from Joint MD to be Managing Director, in charge of all day-to-day management. He organised the company into separate divisions with a comprehensive committee structure.

The struggling North Park factory, under its new manager Jeff Redding, bought Tite and Garfirth, the competitor that had been a partner during the war. He also bought a closing factory in Maltby, Yorkshire and the factory division was renamed Tite & Garfirth, with its own board of directors.

The shoe repair shops (which were renamed TSR – Timpson Shoe Repairs) had their own management committee, capably led by Michael Frank. The repair shops nearly got a new name. Geoffrey wasn't keen on Timpson; he felt the brand had lost its way and was keen to break free from the family connection.

Shoetique, my unwise venture, was seen by others as a bold way to bring the business up to date. So, Shoetique also got its own board, management committee and General Manager, H.G. Wyer, previously a Merchandise Controller on the retail side of Coats Patons.

To complete the management chart, Timpson Shoe Shops also needed a General Manager and Tim Perry got the job. Tim was a Cambridge graduate with a Masters Business degree from the Massachusetts Institute of Technology. Before joining Timpson, he had been a consultant, a regional manager with British Bakeries and, for just over a year, Managing Director of the Clarks shoe chain, Peter Lord.

My father's 'Chairman's Report' in February 1972 does little to hide his annoyance and frustration. He says, "I hope the forward plans will soon be finally formulated and the 1971 period of incessant meetings is now passed. Too many meetings tie down executives, take up valuable time and prevent the team from doing what is so essential – getting out and finding out". Later that year, he got even more heated about the recruitment of so many new executives; "Our Headquarters is reaching the position of having more bodies than jobs." Clearly, there were problems ahead.

The Annual General Meeting in April 1972 brought a poignant moment when a shareholder, Arthur Goulding, in proposing the reappointment of the auditors, started by saying, "I was pleased to see that another William Timpson has been christened (he referred to my son James). In many ways, that defines the company's success. For five generations, the family have been proud of the name William, proud of the company that bears that name and proud of the reputation the company bears, and they have every reason to be proud."

Geoffrey Noakes didn't take any notice; Management by Objectives was put into practice without the slightest hint of compromise. Everything was focused on the next financial year when top-down planning was going to transform the company's performance. Roland Smith encouraged Geoffrey to make some major strategic decisions that included both an acquisition and a disposal.

During 1971, each division producing a detailed budget that delivered the group corporate plan. Figures were produced in amazing detail – by week and by shop, with the total agreeing with the group budget. The theory was that if everybody met their weekly plan, the company would achieve its overall goal. Everyone was forbidden to use the old-fashioned comparison with last year; every figure had to be compared with their plan (which added up the total budget). It took weeks for area and branch managers to produce the detail, making sure individual plans added up to the company target. Everything was ready for the first week of 1972, a new financial year, but the team had a setback; most shops failed to reach the plan for week 1. Senior management spent the year talking about 'slippage' and wondering how to improve the planning process for 1973. However, helped by a good year for shoe retailers, a small profit at the factory and better results in the repair factories, the business was heading for a record year.

Following his appointment as sole Managing Director, Geoffrey Noakes led from the front and hired a public relations company, Pace PR, to get his message across. They made much of his military background at the Army Staff College in Quetta, India, during the Second World War, when he helped guide 1,000 elephants over a mountain range. 'The Colonel Steps up the Profit Pace' was the Manchester Evening News headline when the 1970 results showed an increase in profit from the disastrous £603k in 1969 to £1.08m.

A Guardian profile piece had the headline 'Timpson Responds to Military Rule'. It said, 'in June 1970, the company appointed Geoffrey Noakes Managing Director and, for the first time, the company has shown signs of life. The redoubtable Professor Roland Smith was drafted onto the Board and his thinking, combined with Mr Noakes' leadership have set a pattern for the future. The first thing to emerge is a "group concept" which management talk about as eagerly as converts to a new religion'. The Guardian journalist had clearly been given some frank views; 'the geographical spread of shops is bizarre. It covers all except the most prosperous part of the country – London and the South East. "We've just got eight shops that ring London", joked Noakes cheerfully.'

Pace PR had a positive story to tell when interim profits in 1971 rose 52% to £333k, therefore, like the rest of the shoe trade, Timpson was heading for a record year, helped by lower purchase tax and a 50% reduction in Selective Employment Tax. Geoffrey Noakes' campaign changed city opinion of Timpson. An Observer journalist tipped Timpson in his 'Go Go Portfolio' and said, "Thanks go to Geoffrey Noakes, who has pulled off a remarkable transformation in Timpson fortunes during the last year".

CHAPTER TWENTY-ONE

NORVIC ACQUISITION

DURING 1971, THE PROFIT IMPROVEMENT and positive press pushed the Timpson share price to 98p, more than three times where it was in 1969. But the City was disappointed with the year-end results announced early in 1972. Although profits were a record, up 9.7% at £1,251m, the second half was worse than 1970. Despite the new 'Group Concept' and 'Management by Objectives', little had changed.

While all the restructuring went on, I kept my head down and thoroughly enjoyed the ladies' shoe buying role. It was an exciting part of a new phase of my life, the first four years of my marriage to Alex and the birth of our eldest children, Victoria and James. I was left out of a lot of Geoffrey Noakes' plans and escaped membership of his new committees but the new mood couldn't be ignored, especially when his marketing policies dictated how my buying should be done.

Fashion buying is a glamorous job, but you are constantly open to criticism for buying shoes that don't sell or not buying enough of those that sell quickly. You need a thick skin to have the confidence to buy next season's range, despite any carping from colleagues. But Geoffrey's marketing plan was making life difficult by splitting Timpson shops into two segments – blue and red – with red shops getting sharper fashion and higher prices. It wasn't easy to find higher-priced shoes that would sell in our shops, but the big mistake was taking the successful Penny-Wise range out of the red segment group. Our best sellers were being excluded from the top turnover branches.

I was so convinced that the marketing plan was madness that I paid several early visits to Geoffrey's office to catch him before the start of his meeting schedule and plead for common sense. One day, I was in for a shock. There was a new rug on his office floor, a tiger skin with its teeth roaring at you as you entered – this tiger was to become Geoffrey's trademark as he issued comments and orders from 'The Tiger's Den'. Thankfully, I got Geoffrey to agree to my marketing thoughts but I never felt close to winning the bigger argument.

One worry, raised at these early morning meetings, was regarding Shoetique, my new flawed concept, which had become a separate Division with its corporate plan. Despite mounting losses, Geoffrey included Shoetique in his press interviews and City journalists quoted it as a cause for optimism. This positive publicity encouraged Geoffrey to press on with the project under a new General Manager (Timpson Area Manager, David Wood, who had no fashion experience).

There were more senior management appointments – Bob Kirkman joined from Jute Industries to become Group Financial Director, Geoff Galgut was appointed Group Personnel Controller Designate (prior to the retirement of Bill Simmons) and Rut Moors, with area management experience at Bata and the British Shoe Corporation, became General Manager of Timpson Shops, replacing Tim Perry, who found it difficult to adapt to the Timpson culture. However, if the company was to be transformed, Roland Smith advised Geoffrey Noakes, the Group needed a growth strategy that took the company upmarket and further South.

By the middle of March, the shares had fallen to 75p. So, when Geoffrey Noakes found his acquisition target, he bought the 141 shop Norvic Retail Division for £2.9m. The deal was described in the company press release as 'a further step in our plans to gain a bigger share of the market', but it also took Timpson into some uncharted territory.

Norvic had its roots in Norwich. It was the brand name of shoe manufacturers Howlett and White, who acquired their first retail shops in London in 1927. Norvic became a major women's shoe brand, selling to independent retailers throughout the UK but also with its own chain; most outlets were called Norvic, although some kept the original names of well-known local retailers after they had been acquired. That is how Charles of Exeter and Baber of Harrogate became part of Timpson.

Timpson increased its share of the footwear market and extended its geographical coverage but Norvic catered for a very different market. To be blunt, Timpson acquired an old-fashioned branded retailer that catered for older women. Alan Simmons, who was given the special responsibility to Geoffrey Noakes for the development of Norvic, quickly identified, "By acquiring Norvic, we have secured a sizable chain of shops trading in a market segment which is distinct and different from Timpson".

I visited Norwich to meet their buyer, Les Cass, and work out how the two buying jobs could be combined and it quickly became clear there was a huge gap between the two chains. I was grateful not to be on the Norvic Management Committee. The only person who really understood their business was the long-serving Norvic Retail Director, Eric Cattle, who fortunately joined Timpson as Norvic General Manager heading up the new division within Timpson.

In his editorial comment to the 'Timpsonian' house magazine, under the title 'from the Tiger's Den', Geoffrey forecast that by 1974, Norvic would be making a profit of £450,000 before extra bank interest of £210,000. The objective was to increase Norvic turnover from £3m to £4.6m by 1975, but it was a tough task. I suspect neither Roland Smith nor Geoffrey Noakes knew how they were going to integrate the Norvic shops into Timpson. Yet, the deal was well received by the City when Geoffrey claimed the Group was in a phase of controlled expansion.

CHAPTER TWENTY-TWO

FACTORY CLOSURES

DURING THIS HYPERACTIVE PERIOD of restructuring, manage-ment committees and forward plans, the shoe repair team, who liked to be called TSR (Timpson Shoe Repairs), quietly got on with doing a very good job. Geoffrey made an excellent choice in Mike Frank as the General Manager of TSR. Mike, who had a distant connection to the Timpson family, joined the company as a management trainee. He got to know the shoe repair trade by working on the shop floor and became an area inspector, responsible for up to 20 branches, before joining the Head Office team as a personnel manager before taking control of the day-to-day business, leaving Geoffrey free to spend most of his time changing the shoe shops.

Mike had a hint of the military in his past so the latest management style was easy to accept, but he did the Management by Objectives with a bold hint of independence and a cheeky sense of humour. He had a constant stream of correspondence with branch managers who quite often received a small picture under Mike's signature. His hangman sketch meant 'if you don't get it right next time, it's a final warning', and if he received a letter including comments with which he disagreed, he would simply draw three circles and send it back; the circles meant "Balls!".

After many years of untroubled progress, the shoe repair trade had a terrible time in the late 1960s. Cheap imports, new hardwearing sole materials and the decline of stiletto heel fashion halved the total shoe repair market. In the 1950s, most sizeable towns would have 20 or more cobblers, all making a living. In addition, there were several shoe repair chains, similar to Timpson. Some were part of shoe retailers, including Saxone and Stead & Simpson, while others were specialist shoe repairers like Broughall's based in Luton, Shoecare in Kent, Heelamat in London and Lillywhites in Yorkshire. The biggest chain, Combes, was bought by Ireland-based Allied Leather, who went on to acquire several other substantial chains including Shoecraft, Malones and Paynes.

When the demand for shoe repairs suddenly fell, shoe repairers had to do something else to survive. Most introduced leather goods, hosiery and shopping baskets, which, despite the low margin, produced some helpful profit and extra customers. Timpson shops had a healthy hosiery business which was an ideal addition to TSR. TSR was soon selling much more hosiery than shoe repairs but at a very low margin. Shoe repair demand continued to fall and the merchandise wasn't enough to save several shoe repair outlets. Between 1968 and 1972, 35 struggling Timpson repair shops were closed.

For Mike Frank and his team, the big answer to the shoe repair decline was found in Holland, where a new generation of shoe machinery put all the stitchers, scourers and trimmers into a single line of kit that fitted into a shop behind the counter. This meant that the operatives, who previously had been in a back room, a cellar or upstairs, could work in the shop and also serve customers. There was less need to employ counter girls, so wage costs went down. Customers liked to see the job was being done on the premises so turnover increased wherever the machinery was moved into the shop.

The other change with a lasting impact took place in 1969, when we introduced key-cutting. It took time to be accepted; cobblers weren't keen on cutting keys. But keys came to Timpson at the perfect time, not just because the business desperately needed a new source of turnover, but it was also when ironmongers, the traditional place where keys were cut, started disappearing from the high street.

Gradually, TSR got the message; to survive, cobblers needed to do something else. A year later, a few shops started to offer engraving and Mike Frank had made the first moves in developing a multi-service retailer.

Two years after the profits collapse at North Park in 1969, my father's Report to the Board in February 1971 was still complaining about problems in Kettering; 'For the third year running, we have had a bad result from Tite & Garfirth Ltd. And it would seem there is no end to the number of dead rats dug up that should have been got rid of in the past.' A year later, he was more optimistic, recording a return to profitability and a full order book, but regrettably stated that money tied up in manufacturing should be put to better use.

On July 31st 1972, the closure of North Park was announced. It made the national headlines. The Guardian reported, 'A group of shoe workers, who have increased their productivity by almost 90% over the past three years, were told yesterday that they are to be made redundant. About 650 employees will be affected by the closure of Tite & Garfirth, which was reorganised in 1969, and since then, according to a company statement, has "fought for survival with every means at its command".

'The workforce was trimmed from 1,000 to 650 and output increased from 18,000 to 22,000 pairs a week, however, the company announced yesterday, "Forward projections show that footwear manufacturing will continue to be a big risk area of operation which will, at best, produce only minimal returns on a very large capital investment. We have, therefore, with very real regret, taken our decision. The factory closure is to be phased over five months with the eventual shut down at the end of December".

Unsurprisingly, the news didn't go down well, particularly in Kettering. Bert Comerford, president of NUFLAT, the footwear workers' union, called for a rethink, saying, "This is the biggest blow that the Kettering footwear industry has ever had. I wonder if the Timpson Board gave sufficient thought to the social consequences of closure and the hardship caused to people out of work". £150,000 in redundancy payments and £50,000 in ex-gratis awards did little to dampen the genuine anger in a town that had trusted Timpson as its main employer for nearly 50 years.

It was a big building which dominated part of the town, a factory of which three Timpson generations – William, Will and my father – had been immensely proud. It was the building where my parents met so I, too, had an emotional link. But it wasn't the building that brought my father so much sadness; it was the employees who lost their jobs. He had worked there for three years and walked around almost every month for the last thirty, so he knew the operatives; they were his friends.

The forecast was correct; shoe manufacturing faced a dire future due to foreign competition. North Park would not have survived, but it was tough to take, a decision made harder because we were a family business.

All options to sell the factory as a going concern had been exhausted before the closure announcement was made, so, by Christmas 1972, the building was empty. It was acquired two years later by the British Shoe Corporation subsidiary, Burlington, but they too closed down a few years later and the building, lovingly planned by Tom Mursell and opened in 1923, was demolished to make way for housing.

The closure was announced at the same time as the interim results, which showed a 20% increase in pre-tax profit to £400,000, figures that were well received by the City and the share price went up by 5p.

CHAPTER TWENTY-THREE

FEUDING COUSINS

THE 'CHAIRMAN'S REPORTS' MUST have given the directors a strong hint that my father did not see eye to eye with his cousin Geoffrey. The report in August 1970 included the following passage:

> "During June, we launched a new concept for the Company. This meant a tremendous amount of planning in the team dressing room but, at the present time, there is not enough action on the field of play to score any runs. I look forward with confidence to progress as innovations are introduced but we mustn't go too far too fast; it would be fatal to have change for change's sake. We need statistical controls and targets but every man on this Board should give the priority to our product. We must be careful not to abandon all our inherited characteristics and jettison everything typically Timpson."

In his next report, my father was concerned about the appointment of several new executives and the effect they were having on the Company culture.

> "During the autumn, we completed the appointments in accordance with the new structure. I welcome the new blood, but we must ensure

we are receiving the right injection. I sincerely hope that we shall maintain the Timpson spirit for the good not only of ourselves but also the good of the business itself, a business that is the envy of many."

These remarks, and many more, demonstrated a big difference of opinion, but the breakdown of the relationship went much deeper than a difference of opinion about the drive for Management by Objectives.

In 1971, Geoffrey wrote to my father, "I don't understand some of the sales variances in your visit reports; is this because you are comparing against last year, whereas the party line is that we all use Budget as our measurement, whether it be Plan Sales, Margins, Expenses or anything else, otherwise we shall not attain the budget profit? In your notes on the Birmingham area, did you not say that 107 Aston is £2,500 up whereas they are actually only £142 up on plan?

It is important for me to make this point so that we, when visiting branches, all speak the same language with the same emphasis.

I will put this note in my file for discussion at our next meeting because the principle is of prime importance to our profit aim and will become more so as we develop the Group Corporate Plan."

My father replied:

"I have your letter and again I wonder whether you realise how rude some of your letters read.

I'm not a recalcitrant person. When I call at a shop, I ALWAYS check the planned figures, but also check the progress a shop is making in each department, which is only available against last year.

I would draw your attention to the fact that all our computer reports are based on comparing this year with last year, as are our Company Accounts, which measure our progress in the eyes of the world."

It was hardly surprising that they disagreed; they were opposites in every way – in character, values, attitude and style. Neither suited each other.

My father tried to maintain traditional family values but Geoffrey was tough enough to make life difficult for his cousin. In a poorly disguised political move, Geoffrey wrote his job description for the future Timpson Non-Executive Chairman, making sure my father didn't qualify.

The job definition stated:

1. Time and energy to do the job.
2. Contact with the outside world through other directorships and appointments including leadership.
3. Able to give imaginative, persuasive and forward-looking advice over the whole range of the Group's existing and potential activities.
4. Knowledgeable in management and financial techniques – willing and able to keep up to date.
5. Capable and willing to travel and play a full part in acquisitions, financial evaluations, strategy and hard bargaining.
6. Able to stand back from day-to-day execution and present a detached viewpoint.

The definition was perfectly suited to Professor Roland Smith but certainly didn't describe my father.

On Friday 8th September, Geoffrey Noakes hosted a meeting at his family home on The Avenue, in the leafy suburb of Hale, about 4 miles from the office. The meeting was attended by all the directors apart from my father and myself. The minutes of that meeting record that they unanimously resolved 'to secure a meeting with Mr W A Timpson with a view to proposing that he should retire as Chairman and Director of William Timpson Limited in the near future and that his service agreement be terminated at the Board Meeting on September 14th, and that he might become President of, or consultant to, the company.

On September 14th, the Board calmly discussed current issues in the traditional Board Room on a corner of Timpson House overlooking the executives' car parking bays. Portraits of my grandfather and great-grandfather watched over the 9 directors as they went through the expected agenda.

My father seemed more confident than usual, probably relieved that the traumatic North Park closure was now history. Geoffrey was strangely quiet, Roland Smith said nothing, and new director, Bob Kirkman presented the accounts with Scottish clarity. Bill Simmons had little to say about personnel but his son Alan gave a long update on the Norvic acquisition, Bert Brownhill confirmed that our new computer was doing well and Norman Redfern spread some site plans on the table to get approval for three new shops. I was in a good mood; the autumn shoes were selling well, I was building a strong range for next spring and stock levels were below budget. Perhaps I spoke a bit too much, but, in retrospect, I was more relaxed than anyone else round the table.

After the meeting, we sat round a small table in the directors' dining room drinking sherry while a waitress took our lunch order. Roland Smith leant across to my father to whisper a quiet remark, but I didn't take much notice.

Over lunch, discussions ranged from the high rate of inflation to Manchester City's poor start to the season. After the meal, instead of returning to the armchairs for coffee, my father, the Professor and Geoffrey disappeared, leaving me with the other directors, who peeled off much earlier than usual. Bob Kirkman, the last to leave, asked me to pop into his office.

As soon as I went through his office door, I knew this wasn't a casual encounter. Bob Kirkman was sitting alongside Bill Simmons and Bert Brownhill. They got straight to the point; "While we are meeting you," said Bob, "Geoffrey and Roland Smith are asking your father to step down as Chairman." They explained this would be a great move for the business and suggested my father would be happy to become the President. I didn't hear much more; I was just stunned and my mind was racing; I didn't really trust my fellow directors and that lack of faith had been confirmed.

I didn't wait for a discussion, I went straight upstairs to see my father, but the sign on his door showed engaged. I went back to the directors' dining room, poured another sherry and sat in deep contemplation.

Half an hour later, I was with my father and Teresa Dutton, his secretary for the past 15 years. I have never seen him more determined. He had made it crystal clear to Geoffrey and Roland Smith that he had no intention of retiring. In turn, they clarified that he had two weeks to make up his mind, otherwise he would be forced to go.

The Changing Face of Timpson Shoe Shops

1930s

1940s

1950s

1960s

1970s

1980s

Diversification

Early key cutting display 1975

The big key board – Leicester 1985

Merchandise 1970

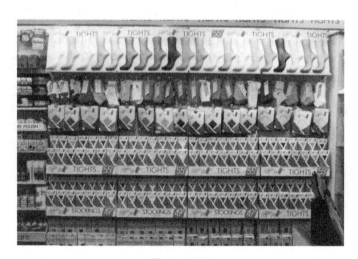

Hosiery 1982

Stunningly successful new service until health problems were revealed

The shoe repair machinery introduced in the 1960s is unchanged today

Early display of key blanks—1976

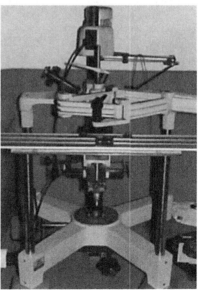

First computer engraver - 1988

The pantograph engraver—1971

Timpson Shoe Repairs in the 1960s—the shoes were repaired behind the scenes and customers were served by 'Counter Girls'.

CHAPTER TWENTY-FOUR

BOARD BUST-UP

I SAW MY PARENTS ON the way home and, as I expected, they were in a state of shock, sat together next to the fire, mostly in silence, occasionally sighing, before telling me how they felt about the rest of the Board. Then we started talking about what would happen next. We had a few options – hand control to Geoffrey Noakes, put the decision to a shareholders' general meeting, or find a buyer who would bid for the company. I left for home knowing my father was determined to make sure Geoffrey didn't win.

Alex was serving supper to our small children, Victoria and James. In a quiet moment, I told her the story of my day. It didn't take Alex long to take it all in. She had a sharp political instinct and was already worried about Geoffrey. "You're going to be very busy," she told me, "and you'd better start straight away." On Alex's suggestion, I went to see Geoffrey at his home that night. After a superficially warm greeting, Geoffrey showed me into his library, where he poured a drink, which gave me the determination Alex expected.

I told Geoffrey he would ruin the business by splitting the shareholders in two. I told him that there was no way the family would support a Board that turned against my father.

He listened quietly and promised to see me in the office, but the next morning, he made it clear there was no going back on the decision. I suspect that Geoffrey thought there was very little chance that my father would stand in his way and, in any event, Geoffrey had enough self-confidence to think he would be the one who would get the family's support.

That day, my father sent all the directors a memo; 'You are a party to the resolution that I should relinquish my position as Chairman. The manner in which this action has been presented to me by Professor Smith, Mr G W Noakes and Mr W H Simmons is a direct insult to someone who has loyally served the Company for 43 years. As I suspect you are unaware of the terms suggested to me, will you please see me in my office when I call you this afternoon, so I can tell you the full facts.' Those that turned up never looked my father in the eye.

That early morning meeting was the last real conversation I ever had with Geoffrey Noakes. I continued with my buying job and, on occasions, appeared in the directors' dining room, but I was a stranger, alienated by the rest of the Board. I knew, from the support coming from most colleagues, that Roland Smith had got it wrong; Geoffrey's PR campaign didn't win round most Timpson employees. My father had already been asked to step down, so there seemed little doubt that I, too, would be asked to go.

I spent the weekend doing what Dads do – went shopping, a walk in the woods and played golf. It gave me time to think and I thought of my father wondering what to do next. I expected he would accept the inevitable consequences of being outplayed in the power game – but he surprised me. While I was back in the office on Monday morning, my father was finding some new advisers.

For the first time in my life, I studied the list of shareholders. The family held 52% which, I assumed, meant control, but I now know you need 100% to control everything.

I am descended from a great-grandfather who had 12 children. In 2006, I held a party for all those of his relatives I could find and over 140 turned up. By the fourth generation, family company shares are held by so many relatives that many might pass in the street without recognising each other.

My father got out of bed on Monday morning with a new spring in his step. By lunchtime, he had found his lawyer, Clayton Flint of Addleshaw Sons and Latham, who had the connections to put our family shares on the market, but the initial aim was to win the argument at an emergency Board Meeting. The meeting was called for the end of the week with a simple but sinister agenda:

1. Minutes of the last meeting
2. Matters arising
3. W.A. Timpson
4. Any other business.

My father spent the week preparing for the Board Meeting. Clayton Flint called in Mike Keeling from the London & Yorkshire Trust to discuss the options. The Board could sack my father as Chairman, but they couldn't remove him as a director; that had to be done by shareholders at a General Meeting, but it didn't seem sensible for the bust-up to be settled in public. The choice was between letting Geoffrey take control or selling enough shares to trigger a takeover bid.

The meeting was scheduled for 10.30 am on Friday 22nd September. I nervously visited the senior executives' lavatory next door to the Board Room where Geoffrey was having a pee. We stood in silence; he stared at the ceiling and I did the same.

My father was already sat at the top of the table, so I sat at the other end and waited for the rest to arrive. They came in together looking uneasy.

My father opened the meeting with his prepared remarks; 'I have in front of me the written suggestion presented to me on the 14th of September, which is signed by you all apart from John Timpson.

Before we can carry out any formal Board business, this matter must be cleared and I have the following points to make:

1. I regard your action as hurtful in the extreme.
2. I do NOT accept your suggestion.
3. If you remove me from the Chair, the protective umbrella of the Timpson family shareholding will be withdrawn and my interest will be to realise my shares at the best price possible, which means a bid. If you cancel my agreement, I will sue for the maximum compensation. You are not entitled to fire me off the Board, so I will remain as a director until I've sold my shares.
4. Now that you have taken this action, a continuation of the present position is impossible. The alternative is that Geoffrey Noakes and Professor Roland Smith leave the Board at once and the Timpson family continue the policy of providing an umbrella by means of our shareholding.

   I think you should understand that I am fully confident at least 30% of the ordinary shareholders will support me. The implications are obvious to any reasonable person and the effect is so profound that I do not think you should be called upon to make a decision now. I suggest that we adjourn and meet again on Monday at whatever time you may wish.'

I seconded the adjournment proposition, fully supporting my father's statement regarding the family shareholdings, but the proposal was lost by 7 votes to 2. It was proposed that 'W A Timpson do cease forthwith to hold the office of Chairman and after the amendment 'that G W Noakes ceases to be Vice Chairman and Managing Director' was defeated by 7 votes to 2, then my father was ousted by the same margin.

It was a dramatic but expected result. The room was full of embarrassed tension as my father stood to make a final statement before he left the Chair. The Board Minute says, 'W A Timpson addressed detailed personal and abusive comments to certain members of the Board and restated the possible effect that the sale of the family shareholding would have on the future control of the company.'

He told Roland Smith that it was a lesson for his students on how not to fire a Chairman. Then he went on to remind Bill Simmons that he had only recently tearfully talked about his pride in working for the company.

After reminding another director about an embarrassing incident when my father came to his rescue, he addressed his final remarks to Geoffrey Noakes, saying, "he may be an able businessman but has been impossible to work with. My predecessor, Allan Booth, told me, 'Look out for Geoffrey Noakes; he doesn't care who he tramples on. His own brother John warned, 'He is out for all he can get, he is all out for power'. My father finished by saying, 'Look at the portrait behind me (Mr Will) who bailed you out of your first venture into shareholding! And yet you have a mania to get rid of the Timpson name, not realizing it is our name on the shops that has created our success.' At this point, he moved away from the head of the table and challenged Geoffrey to take his place saying, 'You are not fit to take the Chair I now vacate.' At this point, Geoffrey took the chair and the final details of my father's sacking were recorded in the minutes – but they don't report that I followed my father out of the Board Room and, somewhat childishly, slammed the Board Room door.

Within half an hour, my father received a letter terminating his contract which concluded, 'you are required, within 7 days, to vacate your office at the company premises, to hand over all papers pertinent to your responsibility as Chairman, and the company car used by you. Although you are technically able to remain as a director until our next Shareholders' meeting, you are to take no part in the running of the company and may only enter one of the Company's shops as a customer.'

The company was never going to be the same again.

CHAPTER TWENTY-FIVE

BID BATTLE

THREE DAYS AFTER MY FATHER WAS FIRED, I joined him in Manchester for a meeting with Clayton Flint to talk about the next move. We decided to contact those family members and close friends who we thought would wish to support my father and sell their shareholding. We discussed a shortlist of three possible bidders, Great Universal Stores (GUS), United Drapery Stores (UDS) and Sears (owners of the British Shoe Corporation). GUS already had two shoe chains – Greenlees and Easiphit – British Shoe had many more including Saxone, Dolcis, Trueform, Manfield, Freeman Hardy & Willis and Curtess. UDS only had John Farmer, a specialist branded shoes multiple, which had just been bought from the Farmer family earlier in 1972. We decided to target UDS, being the one group that was likely to preserve the Timpson identity and protect the future of employees.

News of the board room bust-up appeared in the press two days later. The Financial Times ran the headline 'Chairman quits after Timpson clash' and the Manchester Evening News used 'Boardroom split at Timpson?' The article said that Timpson branch managers received a statement to the effect that Mr Timpson has not only ceased to be Chairman but also ceased to be an employee.

My father received a mountain of letters, mainly from branch managers, all with the same message; 'We were shocked to hear the news, we never thought this sort of thing could happen, we will miss working for a family business.' When my father returned his company car (a Bristol), everyone at Timpson House saw that the curt memo announcing his dismissal had turned into reality. I didn't see that car again until 40 years later when my son, James, tracked it down to the current owner and brought the Bristol back into the family.

On the day my father was officially dismissed, Bernard Lyons, the Chairman of UDS plc, agreed provisional terms to buy our shareholding for £1 a share, which compared with a price of 65p before he made his bid. My father went to London on Monday 2nd October to finalise the details with UDS, and, during the next 24 hours, contacted the key family shareholders. Some signed Powers of Attorney but most, including my father's step-mother, Lillian, his sisters, Ruth and Hester and his brother David, his cousin Kathleen Ollerenshawe and Noel's widow Millie, gathered at 6.30 pm the following evening in the drawing room of Cranoe, my parent's home in Hale-Barns. After an hour's discussion, everyone signed a Power of Attorney, giving my father the right to speak for 3.737 million ordinary shares – 25% of the equity.

At 8.00 am the following morning, in Manchester, the agreement was signed and at 9.00 am, it was announced to the Stock Exchange. A few minutes later, Bernard Lyons arrived unannounced at Timpson House to hand his written offer to Geoffrey Noakes. The directors decided the bid of 100p a share (£17m) was totally inadequate, pointing out, as in all future letters to shareholders, that 'Mr W A Timpson and Mr W J A Timpson, having entered into an agreement with United Drapery Stores, have taken no part in the drafting of this announcement.' The share price rose to 110p.

The Times, along with other newspapers, expected another bidder with most tipping Sears as the most likely. Within a week, after Geoffrey Noakes confirmed that 'Other approaches had been received', the share price rose to 133p. It went even higher after Geoffrey Noakes launched a press campaign including a profile piece in The Guardian, which hinted profits could increase to £1.6m and suggested both Sears and GUS were waiting in the wings. Five days later, the shares were 141p. At this point, UDS increased its bid to 150p (26m) and got the backing of the Timpson directors. Within hours, Sears made an offer of 160p (27.6m) but the Timpson board still stuck with UDS due to concerns that the Sears bid would fall foul of the Monopolies Commission.

The Geoffrey Noakes media campaign included a special edition of 'Timpsonian', the company newsletter – a double-sided broadsheet describing Geoffrey's recent run of success – record profits, the Norvic acquisition, 500 shops nationwide and a corporate plan for continued success. The front page showed a confident Geoffrey Noakes standing on his tiger's rug, promoting his tiger attitude 'leading a sharp team of young executives who have developed a very sharp marketing programme'. This was a plea for support from within the company, but, for many colleagues, ousting my father had undermined Geoffrey's reservoir of respect. However, this bid to win the hearts and minds of Timpson employees was irrelevant, as the only battle was about who would buy the company.

Sears claimed they had nowhere near a monopoly, quoting an Economic Intelligence Unit survey that gave them 13.6% of the number of shoe shops, 15.8% by volume and 19.8% by sales. UDS countered by arguing Sears had 53% of the specialist shoe market. Undaunted, Sears lifted their bid to 175p (£30.4m) and promised they would reopen the North Park factory. The Timpson Board withdrew support from UDS and met the Sears Board who promised no changes would be made in the way the business would be run without approval from Timpson directors, who would be invited to join the British Shoe Board.

This put our family shareholding group in a tricky position. If a Monopolies reference dragged on into February, there was a technical risk that our deal with UDS could revert back to the original price of 100p. We were also desperately keen to prevent BSC from acquiring Timpson, closing down Wythenshawe and absorbing our shops into the

Braunstone culture. For peace of mind, we did a new deal with UDS, agreeing to irrevocably buy the shares from UDS for 150p, come what may. This was a significant tactical move for UDS that put Sears at a distinct disadvantage. But the shares still kept climbing, with Sears acquiring 15% in the market; at one point, the price reached 175p.

Although the Timpson directors no longer backed UDS's bid, they didn't change sides; instead, they sat on the fence and waited until the Department for Trade and Industry made a statement. The bid became a major talking point in the financial press and even during a debate in the House of Commons. The arguments got particularly heated after Peter Walker, Secretary of State for Trade and Industry, announced that the Sears bid would be referred but the one from UDS could proceed. This was the first time only one contested bid was singled out for examination.

Within days, the battle was over. Bernard Lyons was jubilant, whereas Charles Clore and his team at British Shoe felt unfairly treated. Geoffrey Noakes mentioned meaningful talks with another bidder; there was a rumour that Charles Clore was planning to finance Isaac Wolfson to bid, through GUS, on his behalf but no new offer appeared.

As soon as the Sears bid was referred to the Monopolies Commission, it was withdrawn. Sears argued that a 5-month enquiry would create too much uncertainty for both Timpson and Sears. It would put other Sears' plans on hold and put the Timpson business in limbo.

Despite further last-minute hopes that GUS would enter the bidding, helped by Geoffrey Noakes saying a further approach had been received on December 11th, the Timpson directors accepted the UDS bid for a second time, and, a week before Christmas, it went unconditional.

On January 11th 1973, my father wrote a letter to Bernard Lyons; "Following our meeting yesterday, I now formally offer my resignation from the Board of Directors of William Timpson Ltd under the terms we agreed together, namely, that I shall receive £40,000 and a Bristol 411 motor car." (James also found this car a few years ago and added it to his collection).

PART TWO

CHAPTER TWENTY-SIX

PART OF UDS

WHEN UDS MOVED INTO TIMPSON HOUSE, close observers realised that Timpson had joined another family business. There were four Lyons on the UDS Board; Bernard Lyons, the Chairman, his brother Jack, a non-executive director, and his sons, Robert, the property director and Stuart, who had just become chief executive of UDS Tailoring, the biggest and most profitable part of the group that included John Collier, Alexandre and Claude Alexandre (based in Scotland). With a turnover of over £200m, UDS was on equal terms with Sears, GUS, House of Fraser, Debenhams and Burton the Tailor. The Lyons had collected a strong retail portfolio which included Richard Shops, John Farmer shoes and a chain of department stores that included Whiteleys in Bayswater and Allders in Croydon.

Bernard Lyons became the Timpson Chairman, while Mike Frank and Rut Moors joined the Board, but very little changed. Geoffrey still ran the day-to-day business, but not in the way he had planned, issued statements from his 'Tiger's Den' and continued his Management by Objectives. But Bernard Lyons put an arm around everyone's shoulder and promised more capital expenditure for expansion.

Roland Smith quickly retired from the scene to pursue a string of other non-executive directorships, including House of Fraser, British Aerospace and Manchester United.

The Board wanted Timpson to move upmarket and the buying team, led by Alan Simmons, which now included Chris McLullich, a recruit from Saxone who bought ladies' fashion footwear, was encouraged to buy more expensive shoes and provide enough stock to meet the higher sales target.

They believed more attractive displays would increase the number of customers coming through the door and appointed Keith Bramall, a professional marketing manager, as Group Creative Display Executive. He initiated a number of new brand names in both Timpson and Norvic – Royals and Lancers for men's shoes, County Set and Sapphires for women and the resurrection of an old brand, Walk-Right, for children.

The strategy was described by Geoffrey Noakes in his editorial 'from the Tiger's Den':

'Our plans are advancing in three main areas:

1. The new size, style and operation of branches
2. The image and promotional features of those branches
3. The most important move into a tighter and more strictly defined market segment in each of our Operating Companies'

'These changes will not be completed overnight, whether it be in stockholding, shopfitting or site selection, and, in fact, it would be most unwise to try to do so. As we gain experience of the degree of success of each move, so shall we be able to take advantage of what we have learnt and achieve the best overall final result.'

'However, having said this, I am sure you will agree that what is most important is that we do not lose impetus at any stage but combine together to move progressively forward. This brings me to the very important aspect on which our success will be founded, which is that we all understand what we have to do and accept it as being the right way to progress.'

'All past experience proves that fully involved long-term support at all levels is never accorded to a leader whose aims aren't understood or are unacceptable, particularly if they are to be obtained without proper consideration for the welfare and ambitions of those who must inevitably bear the burden of implementation'.

'A written concept and detailed plans have their part to play, but continual personal communication and discussion at Managers' and Staff Conferences and in the Branches is an essential at all levels. All of us work better and with greater satisfaction if we know we are participating in our own future.'

'Please accept that I fully appreciate that our future success depends on your acceptance and involvement in what we plan to do, and your determination to make it successful. A well-led, fully involved and competent team will always succeed. Each one of us has a part to play, from the Chief Executive to the most newly joined assistant. If we all do our very best to play our part to the full, success is assured, together with the benefits that will follow.'

Unsurprisingly, this vague belief in planning and process didn't bring the promised success. Sales fell well short of the plan, and, although the team blamed 1973's winter of discontent when power cuts severely interrupted shopping, it was clear to long-standing Timpson shop managers that Head Office had lost touch with the traditional Timpson culture and hadn't found anything to put in its place.

The move upmarket and splitting shops into different market segments increased stock levels without increasing sales. In an attempt to cover lost margin, the management team increased prices even higher, which pushed sales further below budget. Stock levels became dangerously high and the year ended with an enormous January Sale, with profits way below expectations.

Running Norvic proved to be much more difficult than expected. The average shop turnover was less than half that of a Timpson shop, and, with a much higher average price, stock turnover was low and stock levels unacceptably high. A big proportion of the merchandise was branded (mainly Norvic) with a much lower margin than the unbranded stock sold in Timpson. This all produced a high wage percentage, poor merchandise margins and a business that barely did better than break even. The buyers soon discovered that sourcing merchandise for a branded business is very different from the technique needed for the own-brand High Street shoe multiples.

While the shoe retailers were stuck in endless meetings trying to figure a way out of their current difficulties, the small TSR (Timpson Shoe Repairs) team found a formula for success. Michael Frank was helped by Charles Noakes and Alan Chatterton. Charles, the younger son of Geoffrey's brother John, was a gentle kind-hearted man who had a four-year apprenticeship in shoe repairing, including a year working in the United States. When I was at Nottingham University, Charles was managing the Timpson Shoe Repair unit in Loughborough. Alan Chatterton was a self-taught, dynamic multi-tasker, who emerged from an administrative role to become the director responsible for development. The TSR team created a strong and profitable chain by bringing in key-cutting and engraving, developing a successful merchandise business based on hosiery, leather goods and shoe care, while dramatically redesigning the branches. Michael Frank found favour with UDS, who were keen to help him expand the business.

While TSR had a good story to tell, the rest of Timpson still struggled to find its feet. A new approach was promised following a change in senior management. Alan Simmons and Norman Redfern both left to join Edwards the Butchers, a family business with strong connections to Manchester United and Professor Roland Smith. Timpson appointed Dennis Fleischer, an experienced Merchandise Director from British Shoe, as the Group Deputy Managing Director. He quickly changed the stock control systems, computerised the Norvic business and reorganised warehousing and distribution. Bill Jones, previously chief executive of Curtess Shoes, became General Manager of Timpson Shops replacing Rut Moors, and long-serving Timpson area manager, Bill Dawes, was given the General Manager job for Norvic, with a brief to improve basic retailing standards.

Bernard Lyons handed over the Timpson Chairmanship to his son Stuart, who was more hands-on than his father. The new team had a fresh look at the way Timpson was being run. Stuart wasn't intimidated by Geoffrey Noakes's blustering style. Management by Objectives was abandoned and replaced by the disciplines used at British Shoe.

CHAPTER TWENTY-SEVEN

SWEARS & WELLS

WHEN THE LYONS FAMILY came to Timpson House the day their bid became unconditional, they toured the building, spoke to lots of colleagues, but didn't speak to me. So, I wrote to Bernard Lyons asking for a meeting. I was in London for a two-day break with Alex when we arrived at our hotel to find a message asking me to ring Bernard Lyons; within an hour I was in his office. Bernard suggested I should meet his son, Stuart, which I did the following week. Stuart proposed that I should leave Timpson and join John Collier. I started working at their headquarters in Leeds the following Monday.

For three weeks I went on an induction tour, visiting the warehouse and most of the offices. Morale at John Collier was sky-high. There was an air of arrogance, market share was being gained from the Burton Group and UDS Tailoring (John Collier, Alexandre and Claude Alexander) was providing a substantial proportion of UDS profits, from over 600 outlets, with a very strong 'Made-to-measure' men's suit business, helped by successful television advertising – 'John Collier, John Collier, the Window to Watch.' Most of the turnover came from two or three-piece suits, measured in a shop, made in factories in the North East of England and available for collection within a fortnight. The shops had

enormous window displays and a big arcade with a 'pattern table' display-
ing the range of cloth available – a salesman lingered, ready to pounce,
if a passing pedestrian showed some interest. The entire ground floor
was devoted to suits. Ties, coats, knitwear and anything ready to wear was
displayed on the first floor or in the basement – even the biggest shops
sold less than 10 shirts a week.

To find me a job, I was given responsibility for developing the sale of
shoes, taking on a business that, in a good week, sold 300 pairs, a sharp
contrast to the 100,000 pairs a week I had been managing at Timpson less
than two months before. I did the job in one day per week and filled the
rest of my life with golf and gardening. After six months, I was fed up with
having nothing to do. Other jobs offered within UDS (at John Myers Mail
Order and UDS Department Stores) didn't appeal, so I went to London to
hand in my notice. I didn't have a clue what I was going to do next, apart
from a vague idea that I would open my own shoe shop (which, in retrospect, would probably have been a disaster). I think a feeling of grief was
kicking in following the loss of our family business and I needed a goal
break from work. But it would have to be a short break; with Alex planning
to add two more bedrooms to our house, I was running out of money.

I never got the chance to resign. Bernard Lyons called me into
his office and asked a strange question; "Do you live anywhere near
Liverpool?" Wilmslow seemed to be near enough for him so he continued, "We have a 60-shop business based there called 'Swears and Wells',
which also trades as 'Suede Centre'. We have just parted company with
the buying director, finance director and chief executive, so will you run
it until we can find someone decent?"

Ten days later, I arrived at the office in Bold Street, Liverpool and
quickly discovered why the previous manager had gone. In the week
before I arrived, the total turnover of sixty shops selling leather and fur
clothing was only £25,000, of which over £10,000 came from the two
shops in London's Oxford Street. Sales were less than half those of last
year and the company was running up a substantial loss.

I didn't know where to start, but fortunately, one director remained – Margaret Broadley, the Personnel Director who controlled five area managers. I followed my father's example and visited lots of shops. The colleagues were quick to tell me that the stock was overpriced so I launched a sale and turnover doubled. I was aware that Bernard Lyons regarded me as a stop-gap, a temporary manager who, at best, would keep the shops trading, so I wasn't surprised that I was summoned to Marble Arch for further instructions. He had heard that I was planning to visit some of our suppliers and wanted to give me some tips on the rag trade.

"It isn't the same as buying shoes," he told me. "These guys go for big margins so drive a hard bargain; if you haven't chipped 20% off their asking price, you have failed." I innocently followed his advice and, on one occasion, got 15% off the price of an order for leather coats; no doubt the manufacturer recovered his loss on our next deal.

Suddenly, I had a big stroke of luck. The Suede Centre shop in New Street, Birmingham, caught fire and all the stock was smoke-damaged. Margaret Broadley telephoned from the site to report that the shop could reopen within three days. Remembering the successful Timpson fire sale in Wilmslow in 1971, I asked Margaret to keep the branch closed for at least a week, with big posters announcing 'Fire Sale starts Friday 10.00 am'. When the shop reopened, there was a significant queue and we took 15 weeks' turnover in 2 days. As a result, my business was easily top of the UDS weekly turnover league – the job was mine for the foreseeable future.

A few weeks later, I was joined by a Finance Director, Ken Martindale, who proved we were marginally profitable, but it was unclear who was on the Board. Neither of us was a director and no one held a board meeting. We thought Bernard Lyons was Chairman although another UDS director, Peter Sheldon, was the only person from Marble Arch who came to visit. I was still paid by William Timpson Limited at the salary of £7,000 a year, which I received at the time of the takeover.

It was very casual, but I didn't care. I enjoyed the job and it became my number one hobby. My commitment was demonstrated at Christmas

1973, when the Belfast store was hit by a terrorist bomb. Our third child, Edward, was born very early on Boxing Day, so Alex was still at the Nursing Home in Knutsford when I went to Belfast to deal with the insurance and trading problems. To make sure Alex never knew, I hired a plane from Blackpool and got back in time for the visiting hours. The bomb-damage sale, four weeks later, cleared every garment in three days.

We had 300 employees but only 4 men – the manager of the Belfast store, our van driver, Ken Martindale and myself. None of the area managers had a car so the shops were grouped according to the railway network, which is why Blackpool and Chatham were in the same area. I struggled to persuade every area manager to accept a car; one needed to pass her driving test while others insisted that they did a lot of work on the train. It worked pretty well so they might have had a point.

The business was very seasonal; there was a healthy demand between September and February, but the rest of the year was devoted to survival. Much depended on salesmanship and a good manager made a massive difference, so I spent at least two days every week visiting branches, talking to colleagues. Price promotions played a key role and I had a lot of fun at advertising agents, Stowe and Bowden, in Manchester where Jim Reece and John Wood helped me combine cut prices with a bit of humour – 'Save a packet on a jacket' worked well but was overshadowed when I took in 1995 sheepskin coats before Christmas 1994, cut the price in January and advertised 'Styles you've never seen before at prices you'll never see again!'. Big discounts were the secret to success in leather and fur retailing.

I had another call to visit Bernard Lyons; this time, he wanted to talk about imports. "Go to Eastern Europe," he said as I walked through the door. "The merchandise is bound to be cheap, and, with so much cold weather, they will be full of factories making sheepskin coats and warm-lined leather jackets". I had no choice; together with our buyer, Ann Hennessy, and Max Sandler, brother of a UDS director, I went to Hungary, Romania and Bulgaria. It was my first experience of communist countries and lived up to expectations. Our restaurant table was bugged in Budapest and a prostitute knocked on my bedroom door in Bucharest. Bernard Lyons was wrong about the bargains; I was so disillusioned by the time I got to Sofia that I caught the first plane home and didn't bother with Yugoslavia.

My job felt more secure after Bernard handed over Swears & Wells to his son, Stuart, who made Ken Martindale and myself directors. Despite the national three-day week, leather prices rising by over 20% and other costs rising even faster, we increased turnover to £5m and profits reached £375k.

With Stuart Lyons spending several weeks contesting Halifax for the Conservatives in the second general election within 20 months, I was left to develop the business with Margaret Broadley and Ann Hennessy, whose extrovert approach to buying transformed the look of the merchandise. Following market research, carried out by the Specialist Research Unit (SRU) run by Dennis Stevenson (now Lord Stevenson), we abandoned the Swears & Wells name, apart from the two stores in Oxford Street, and called all the shops Suede Centre. At the beginning of 1975, using the experience of the two fire sales, we started a sequence of Swears & Wells closing down sales followed by Suede Centre opening offers. This brought queues of bargain hunters and kept us top of the UDS turnover league.

Stuart Lyons lost the election in Halifax and returned to his career in UDS. In February 1975, his father appointed him Chairman of Timpson, so I wasn't surprised that he didn't have time to visit Liverpool. However, towards the end of the month, he telephoned. "Are you sitting down?" he asked. "Would you like to return to Timpson as Managing Director?" It was an easy question.

CHAPTER TWENTY-EIGHT

BACK AT TIMPSON

I DIDN'T START MY NEW JOB for three weeks. The waiting time was spent talking to Stuart Lyons about our future plans. Stuart sent me to London to meet the UDS Advertising agency, Young and Rubicam, and their Public Relations arm, Burson-Marsteller. I caught the Pullman from Wilmslow Station and spotted Geoffrey Noakes at the far end of the platform; perhaps he knew he was heading for his last meeting at UDS.

The three weeks felt like three months, Alex was the only person I could talk to, but she, as always, kept my feet firmly on the ground. I was to be appointed at a Timpson Board Meeting scheduled for the last Friday in March, so to make it easy to keep our secret, we turned down social invitations and spent our evenings at home. However, on the night before the meeting, we went to an amateur dramatic society performance in Knutsford. Sat in the next row, immediately in front of us, were Mike Frank and his wife Chris. Mike didn't know that we would meet again within 12 hours and work closely together for the next 14 years.

I had breakfast at the Midland Hotel in Manchester with Stuart, UDS Finance Director Brian Wilson and Bob Kirkman, one of the Timpson directors who ousted my father (he became UDS Company Secretary a year later). When we arrived at Wythenshawe, the directors were waiting in the Board Room – Dennis Fleisher, Mike Frank, Bert Brownhill, Peter Lomas and Bill Jones.

It was a one-sided meeting; Stuart spoke, the rest of the Board listened. After announcing my appointment, Stuart outlined his new strategy, which included the closure of Norvic Retail and a change in style from British Shoe Corporation systems and 'Management by Objectives' back to a more people-based family business. He also announced, without asking my opinion, that I would still be controlling Swears and Wells, with their Head Office moving to Wythenshawe. He liked the idea of saving the cost of an extra head office and a new chief executive.

Another decision Stuart made on my behalf was the appointment of my secretary, Teresa Dutton. Teresa worked for my grandfather before becoming secretary to my father. It must be rare for any PA to work for three generations.

I had no plans to change the management team, but my appointment wasn't good news for some round the table, particularly Dennis Fleisher, who had seemed almost certain to succeed Geoffrey Noakes. I was disappointed when Dennis handed in his resignation, as I would have learnt a lot working with him. He was soon running Barratts for the Ziff family. When he left, I appointed Jim Taylor to head the buying department.

Geoffrey Noakes retired to spend much of his time at his weekend home near Malpas in the Cheshire countryside. Despite the overpowering influence he had during the previous 7 years, his regime was quickly forgotten by the colleagues he left behind.

Bill Dawes was desperately upset when he heard about the Norvic closure but, a few months later, it left him free to fulfil his dream, replacing Bill Jones as the Timpson Shops General Manager.

The business had suffered from a succession of management changes over the previous 4 years and we needed a period of stability. I even kept IT manager, Bert Brownhill, on the Board, despite his part in my father's dismissal – his son-in-law, Mike Williams, also got a senior role as

Property Manager, shadowing the work done centrally by Robert Lyons at UDS Properties.

The only significant change during the next 8 years followed Peter Lomas's promotion to become the UDS Tailoring Finance Director (he later moved to Gratton and then Next). We found the perfect replacement, Peter Cookson, who was in the Timpson finance department before I went to Swears and Wells, but disillusioned by the way the company was being run, he joined Gateway supermarkets.

I interviewed Peter Cookson at the nearby Post House hotel – one of the ugliest buildings in Manchester – we got on well and started a partnership that continued for fifteen years.

TSR was tightly controlled by Mike Frank, who fiercely protected his subsidiary from outside interference, and, for some time, I was one of the outsiders. I was probably better spending my time on the retail shops that were heading for a loss.

I was never taught how to run a business. You didn't get many practical hints studying Industrial Economics at Nottingham University, so, apart from a three-day course at Ashridge and the teachings of Roland Smith, I learnt everything through experience. Perhaps that is why I am a bit of a maverick. However, in my first year as Managing Director, I tried to stick to the rules. I even supported a full appraisal programme, which I now recognise did more harm than good. Apart from persuading me to do appraisals, the personnel manager, Geoff Galgut, like many other meticulous colleagues (including Fred Potts our hyperactive warehouse manager), kept looking after the detail and protected me from a tendency to play things by ear.

I ran the business by running about – meeting all the area managers, visiting Italy, Paris and Düsseldorf to check out fashion trends, getting involved in the trade associations, doing a bit of broadcasting, and visiting as many shops as possible. I was helped enormously by a six-foot-four ex-policeman, Ben Potts, who became my driver. A dry raconteur and expert cryptic crossword solver, Ben spent much of his free time with his wife Kath (referred to as 'the bride') holding hands whenever they walked near their Wythenshawe home. With three small children and a busy business, Alex didn't see how I could find time for golf, hockey, cricket or squash so I settled for one or two games of squash a week and put the rest of my sporting life on hold.

My initial success came from an unlikely source. We turned the Norvic shop closure programme into a major profit earner, by using the experience I'd gained from the fire sale in Birmingham, the bomb sale in Belfast and the closing down sales when we converted Swears and Wells to Suede Centre.

One hundred shops had to close, so we took our time, shutting 3 or 4 each week. Before each sale started, we closed the shop on a Saturday night and plastered the windows with posters – 'Closing Down Sale Starts Friday 10.00 am'. Over the next few days, chairs were removed from the sales floor, the shop was filled with sale racks and extra reduced stock transferred from elsewhere. Every sale started with a long queue, and in the first two days, takings could be 15 times an average week. Despite the cut in margin, Norvic shops were making more money than they had seen for years.

The sale technique worked everywhere, but the long-serving manager in Windsor insisted it wouldn't work across the road from Windsor Castle. "Our customers demand personal service, even in a sale," he insisted. We ignored his advice, took out the chairs, filled racks with cut-price shoes and waited for the usual miracle to work. The manager still complained, "It won't work without chairs", making a final desperate plea; "What will happen to one-legged folk if they can't sit down?!"

The Windsor sale attracted a bigger queue than normal, and, well before opening time, success was assured. But the manager was right; towards the front of the queue was a man with one leg.

Some of the Norvic branches were converted to Timpson shoe shops, a few became Timpson Shoe Repair units and many were transferred to UDS's Farmer shoe chain, but most were closed.

I got 'corporate communications' advice from Michael McAvoy of Burson-Marsteller, but also received guidance from Alex, whose sound judgement was based on common sense. When in Manchester, Stuart Lyons stayed at the Midland Hotel, where we had dinner in their French Restaurant. I usually left the conversation to Stuart and Alex. After a couple of years, Stuart started staying at Merithorn, our house in Wilmslow. By then, we had become foster carers and Stuart enjoyed having breakfast surrounded by young children. Alex was never overawed by big business and certainly wasn't bothered by big businessmen. She helped me forge a strong relationship with Stuart which was good for both me and the business.

Alex also taught me the secret of groupmanship. If you are part of a conglomerate, make sure another part of the group is doing worse than your bit.

CHAPTER TWENTY-NINE

CUSTOMER CARE

WITH THE LONG-TERM BENEFIT of hindsight, your major mentors are put into a proper perspective. Alex was my major game-changer, but Stuart played an important role. Stuart is a clever guy; few would attempt to learn Mandarin Chinese while heading up a complex multi-million-pound business. He put into practice a definition of intelligence I learnt at University – 'The ability to discover the relationship between relationships' – he was able to turn two plus two into five.

Stuart decided to turn Timpson back into a family business. With a Timpson back in the Board Room, Stuart saw no reason why it couldn't, yet again, feel like a caring family company. He spotted an opportunity. The market leader, British Shoe Corporation (BSC), was supreme in almost everything it did, but there was an Achilles Heel. BSC didn't particularly care for their customers.

The problem was faulty footwear, made worse by the mid-70s fashion for platform soles with high bulky heels, many made in Italy. They followed the latest fashion but weren't built to last. For some styles, over 15% fell apart within a fortnight and the overall customer complaint rate reached 5%. BSC controlled the problem at branch level by setting a 2% limit on complaints.

Shoe shops got so much stick from the media that the newly created Office of Fair Trading forced footwear retailers to agree a Code of Practice alongside Funeral Directors and Betting Shops.

Stuart Lyons saw this woeful weakness as our big chance. Within a month, we launched our 'Money Back Promise', with a poster in every shop window – "If you have any good reason to be dissatisfied, we will give you your money back – and that's a promise". The poster carried my picture and signature. We withdrew styles with a complaint rate higher than 4% and gave total authority to branch managers to settle complaints. Our competitors looked on with mild amusement. The BSC Chief Executive told us our poster was like 'giving petrol to an arsonist'.

To emphasise our family credentials, Stuart persuaded me to put our children's pictures on display with the caption 'my mum loves Timpson'. He also wanted to advertise; TV worked for John Collier and he felt it could do a similar job for Timpson. Young and Rubicam produced a jingle some people still remember. The commercial had shoes dancing on the Timpson logo singing, 'T-I-M-P-S-O-N, Timpson are 110 . . . .' and to celebrate, they are giving you a present – 110p off 110 styles – and it repeated our guarantee, "If you are dissatisfied, we will give you your money back – and that's a promise" – sales increased by 20%.

Stuart and Alex boosted my confidence, but I was apprehensive at my first meeting of the Multiple Shoe Retailers Association (MSRA), a Council made up of major competitors. I was the youngest by 20 years, so felt it best to be seen and not heard. I kept particularly quiet when they discussed the Code of Practice because Stuart had a plan.

Stuart arranged a meeting with Sir John Methven, the OFT's first Director-General. When we revealed our purpose, with undisguised emotion, he revealed, "You are the first business to offer help. Everyone else seeks confrontation; you want a better deal for consumers."

We were given the latest version of the OFT footwear code. Over the weekend, I converted it into a Timpson Code of Practice which we took back to the OFT three weeks later. It was the ideal way to make our service-centred family business stand out from the competition, so I never told the MSRA what I was doing with the OFT.

Creating an individual approach to customer care and turning Timpson into a consumer champion was an exciting, enjoyable and fulfilling project, made possible by our Manchester-based advertising agency, Stowe and Boden. They created 'The Shoe People' – cartoons of shoe characters who brought our customer care approach to life. My main contribution was a classification system which categorised each shoe according to durability: 1. Waterproof. 2. Heavy Duty. 3. Everyday. 4. Lightwear. 5. Occasional. 6. Indoor. Within four months, every shoe had been labelled and a 'Shoe People' leaflet promoted our Code of Practice.

Advised by Michael McAvoy, I became a mini consumer champion, talking to local consumer groups and phone-in programmes on local radio. Thanks to Stuart Lyons insisting that I treated Timpson like a family business with customer care at the heart of what we did, I found a way of running the business that has guided what we do for over 40 years.

CHAPTER THIRTY

CONSUMER CHARTER

THE CUSTOMER-LED APPROACH seemed to be working and, thanks to the 110th birthday promotion, sales were good, but I still had too much old stock, so I had a bold idea.

Encouraged by the dramatic sales when we closed Norvic, I decided to try a similar trick for all the Timpson shoe shops. Closing the shops while preparing a sale was the magic ingredient, so I decided to close every Timpson shop for two days (Wednesday and Thursday) before launching the July sale at 10.00 am on a Friday.

In 1975, every retailer just had two sales a year. The January Sale had been brought forward to either December 27th or 28th (everyone was closed on Boxing Day). Summer sales started around July 15th. I made my big splash in the first week of July with all the competitors on full price. To add more drama, we booked television advertising on Tuesday and Wednesday night.

I was in my office on the Wednesday (no point in visiting the shops as they were all shut); I was a bit nervous but supremely confident the sale would be a great success, when I received a call from Bernard Lyons.

"Have you gone mad?" he started, in an angry tone. "Tell me this isn't true? No one in their right mind would shut shops on a weekday and to shut the lot is just crazy!" I explained my plan and promised all would be fine, but he wasn't convinced. He put his phone down with a veiled threat; "I hope for your sake you know what you are doing."

I was in Sheffield before 9.00 am on Friday morning, going from one Timpson shop to another (we had five in the city centre). It didn't look promising. Inside each branch, colleagues filled racks with shoes but pedestrians didn't stop to look. It was 9.35 am before I saw a customer queuing, but by 10.00 am, we had queues outside every shop – not just three or four standing in line, but at least 30 and our biggest branch in Haymarket had over 100 queuing right round the block. I didn't need to call Bernard Lyons; he would get the message when we submitted our sales. Despite being closed for two days, we beat the record set at Christmas.

A week later, I had lunch with Stuart Lyons and Sir John Methven, who wanted us to launch our company code of practice with public approval from the OFT. It was a dream opportunity, bound to upset our competitors, but giving the right impression to our customers. The OFT, keen to shame other shoe retailers into agreeing a national code, wanted as much publicity as possible. It wasn't on the front page but we hit a few headlines and I was interviewed by Jimmy Young on his lunchtime radio programme.

Care for customers became central to everything we did. We wrote a Code for Shoe Repairs and a Children's Charter. We designed our own foot gauge and had the width fitting of every children's shoe calibrated at the Shoe and Allied Trades Research Association (SATRA) in Kettering. We aimed to do what Clarks did at much cheaper prices. Our advertising claimed 'There's no need to pay more for correctly fitted children's shoes'.

I kept looking for ways to help us stand out from the crowd and give customers something special, but lost my nerve before launching one of my wilder ideas. My plan was to end '99p' pricing, which many consumers, wrongly, thought was an evil plot to charge more money. Everything was ready to go – price change circulars had been printed and our warehouse held 500,000 new price tickets – £1.76, £4.33, £2.81, £5.67 and many more – but none that ended in 99. With little more than a week to go, I lost my bottle, scrapped the scheme and have never been tempted again.

Another good idea got blown off course by our field management team. We developed a few adventurous children's shoe departments. Alex took a keen interest and introduced a ball pit in the Wilmslow branch. It was a great success; children loved it, but middle management didn't and raised a long list of concerns including the chance of children peeing in the ball pit. It was a small battle that wasn't worth fighting.

Despite these setbacks, we kept developing the consumerism theme, and even appointed our own internal Consumer Affairs Manager, Colin Adamson, who came to Timpson from the OFT. As well as promoting new consumer-based ideas, he monitored our performance and edited an Annual Review of the Timpson Code of Practice. This groundbreaking approach to consumer issues helped Timpson become a better and more caring business. Customer service improved, our range of shoes got better and profits for 1976 were well over £1m.

CHAPTER THIRTY-ONE

GROWTH AT TSR

IN THE 1970S, SHOE REPAIRING was still very competitive. Despite the rapid decline in demand, lots of independent cobblers survived. Most occupied their own freehold premises or paid very low rent and rates and could earn a reasonable living, especially the many that traded below the VAT threshold and avoided other taxes by paying wages and expenses in cash.

There were also enough multiple shoe repair chains to form a lively trade association, The National Association of Shoe Repair Factories (NASRF). Our biggest competitor, Allied Shoe Repairs, had over 500 shops operating under a number of different fascias – including Paynes, Combes and Malones. Timpson was the second-biggest with 180 outlets and the next most significant, Automagic, was a publicly quoted company with 100 shops, many sited in central London.

At the end of the 1970s, a new competitor made a significant but brief impact. Sketchley, the dry cleaners, introduced heel bars into over 100 shops and did it very well because their new service was run by a team of experienced shoe repairers. Ten years later, when the core Sketchley business was struggling, to save costs, Sketchley disbanded the shoe repair support team. Within four years, 75% of their recently acquired extra sales disappeared.

Almost every cobbler realised that to survive, they had to add something else; most sold leather goods – purses, suitcases, wallets and even five-year diaries. A small number of smart operators added key-cutting, but it was several years before most shoe repairers worked out the answer to the trivia question 'Why do cobblers cut keys?' Fortunately, TSR was ahead of the game. Key-cutting, first trialled in 1969, was given a big boost after the company joined UDS.

At first, we cut a limited range of the Yale-type cylinder keys; most mortice keys were pre-cut. Sales were little more than £10 per shop per week. That changed when key blanks were displayed in the shop window. Within a year, average shop sales rose to £40 a week and even diehard cobblers started taking key-cutting seriously.

But the big growth business in TSR was merchandise. Some shops looked like an Aladdin's cave, cluttered with shoe accessories, leather goods, shopping bags, wickerware, Alibaba baskets, tote bags and a wide range of cheap gifts at Christmas (it was three years before we discovered that our five-year diaries only had 28 days in every month). The biggest turnover came from hosiery – at a poor margin but a big traffic-builder. Busy shops like Bradford, Kirby and Tib Street in Manchester sold over 2,000 pairs of tights a week.

TSR outlets weren't in the busiest part of town; the TSR team looked for secondary sites where rents were cheap. Shoe repairers were regarded as second-class citizens so landlords seldom offered them units in smart new shopping centres.

Mike Frank and his senior team, Alan Chatterton and Charles Noakes, kept TSR under tight control. I chaired their management meetings, but the TSR trio had a full dress rehearsal before we met in an attempt to control the agenda. Their shops were managed with military precision using a detailed list of 'Standing Orders for Shoe Repair Factories' (SOSRF). Critical to TSR's success was the control of wage costs, which was helped by a weekly branch bonus. There were two calculations, one for the colleagues working in the factory and another for those behind the counter.

Each week, the total wages paid in each branch was multiplied by a factor that set a sales target for that week. A bonus was earned on all sales over the target, with no limit. To earn good money, the branch colleagues needed to push sales up and keep staff levels down (reducing the target and spreading the bonus amongst a smaller number of colleagues). This has evolved into today's elegant bonus scheme that provides the adrenaline which puts a buzz into Timpson outlets.

Mike Frank was a good manager, who visiting nearly every branch twice a year. He had an old-fashioned relationship with his shop staff, calling a junior 'young lad' – as in, "How long have you been with us, young lad?" – and sending memos that started 'Dear Smith' or 'Dear Robinson'. He got away with this slightly aloof approach with an engaging smile. He was a genuine character who truly loved the business and everyone in it.

In 1979, when Mike Frank attended a three-month management course at Ashridge, I got a rare chance to take a closer look at TSR and was disturbed by the housekeeping. We were no better than the cobblers down the road. My response was to change the uniform, replacing dull grey overalls with a blue apron, worn over a check shirt with a tie.

The tie was probably my biggest contribution to the development of TSR. At a stroke, the tie set us apart from our competitors. A new set of housekeeping rules prohibited eating, drinking and smoking in front of customers and banned radios. It was big a culture change, which some shoe repairers found difficult to understand, but after three years, even the most rebellious cobblers realised that our dress code was here to stay and everyone was looking the part.

The TSR team took pride in meeting their annual budget, so, while Mike Frank was on his training course, I hid an extra £100,000 in his overheads. Sure enough, on his return, Mike and his team achieved the budget and the total Timpson profit was £100k better off.

TSR opened a heel bar in every UDS department store, a departure that caused a few difficulties with Bernard Lyons, whose chauffeur took a pair of crocodile shoes into our outlet in Whiteleys, their local store. The shoes were never seen again – we lost them!

Bernard never forgave us but recognised TSR made good margins and was keen to see the new TSR unit in Allders of Croydon. He went there on the evening when Alan Chatterton was putting some finishing touches to the layout. He nipped around the corner for a coffee and left the roller shutter half-open. Having second thoughts about security, Alan Chatterton went back to close the shutter. In the meantime, Bernard Lyons went in to take a closer look and was locked inside the shop.

Trading inside the department stores involved an ongoing battle with the security team who questioned the honesty of our cobblers and forced us to display shoe care products behind glass to prevent theft (and reduce sales by 60%). Things took a turn for the better when the all-powerful head of security was found, after hours, in the bedding department of Arding and Hobbs in Chatham, with a girl from lingerie. His successor was much more reasonable.

At about this time, I spoke at the Multiple Shoe Repairers' annual conference in Jersey. I used charts to illustrate the inevitable decline in demand for shoe repairs, helping the industry to face up to reality. In the bottom right-hand corner of every chart were the words 'Source – Imaginary Research Limited'.

A few weeks later, I was contacted by the Financial Times. The journalist wanted to talk about shoe repairs. "I understand," he said, "you have some recent statistics." "That's true," I replied, "but I made them all up." Undeterred, he continued, "That's a pity, but they're the only figures I can find so I might as well use them."

In the middle of the 1960s, our repair business was closely connected to Timpson shoe shops. Nearly half the factories were located on shoe shop premises – upstairs, downstairs and, in some cases, in the shop itself. Every shoe shop took in repairs which they sent to the nearest factory using a network of delivery vans.

When the demand for shoe repairs declined, stand-alone repair branches made up some of the lost turnover by cutting keys and selling shopping baskets, but the shoe shops couldn't cut keys. By 1978, most workshops on shoe retail premises had been closed. The future for TSR was to open modern high street shops and, if possible, grow by acquiring competitors. In 1978, we spotted the ideal candidate.

'Shoe Care', a 14-branch business based in Kent, was up for sale. It was a good business with profitable shops in busy Kent shopping centres, including Canterbury, Maidstone, Ashford, Sittingbourne and Gravesend, a new unit planned in Hempstead Valley and a factory in Aylesford, near Maidstone, that made moccasins which sold remarkably well in every shop.

I met the owner, Brian Smith, at his lawyer's office, just off Oxford Street, London, and, within three hours, we agreed a deal. He was happy to sell the business with no strings attached for £175k, which I thought was a really good price. Over the moon, I walked to the UDS Head Office at Marble Arch to get their approval, but Finance Director, Brian Wilson, told me to get a better deal. He thought I could buy the business for £150k. Brian Smith and his lawyer refused to budge, so the first deal of my life never happened.

A year later, we found another opportunity in Broughall's, based in Luton. They had 35 shoe repair outlets from Norwich to Cheltenham with some great sites including Witney, Welwyn Garden City and Dunstable. This time, I let Stuart Lyons do the deal, which was agreed over a beer-filled lunch in a Dunstable pub. It was a family business that funded the family lifestyle, including gambling trips to Monte Carlo. One weekend, their field director, Ralph Young, got an urgent call; he was told to visit as many shops as possible, take cash from the tills and catch the first plane to Monaco. Ralph did just that, handed over the money and was told to catch the first plane back home.

Broughall's, suffering from poor leadership, struggled to make money, so we bought the 35 outlets for £275k. Many of the shops still trade today and make a combined annual profit far in excess of the original purchase price.

A few months later, Shoe Care came back on our agenda, but this time, Stuart Lyons did the negotiations and agreed to pay £250k, plus an annuity to Brian Smith and his wife of £15,000 a year, index-linked. As Brian suffered from poor health, he insisted the annuity should also apply to his wife when she survived him.

Sadly, Brian's wife died within six months of the deal, but Brian, who was fitter than we all thought, survived for another 20 years. Just before he died, he was receiving an annual payment of £57,000 a year. The company, which I originally agreed to buy for £175k, finally cost us nearly £1m.

CHAPTER THIRTY-TWO

GROUP POLITICS

STUART LYONS' STRATEGY OF turning Timpson back into a family business and taking up the consumer cause worked well. Day-to-day running of the shoe shop business was in the hands of loyal colleagues with a wealth of experience. Men's footwear was managed by Jim Taylor, whose father had been the leather buyer at North Park. Jim worked as a shoe shop assistant before learning to be a shoe buyer. Tom Hardman, whose brother Jim was a Timpson shoe shop manager, worked in the warehouse and the distribution department, before becoming women's footwear buyer. Tom was a talented shoe man with a wicked sense of humour.

Tom Howell, one of many Timpson employees with a military background and continuing involvement in the Territorial Army, bought our children's shoes. His brief was to match the Clarks' offer at two-thirds of their price. He played a major part in building the Timpson reputation for being a proper family shoe shop.

The warehouse and transport fleet were managed by Fred Potts, previously a shop manager, whose eccentric enthusiasm and attention to detail made him a larger-than-life character. Fred was always on the move, walking quickly from one end of the warehouse to the other, carrying a big bunch of keys, which were his badge of authority.

Bill Dawes, who, for many years, managed the Timpson shop on Union Street, Glasgow before becoming an area manager, was appointed General Manager of the Timpson shops after he had completed the Norvic closure programme. Bill was as dour as a Scot is meant to be, one of life's pessimists, passionately risk-averse for all the right reasons. He was well respected by his area managers, most of whom joined as junior assistants in a Timpson shop.

The tension created by the Board Room bust-up had disappeared, fewer politics were being played and there was a positive atmosphere throughout the business.

The approach to customer care, with our generous handling of complaints and the Timpson Code of Practice promoted by the 'Shoe People', helped to make us stand out from our competitors.

It seemed we could do no wrong. Every Timpson shop got a refit with a yellow fascia and a new style of window display. I fell in love with press advertising. Television was probably more effective, but we found a format for half and full-page press ads that was easy to develop, considerably cheaper and worked well. It was a joy to go to work with profits improving month after month.

My days at Swears & Wells taught me how price reductions can create more business, so all our adverts had a value appeal. 'Back to School' adverts worked particularly well under the headline 'No Need to Pay More for Correctly Fitted Shoes'. Alongside our SATRA-calibrated fitting shoes at everyday prices, we advertised black gusset plimsolls (a must-have in every school bag) for 99p and football boots reduced to £2.99.

The most successful adverts appeared in 1979 when we repeated a Swears & Wells ploy by taking in autumn shoes at a generous margin before reducing the price. '£2 off Loafers' lifted total sales by nearly 15%. In November, a similar price offer for boots appeared in the press on the same day as a significant snowfall covered the country. It was my lucky year; we ended with a record profit of £3.5m and, feeling pretty smug,

I did what arrogant managers do, I organised a management retreat; two days in Southport, designed to discover ideas for the next few years.

Like most forward-planning conferences, the feeling of bonding enhanced by late nights in the bar and serious papers presented during the daytime debate didn't produce the hoped-for magic. 1979 was the peak year for us and most other shoe retailers too, but none predicted the turbulent times ahead. An increase in VAT, announced by Chancellor Geoffrey Howe in July, unsettled shopkeepers, but sellers of shoes had a special problem – more shops were starting to sell shoes, especially the fashion chains.

The British Shoe Corporation (BSC) opened concessions in Miss Selfridge, Debenhams, House of Fraser and the Burton brands – Top Shop, Dorothy Perkins and Top Man. We put shoes into 200 John Collier shops. They didn't do much better than my small attempt at John Collier in 1975.

We sent each shop a basic range of footwear and a functional display unit. We expected John Collier staff to do the selling, which they did reluctantly, producing an average turnover per shop of £200 a week. After six months, the displays were shabby, sales had slowed down and we had to mark down the damaged stock.

We didn't find another initiative like the original 'Money Back Promise' and the 'Timpson Code of Practice, but that didn't stop us from issuing press releases. A 'Buy British' campaign brought an invitation to 10 Downing Street and an intense conversation with Margaret Thatcher. Our footwear fact sheet revealed that the nation's smallest feet are in South Wales and the biggest are in Plymouth. There was no research behind these revelations but the press release hit a quiet news day; journalists scampered to Swansea and Plymouth, and our footwear facts made the headlines.

In 1980, inspired by the first London Marathon, four of us from Timpson entered the Greater Manchester Marathon, a five-and-a-half-hour ordeal that didn't deter me from running in the 1981 London

Marathon. The many hours of early morning training helped my mind wrestle with the increasing challenges of shoe retailing. A poor season left us with more slow-moving stock than usual. It was difficult to remember how well the business had been doing in 1979; it doesn't take long for a retail business to swing from success to survival.

We found a more positive twist when Stuart Lyons introduced me to Rodney Fitch, whose design consultancy was already changing the look of the Burton Group, helping Ralph Halpern turn Top Shop, Top Man, Burton and Dorothy Perkins into the modern theatre of retailing. I spent 18 months with Rodney Fitch and his assistant, Richard Austin, designing a new look for Timpson.

Through the connection with Fitch, I met Tony Coleman, Burton's Concession Director. The discussion led to our first department in Dorothy Perkins. Unlike our move into John Collier, Timpson sales staff became part of the package and the first three Dorothy Perkins concessions were pleasingly successful.

In addition, Timpson opened 22 new shoe shops, taking on leases from other parts of UDS. These new Timpson outlets had traded as Van Allan, Grange Furnishing (a small group of shops in Scotland that UDS closed) and some UDS tailoring shops that were culled in a major reorganisation.

Despite our expanding portfolio, trading got tougher; profits slumped from £3.5m in 1979 to £1.6m a year later, but, thankfully, went back over £2m in 1982.

Although the secret of survival in a conglomerate is to make sure at least one other company within the group is doing worse than your bit, with so many poor performers, the overall weakness of UDS became the biggest threat to our survival.

CHAPTER THIRTY-THREE

TROUBLE AT UDS

WHEN MY FATHER APPROACHED Bernard Lyons with the offer to acquire our shareholding in 1972, UDS had just announced record profits and were one of the UK's biggest retailers, alongside Sears, Great Universal Stores (GUS) and the Burton Group. The company, founded in 1927, had grown through a series of acquisitions, including, in 1954, Alexandre, a Yorkshire-based men's tailoring chain which was the Lyons family business. Over the next 15 years, Bernard Lyons transformed United Drapery Stores. His biggest move was the purchase of Prices Tailors, a 350-shop chain founded by Henry Price in 1905 and originally trading as the 'Thirty Shilling Tailors'. The name was changed to 'Fifty Shilling Tailors' and later converted to 'John Collier'.

Bernard Lyons brilliantly developed the UDS tailoring shops, John Collier, Alexandre and shops in Scotland trading as Claude Alexander, into the UK's market leader. 90% of the turnover came from made-to-measure suits, made in factories located in Yorkshire and the North East of England and delivered back to the branch within 10 days of the order being placed. Every man needed a suit for Sundays, special occasions, high days and holidays. John Collier had the best range, the fastest service and beat everyone else on price. The television advert 'John Collier,

John Collier, the Window to Watch' made it one of the best-known names on the high street.

In 1967, Bernard Lyons made his biggest and boldest move when he bid for his major competitor, Burtons, a move that would have created a tailoring chain of over 1,000 branches. The deal was blocked by the Monopolies and Mergers Commission so Bernard had to expand into other parts of the high street. UDS acquired Richard Shops, a leading womenswear chain with 250 shops run from an office near to Euston. They also bought John Myers Mail Order, with a big warehouse in Stockport, the fur retailer Swears & Wells, discounter John Blundells and a number of department stores including Whiteleys in Bayswater and Allders of Croydon. They also acquired a license to trade in duty-free goods at Heathrow and Gatwick, the start of a venture that developed into Allders International, which opened duty-free shops in airports around the world. The shoe retailer, John Farmer, became part of UDS in 1972, just before Bernard Lyons started talking to Timpson.

With profits approaching £30m, we had every reason to believe that Timpson was joining a growing business with a good track record.

My initial experience with UDS confirmed all I had heard, although the casual way I was treated at Swears & Wells should have given me cause for concern. However, I was happy to have a job and delighted to be left on my own. I certainly had no cause for concern when Stuart gave me the job running the Timpson business; he gave me the sort of support that I now describe as Upside-down Management. The first seeds of doubt were sown when the UDS share price fell following their unwise investment in Biberhaus, a German department store, and the failure of London & County Securities Bank that had trading links with the UDS department stores. These blips were quickly followed by news that advertising agency, Young & Rubicam, had ceased doing business with UDS. I was never told why, but, at a stroke, we lost the creator of Timpson's only memorable television jingle.

I put these bits of unfortunate news down to bad luck, thinking some little things are bound to go wrong in a big business, but the next event was more worrying. John Myers Mail Order was closed down with debts of £30m. We had to clear some of their redundant shoe stock in our January Sale.

In 1977, I helped with another closure. Suede Centre stayed under my control for a year after I moved back to Timpson but was then handed over to Jack Maxwell, who ran Richard Shops. I found the move hard to accept, having worked with the team for three years and increased profits to £400k. Jack Maxwell never came to terms with the promotional pricing technique – the magic wand that made the money. Within a year, the Richard Shops team gave up and Suede Centre was scheduled for closure (UDS never seemed to sell anything). I was drafted in to organise the closing down sales following the same ploy that worked so well when we closed Norvic.

When Stuart Lyons succeeded his father as CEO, he established an executive committee which met at the various subsidiary offices in rotation. Timpson hosted the inaugural meeting and Alex masterminded the entertainment. They all came to our home for dinner on the night before the meeting. Alex did her research; fortunately, our daughter had a close school friend from a strict Jewish family and her mum told Alex all she needed to know about serving kosher food and wine. As the home team, we put on a presentation about our business and the star turn was Michael Frank with a clear explanation of TSR, delivered with pictures, his dry wit and endearing smile. Thanks to Mike, and particularly Alex, the visit significantly improved our standing in the UDS pecking order.

At these chief executive meetings, no one had the courage to put their finger on the group's biggest problem – the misplaced strategy at UDS Tailoring. We were conscious that this was the original Lyons family business and it seemed presumptuous to point out that they had lost the plot in the part of UDS they knew so well.

From the early 1970s, made-to-measure suit sales declined rapidly and all but one of the UDS Tailoring factories was closed. In 1978 the Alexandre and Claude Alexander fascias were phased out and 100 shops were closed, leaving John Collier, the only UDS menswear brand, trading from 400 shops. This was in sharp contrast to Burtons, the business that UDS had failed to acquire only 10 years earlier. Under Ralph Halpern, Burton was transformed from a traditional tailor, facing exactly the same challenges as John Collier, into a vibrant business that dominated the high street for the next 15 years. While Halpern was designing a new type of retailing with the help of Rodney Fitch, UDS continued to promote made-to-measure suits and closed another business. Whiteleys of Bayswater was deemed to be a basket case and was the next part of the UDS portfolio to go.

1979 wasn't just a good year for Timpson; the whole of retailing, including UDS, did well. Encouraged by this upturn in fortune, UDS launched a £35m rights issue, in order to expand Richard Shops and buy another womenswear fashion chain. They spent £19.5m of the money buying Van Allan, a fast-fashion business that was competing with Top Shop and Chelsea Girl (later converted into River Island) rather than the more stylish and sophisticated Richard Shops.

Van Allan was a culture shock for the UDS directors, as the best sellers in their new business were hot pants and boob tubes. Van Allan had the freedom to develop a niche market under the previous two owners, Tootal and Combined English Stores, but CEO, Gordon Brown and his team had closer supervision after joining UDS, where they reported to Jack Maxwell, who ran Richard Shops.

UDS had no idea how to make Van Allan any better and the influence from Richard Shops made it worse. Amazingly, in 1982, Van Allan was wound up only three years after it had been acquired and, yet again, I was asked to help organise a closing- down sale. Some of the shops were converted to Richard Shops and three became Timpson, but UDS got little back from the money paid for Van Allan.

The rest of the £35m raised in the rights issue was mostly used to shore up company cash flow as trade quickly deteriorated from the 1979 peak. A proportion was invested in property, although some of the major property schemes were ill-advised, particularly the purchase of a block of shops in St Edward Street in Hull, which was redeveloped, then filled with shops from the UDS portfolio – John Collier, Richard Shops and Timpson, which all lost money. Even today, the shoe repair shop we have on St. Edward Street is one of our few loss-makers.

A few parts of UDS did well. Ocean Trading, the duty-free business, grew rapidly and the other shoe business, John Farmer, outperformed the market. But a small proportion of successful subsidiaries couldn't make up for a stream of bad news elsewhere.

In 1980, UDS launched a group-wide credit card called Vantage, in conjunction with Citibank. The idea was to create cash by handing over the debt from existing credit schemes in John Collier and the UDS Department Stores. Vantage card was a disaster; UDS replaced John Collier's successful credit scheme with higher interest rates and inferior service. The Big Crunch came when Citibank discovered an enormous number of bad debts, due to inadequate screening of new customers, many of whom didn't have a bank account; the £10m loss was shared between UDS and Citibank.

Even Richard Shops (the 1970s market leader) was losing market share, left behind by Top Shop, Miss Selfridge and River Island, who all redesigned their shops to attract a new generation of shoppers.

In spring 1982, UDS was trading poorly; the Rights Issue had been squandered on Van Allan, and, yet again, the Group had cash flow problems. I was becoming disillusioned; the low point came during a short holiday in Portugal with Alex. Bernard, who decided to take a closer interest in day-to-day business, had been round several of our London shops on Easter Monday and found some were shut. A message reached me in Portugal demanding an explanation. Based on past experience, most of those outlets, on a Bank Holiday, would have a wage bill bigger than the takings. I spent much of my holiday on the 'phone preventing panic amongst my team.

UDS, one of the UK's strongest retail groups when it bid for Timpson in 1972, was now a weak shadow of its former self and the future of Timpson business was, yet again, in doubt.

CHAPTER THIRTY-FOUR

TALK OF A BUYOUT

IN MARCH 1982, ALEX AND I went to a local charity dinner near Wilmslow, an occasion when we would happily have handed the ticket price straight to the charity and settled for a quiet evening at home. Out of my earshot, Alex sat next to a near neighbour who she had never met before – a company lawyer, Roger Lane-Smith. By the end of the evening, without asking me, Alex had invited Roger to visit my office. "Frankly, I hadn't a clue what he was talking about," Alex said as we drove home, "But I just know you should listen to what he has to say."

Roger was in my office three days later, talking with enthusiasm about a management buyout. I tried to look knowledgeable, but didn't know what a buyout was and, when Roger tried to explain, didn't understand how someone with no money could contemplate buying a business.

In May 1982, I nervously visited the Candover office to meet CEO, Roger Brooke, a bouncy character, a slightly taller version of Ronnie Corbett, who explained how management buyouts usually work. Venture Capitalists find the finance but, typically, offer the management 12.5% of the equity for a small investment (often lower than £100k). That stake can rise to 25% if targets are met by the time the company is sold or floated on the Stock Market.

Roger Brooke was pessimistic, due to our fall in profits since 1979, but profit wasn't the only thing that mattered; Wm Timpson Ltd still owned a significant number of freeholds bought by my grandfather between the two World Wars.

Roger Brooke wanted to discuss our portfolio with Paul Orchard-Lisle, from Healey & Baker, but I was worried about confidentiality and breaking my service contract, until Alex told me, "You won't get anywhere in life if you don't take a few risks".

Paul Orchard-Lisle, tall, fresh-faced and full of confidence, estimated our freehold and long leasehold properties were worth over £30m and I was despondent – how could we afford a business worth so much money? However, Roger Brook saw the portfolio as a positive advantage; it could provide UDS with an attractive pile of cash. Candover asked me for a Business Plan, so it was time to tell Peter Cookson as I couldn't continue without his help.

I met Patrick and Tim Farmer, who ran John Farmer, the other shoe chain within UDS, over dinner on their home ground near Farnham in Surrey to ask whether we should approach UDS together. They were nervous; we shared similar views but agreed to act independently.

In June 1982, Bernard Lyons announced that, at the end of the year, he would hand over the Chair of UDS to Sir Robert Clark, Chair of UDS's merchant bank, Hill Samuel. In early July, together with the other chief executives, I was invited for dinner at the Carlton Club to meet Sir Robert. Earlier that day, Gerald Ronson, of the Heron Group announced that he held over 5% of the UDS equity.

At the end of July, I took our business plan to Candover. Roger Brook was on holiday so, for the first time, I met Stephen Curran, Roger's number two. Stephen was a serious-looking composed man with a thorough knowledge of our business and a sharp sense of humour. Stephen calculated we could pay £35m and suggested it was time to make an offer to UDS.

Talking about the buyout had been fun but, now, it was about to get serious. I met Stuart to raise my concerns about UDS. He said the bid from Gerald Ronson would never happen, and there were no plans to sell Timpson. Before the meeting ended, I said that if circumstances changed, I would like the opportunity to purchase our business.

To register my interest, I sent Stuart a letter.

'Dear Stuart,

I was pleased to have your reassurance that there is no truth in the current rumours regarding Timpson. I hope that you appreciate the reasons for my concern. For the record, I would like to reiterate that if there were a change and we became a candidate for asset realisation, I should hope to be kept informed and despite the substantial sums involved, be given the opportunity to raise the finance necessary to purchase the Timpson business.

I sincerely believe that my style of management is the best way to produce a good profit performance for Timpson shops and Timpson Shoe Repairs, something I'm sure we will prove in the second half of this year'.

I didn't expect a reply to my letter and didn't get one. I already knew the buyout plan was an unrealised dream.

July was a busy month at home. We moved house. When UDS acquired Timpson, I received about £25,000 in cash, which attracted a fair amount of tax, but, unwisely, converted most of my Timpson equity into UDS Shares. We were living in quite a big house on Hough Lane, a posh part of Wilmslow, in a house which Alex made bigger by adding two bedrooms and a swimming pool. It was the only time in our married life when Alex's expenditure plans ran ahead of my ability to pay. To give us financial peace of mind, we bought a more modest property, using the price difference to pay off our mortgage.

Despite moving to a smaller house, Moss Farm in Alderley Edge, we increased the size of our family. Not just the foster children, who seemed to arrive in ever-increasing numbers, but also Oliver, a six-year-old who came to live with us with a view to becoming our adopted son.

CHAPTER THIRTY-FIVE

TAKEOVER BID

ON JANUARY 4TH, BEN POTTS AND I set off at 6.00 am to visit most of our Greater London shops – Clapham, Peckham, Tolworth, Feltham, Slough, Hammersmith and Hounslow, where I received a message to ring Patrick Farmer who told me, "An offer has been made by a bidding vehicle called Bassishaw, backed by Gerald Ronson's Heron Group, The Coal Board Pension Fund and Barclays Merchant Bank – the offer was 100p a share, valuing UDS at about £170m." By the time I got home to Cheshire, the bid was headline news and I was summoned back to London 36 hours later for a UDS Executive's meeting.

The meeting didn't amount to very much. We were all handed a letter from Sir Robert Clark, regretting the bid had been made but expressing confidence that it would be defeated. But the Sunday papers suggested another bidder was waiting in the wings, and the name most mentioned was Burton.

You feel somewhat helpless when your holding company is threatened by a takeover bid, but I reckoned whatever the outcome, we must be in a stronger position if our company produced good trading figures. For the last three years, we had never been able to match the record year in 1979. We were held back by UDS, who thought our stock levels were far too high. People with no experience of the shoe trade find it difficult to accept that specialist shoe shops only turn over their stock three times a year. Life would be easier if feet didn't come in so many different sizes.

As soon as UDS became distracted by the Bassishaw bid, day-to-day controls disappeared and we were left to run our own business. We steadily increased stock levels in the first three months of 1983. Almost every week, 200,000 pairs were delivered to our warehouse when we were selling little more than 100,000. The policy paid off; by the middle of February, sales were well above expectation.

I returned to London for the fourth time in just over a week for another UDS Executive Committee meeting, which turned into a presentation by the Chief Executives of each subsidiary for the benefit of the bid defence team – Trever Swete and Robert Dutton of Hill Samuel (UDS's merchant bank) and PR consultants, Street Financial.

Stuart Lyons chaired the meeting but Trevor Swete ran it. We each described our business, reported on recent trading, prospects for 1983 and our future plans. Patrick Farmer, Eddie Simes, a shrewd operator who ran Ocean Trading, and the vastly experienced Peter Slaymaker of Allders department stores all delivered concise reports that made commercial sense and I hope I did the same. Jim Sneddon, Managing Director of Blundells (a credit 'tallyman' business), an engaging man with an attractive sense of humour, had a more difficult job. It was an old-fashioned company that needed to change, but Jim skillfully made a convincing presentation. The mood shifted when we moved on to John Collier and Richard Shops.

Both the clothing chains had recently appointed new chief executives – Tony de Keyser had replaced Jack Maxwell at Richard Shops and David Hall took over John Collier from Mark Dixon. Both reported poor trading and were making a loss. In the discussion that followed, it became clear the UDS Board had absolutely no idea what to do.

At the end of this strange and inconclusive meeting, I spoke to Robert Dutton of Hill Samuel, who quietly admitted to me, "Whatever happens, UDS will never be the same again".

CHAPTER THIRTY-SIX

GAME ON

I FAILED TO FULFIL MY USUAL two full days a week of shop visits but since the beginning of January, I had already been on a three-day buying trip to Venice and Lake Garda and hosted our annual long service awards, a continuation of the presentations started by my grandfather in 1956 to celebrate his 60th year with the business. I usually used the long service lunch to give an update on our business prospects, but the UDS bid made this a difficult task.

During a bid battle, attention is focused on the board room drama, taking little account of the feelings or future fortune of people working on the shop floor. While the UDS Board was negotiating for its survival, the subsidiaries were left to fend for themselves. Fortunately, bigger and better ranges in the shops brought a strong start to the spring, so, despite the air of uncertainty, morale at Timpson was reasonably high.

From the day he was ousted as Chairman, my father ceased to show much interest in the business. Once he'd agreed compensation with Bernard Lyons and taken delivery of the new Bristol, his life was spent on the golf course or on holiday with my mother. I always invited my parents to the long service lunch, but this year my mother couldn't attend; an illness, treated in hospital before Christmas, left her feeling anxious and depressed. Her condition deteriorated rapidly and she was admitted to a nursing home. It was the start of a long period of dementia that lasted for 14 years.

There was an easy way to combine my frequent trips to London with the maximum possible time back home with Alex and our family – Victoria, James, Edward and now Oliver, together with sometimes as many as four foster children. My lifesaver was the Shuttle to Heathrow, which transformed business travel in the days before airport security. If Ben Potts picked me up from home before 7.00 am, as long as I got into Manchester Airport before 7.20 am, I was guaranteed a seat on the 7.30 shuttle – no booking, no ticket, no security – you just paid by credit card during the flight to London. From Heathrow, the Piccadilly line stopped at Hyde Park Corner where I got a bus down Park Lane, walking the last 300 yards to the UDS Office. My personal record was 2 hours 10 minutes, door to door.

My next Shuttle journey took me to the Hill Samuel office to discuss our figures with Trevor Swete and Robert Dutton who were masterminding the bid defence. The chat about Timpson didn't take long, but we spent an hour talking about the rest of UDS and the quality of senior management. They were highly critical of the UDS Board and despondent about John Collier and Richard Shops. I started to realise that UDS was no longer controlled by its Board; the big decisions were being made by their Merchant Bank.

I wasn't surprised to see the weekend papers reporting that the Burton Group were on the point of agreeing a deal to buy Richard Shops and John Collier. It was time to catch up with Candover, who thought it was possible to finance a bid of between £35m and £37.5m, but now, with the takeover saga developing, we needed to consider a serious offer.

Before meeting Candover, I went for a walk in Hyde Park with Peter Cookson, following the same route I covered 10 years earlier before deciding to hand in my notice to UDS. This time, we considered whether to risk an open approach to Hill Samuel. We could be going against our service contract and damage our future with UDS. It was a 'no brainer'.

At Candover, we ran through the figures. The cash from sale and leaseback deals looked like £32m, reducing our annual profit from £2.2m down to £1.4m due to the extra rent. At the year-end UDS owed William Timpson Limited £6m, but we assumed, if a deal was done, inter-company debt would be wiped out. It was agreed we could pay at least £37.5m and should make an initial offer of £35m.

With our minds made up, Stephen Curran met Trevor Swete later that evening but got a lukewarm response – our offer was noted but couldn't be taken any further. I rang Trevor Swete the following morning and he confirmed "Timpson is not for sale". He acknowledged that we could make a legitimate offer but the sale of Timpson wasn't part of their defense plan. He concluded by saying "Say nothing to Stuart Lyons"

That conversation ended any immediate buyout plans and with no more trips to London, I went back to running the business.

CHAPTER THIRTY-SEVEN

UDS ON THE RUN

UDS WAS FEATURED IN SO MANY PAPERS that I came to a handy deal with my local newsagent. To get fit for the London Marathon, I went running every morning and called at the shop just before I got home. I was allowed to flick through every paper as long as I bought all those that mentioned UDS.

Although press rumours dried up regarding Burton buying Richard Shops and John Collier, I knew negotiations were going on when Stuart Lyons asked for details of our shoe concessions. My suspicions were confirmed when Robert Dutton rang to tell me that rumours about Burton were true but negotiations were at an early stage and our conversation should be treated as highly confidential – so confidential the rest of our call was conducted in code.

I was told to use 'Blue' for Burton, 'Red' for Richard Shops and 'White' for John Collier. 'Blue' (Burton) were willing to discuss concessions with Timpson (although no one gave us a colour code!). Concession terms would not be part of any acquisition agreement so I was told to contact Burtons to make our own arrangements.

As the UDS bid developed, I became more committed to our buyout. At the beginning of February, we decided to contact Bassishaw. Roger

Lane-Smith told Rothchilds (Ronson's Merchant Bank) that if they bought UDS we would offer £35m for Timpson.

For the first time in four years, I was home alone for the weekend. The most recent foster children had gone back to their mum, Victoria was skiing with friends and Alex took James, Edward and Oliver to visit a goddaughter on Guernsey, so I was looking forward to playing golf. Sadly, the weekend didn't go to plan. My mother was due to be discharged from hospital and we organised a nurse to look after her at home, but it wasn't to be; mental illness defies expectations. Instead, she went to a nursing home, and, for the next 14 years, my father, my sister, her children, my children and myself, alongside a dwindling group of amazingly loyal and faithful friends, went to visit a loved one we hardly recognised and who seldom, if ever, recognised us.

It was a sharp reminder that, whatever issues surround your business, colleagues, your boss, suppliers, customers and even you yourself all have major personal issues that are more important than the day job.

Everything changed the following week. Robert Dutton called to tell me, "UDS are recommending a bid of 125p from Hanson Trust". While I was on the phone, Stuart was trying to ring. When we eventually spoke, he was very upbeat; "I have wonderful news. James Hanson will keep the business intact; at last, the future looks bright". However, when I met Patrick Farmer later in the day, we were both despondent. Our chances of doing a buyout seemed to have disappeared; Hanson already had 700 shoe shops in the USA.

The ever-optimistic Roger took a different view. He had met Sir Gordon White, the Hanson CEO, at a drinks party in New York and felt that the two-minute conversation was enough to make direct contact and declare our interest. Sir Gordon didn't reject our idea out of hand. With rumours that Gerald Ronson was working with Philip Harris, the carpet retailer, who was interested in buying Timpson and John Farmer, perhaps Hanson was the better option.

169

There are quiet periods during every bid battle, usually when the bidder is preparing a circular and the target considers their response. After the Hanson offer, I had time to concentrate on our business.

I was having fun with the Fitch team designing a new Timpson shop. I was impressed and seduced by Burton's spectacular success. Ralph Halpern transformed Burton, Dorothy Perkins, Top Shop, Top Man and Evans, and, in doing so, gave the high street a massive boost. He did all the things UDS should have done. He abandoned most of the made-to-measure men's suits and catered for a generation that regarded fast fashion as a fundamental part of their lifestyle. It wouldn't have worked without the right stock, but the Fitch shopfitting and graphics created a modern retail theatre that made every competitor look dull.

I looked to be part of this new wave of shop design, especially as Tony Coleman wanted Timpson concessions in the main Burton brands, (which could include John Collier). Working with Fitch seemed to be a perfect opportunity.

Fitch designer, Richard Austin, managed the Timpson account; a good choice, since we got on well. All retail designers seem to follow the same path – they ask lots of questions, identify major merchandise groups and design an identity for each category with appropriate brand names, typestyles and colours. I enjoyed watching the new Timpson emerge with 'PACE' for men, 'INSTEP', 'Charles Reynier' for women and the children's brand, 'Walkright'. It all felt so exciting in the design studio, but the real test is when you refit the first shop. That was about to happen in Wigan.

CHAPTER THIRTY-EIGHT

BIG BET ON WIGAN

ON MY 40TH BIRTHDAY, I wasn't able to visit my mother; she was so confused that no visitors were allowed.

We didn't give colleagues their birthday off in those days, so I was at the office when I heard that Bassishaw had increased their bid to £1.30; probably not good news.

The following morning, Hanson offered 145p and the press expected a Hanson victory.

I received the news on the way to meet the tall and charming Paul Orchard-Lisle, at his home, to discuss our property portfolio. Paul was on top form, studying my list with assured confidence, raising the occasional smile and making encouraging noises. I left feeling much more optimistic and Ben Potts drove me straight to Wigan where Richard Austin was waiting.

I walked into an air of despondency. Sales for the whole day were only £100, worse than normal. I expected the shop to be filled with excitement but all I could see was bewildered disappointment. Every shoe was in the right place, the shop looked exactly the way I wanted, but there were no customers.

I felt like creeping into a cupboard and having a good cry, but there was a better plan in my diary. I was booked to play squash with my friend and head-hunter, Alan Percival. Being of a similar standard and both a bit competitive, the 40 minutes on court worked off some of my frustration, but in the evening, I had plenty of time to think.

A few months before, I had become a Governor of Brookway High, a Secondary School across the road from our Head Office in Wythenshawe. That night, Alex and I went to see 'Kes', the school play. Alex said it was a highly impressive performance but I hardly heard a word. I could only think through a day that started with great hope (my preferred bidder edging ahead and a property valuation way beyond expectations), but which was wiped out the moment I walked into Wigan. Seven months' work, £35,000 in design fees and £75,000 in shopfitting costs invested in a scheme that didn't seem to work. Its success was the key plank of my business plan; it was meant to increase sales by 15%, not make them worse – how could we win when my magic refit failed to hit the spot?

On the way home, Alex said, "You were very quiet". "I was just thinking about my day," I replied. "It's been a bit of a rollercoaster, but I'm beginning to realise this buyout won't happen." Alex pulled into a layby, held my hands and looked me straight in the eye. "Listen to me," said Alex. "I'm telling you it will all work out in the end."

Alex, four children and our role as foster carers had reshaped my Saturdays, which, before I got married, were wall-to wall-sport – golf in the morning and either hockey or cricket in the afternoon. Now, my main exercise was running, with the London Marathon only a fortnight away (that Saturday, the paper shop revealed the Richard Shops team were hoping to achieve a buyout).

Just before lunch, I visited Aunt Ruth, my father's elder sister, who was in her mid-70s, an addictive cryptic crossword-solver with a mind as sharp as a pin. If Ruth had taken over the running of our family business from her father, it could have been a different story. She had a severe hearing problem, but her main barrier to employment was being a woman; the family's ideal candidate was ignored because of her gender. As well as having a sharp brain, Ruth was tough. Her husband had died before she was 60 and they had no children, but she remained fiercely independent, living in the same house on Manchester Road, Wilmslow until she died in her 90s.

I needed Ruth's help. We talked about the business and I outlined my buyout plan and then nervously asked if I could borrow some money. If the buyout went ahead, I needed up to £130,000 and, without going to the bank, I was struggling to find more than £40,000. Ruth was fascinated by my plan and was keen to help. She became a true mentor, demonstrating the latent business expertise that should have been used in the Timpson Board Room.

Alex hated cooking. She tolerated cooking for the children – regarding fish fingers as the perfect timesaver for young mothers – but seldom cooked for the two of us. Whenever I got home, I was sent out to buy a takeaway or find a babysitter. (With the continuous flow of foster children, we relied on babysitters for 40 consecutive years).

Usually, we went to a local restaurant for a chat – we ran our life across a dining table or over a morning cup of tea in bed. They were the precious moments when I off-loaded my news and Alex provided a heavy dose of common sense. We favoured several restaurants over the years, but by 1983, our first choice was the No 15 Wine Bar in Alderley Edge, owned by Shirley Eaton, who helped Alex with the interior design of our home. We went to the Wine Bar's opening night and must have been their most frequent customers – four nights in a week wasn't unusual. Our children claimed they ate more meals at the Wine Bar than they had at home.

We seldom went straight home, dropping in at the Moss Rose, a traditional pub at the end of a cul-de-sac, with a crown bowling green and a limited menu of crisps, pork pie and pickled eggs. It was run by Ken and Ira Crossfield, mother of our housekeeper (and Alex's best friend), June Kent. The Moss Rose, also referred to as the Drum and Monkey, had three main rooms. One for darts and dominoes, another for the general public and a small snug reserved for Ken and Ira's friends and relations.

After a bit, we were welcomed into the family, ignored closing time and enjoyed nightly lock-ins until midnight. It suited us much more than the Cheshire set dinner party circuit.

That Saturday, I had booked our regular babysitter, Robbo (Vi Roberts, our ironing lady), but there was always a major obstacle on Saturday nights. Sometime between 7 pm and 8 pm, I would get a phone call from Bill Dawes giving me figures for the week. Alex found it intensely irritating, waiting for the phone to ring before we could go out. I started getting these calls in 1973 when Margaret Broadley rang about Swears & Wells and Alex found them just as annoying 10 years later.

That week, Bill Dawes reported a very healthy 15% sales increase and, of major significance, a very good week in Wigan (60% up). Even Alex appreciated the phone call that night as it made for a convivial evening; the fish pie at the No 15 Wine Bar never tasted better.

CHAPTER THIRTY-NINE

COMMITTED TO CANDOVER

WHEN MY NEXT TRAINING RUN finished at the paper shop, I discovered plenty of new developments. The UDS Board continued to be split 6-2 with Hill Samuel in the minority. The executive team backed Bassishaw saying their bid was 'in the best interests of UDS employees.'

There were several rumours about Richard Shops and John Collier. Some said Burton was negotiating to buy both clothing chains, others thought both were seeking a buyout, while the Daily Telegraph said that Gerald Ronson, if he lost, would use his 15% stake to buy the clothing chains. During a telephone call with Roger, Sir Gordon White said these were simply rumours coming from Ronson.

I had good news on the property valuation. Paul Orchard-Lisle estimated £32.66m could be raised on a leaseback rental of £1.71m, giving a funding rate of 5.05%. It was the highest estimate so far, well over the £30m I was expecting. We talked fees; Paul wanted 1%, which could have given him £325,000, but I spoke to him two days later, dropping the fee to .75% with a maximum of £250,000, which he agreed without quibble within 10 seconds.

The property news was just what Candover needed to make the next move. Sales at Timpson were good, our forward plan was well received and with Paul Orchard-Lisle's latest valuation, Roger Brooke thought we could offer up to £40m. He arranged to visit Wythenshawe and meet our management team, Bill Dawes, Michael Frank and Jim Taylor.

Michael and Bill took Roger around some shops, and, back in the sample room, Jim described our merchandise. Roger left, impressed with the team and keen to press ahead.

I asked Roger to outline the financial deal each director would be offered. He talked about a management investment of £200,000 (lower than the £250,000 he first mentioned, but a figure I held him to). This would give the management 12.5% of the equity, rising to 25% if performance targets were met. The institutional investors would hold the remaining shares and loan the fixed interest capital.

While driving back to the airport, we discussed the choice of non-executive Chairman. I suggested Trevor Morgan, once Chief Executive of Turner's Shoes and then a director of Hepworth, respected amongst fellow footwear retailers, with a shrewd analytical brain and design flair. Roger was intrigued; Trevor's name had already been suggested by Michael Stoddart, Chief Executive of Electra Trust, who was taking a close interest in our deal. Progress was being made.

CHAPTER FORTY

END OF TWO MARATHONS

EVERY YEAR, WITH MILLIONS OF OTHERS, I visited the local
betting shop – on Grand National Day, 1983, the family picked 6 horses.
I placed our bet with John Peel in Alderley Edge, a dingy little side-street
shop that had none of the comforts that bookmakers have today. No television screen, no restroom, no seats, no copies of Racing Post on the wall
or any gambling machines that can ruin people's lives. Betting shops were
hardly retail shops in those days but they certainly are now – another part
of the changing high street, which was about to be changed even more
by the battle for UDS.

I enjoyed a real bonus that day – not particularly on the horses,
although first, third and fourth won me over £30. The unexpected pleasure was provided by my mother, who, for the first time in months, agreed
to go out in my car. I took her to Dunham Massey where there was a
spectacular display of daffodils. She made me stop and she smiled; it was
the last smile I ever saw on her face, but I didn't know it at the time. We
didn't say much because, by then, my mother hardly spoke, but we held
hands and she managed a gentle squeeze. Little things can mean a lot.

There was a lull on the bid front, but my diary was full for the rest of the week. The following Sunday, I was running in the London Marathon. Saturday was my last long training run – 13 miles. It went so well that I ran another 7 miles the following morning and disaster struck. I jarred my knee so badly I had difficulty walking home with the Sunday papers. I dared not tell Alex, who would have sent me to the doctor, who, in turn, would have made me withdraw from the Marathon. My answer was to play 54 holes of golf.

Before I met Alex, I founded a golfing society that initially took 8 and then 12 golfers to Castletown on the Isle of Man. The society is still going but I don't go anymore. Alex hated the whole idea of me on holiday with a load of men, while she was at home looking after our children, and, latterly, a few other people's children. She had a very good point, but backing down from the Shanks Golfing Society was always the defining line in our relationship. This year, I thought Alex wouldn't mind if I joined the group for a day and a half – I was wrong.

That year, the society played at Holyhead on Anglesey, a seaside course with challenges for most golfers but friendly enough for average players to enjoy their round. I played on Sunday afternoon and all day Monday, with no bad reaction from my knee. I left the Dormy House very early on Tuesday morning to pick up my mother-in-law from her cottage near Caernarfon, so she could join us for an important family event – Oliver's adoption.

The legal ceremony took place in the courtroom at Macclesfield. For the Court, it was just a paper exercise, but everyone was very nice to Oliver and made it a special occasion. We were outside in the car park after 20 minutes, taking photographs, before a celebration lunch back home.

Living with Oliver taught us a lot about looking after children, particularly those who lack a loving bond in the early years. New adoptive parents and foster carers are unprepared for the special needs of a child who lacks the security that comes from a strong attachment as an infant. We had a lot to learn.

While I played golf, the papers continued to speculate about UDS. The Board Room split became more acute. The Guardian criticised the Lyons family and Executive Directors for failing to take account of the shareholder's interests, but they continued to back the lower Bassishaw bid.

I had the rest of the week off and took the family to London for some sightseeing before registering for the London Marathon.

Not many marathon runners set off from the Montcalm Hotel, near Marble Arch, but once on the train to Greenwich, greased against jogger's nipple, you are just one runner in a very big race.

The marathon story has been told many times, about the thrill of the occasion, the buzz of the crowd, hitting the wall at 20 miles and the relief of getting to the finish – job done – a personal best but I still didn't beat 4 hours. The knee was my excuse – the pain started just as I passed the Cutty Sark and constantly niggled all the way to the Mall, where I spotted my family, desperately wondering whether I would ever appear.

I presented a cheque for £3,500 to Kilrie, the Children's Home where we first met Oliver and this was also home to our first two foster children. Little did I know that Kilrie would become the subject of an investigation into child abuse. I now view that marathon with mixed emotions.

Still limping four days later, there was a message when I got home – "Ring Mr Alexander of Hanson Trust". 1 rang immediately, hoping to discuss our buyout. He soon put me right. "James Hanson has sent you a letter explaining that Hanson Trust wishes to develop UDS and refutes any claims made by UDS directors in various newspaper advertisements. I am ringing to assure you that Hanson values your business and your cooperation."

It all came to an abrupt end. Two days later, the Teletext on my television stated 'Hanson Trust has 50% of UDS and their offer is unconditional'.

CHAPTER FORTY-ONE

LIFE WITH HANSON TRUST

THAT WEEKEND WAS AN ANTI-CLIMAX. After four months of exciting uncertainty, everything was suddenly settled. A quiet weekend wasn't helped by watching a further chapter in Manchester City's slide towards the Second Division.

By Monday, the bid was history. It was Alex's birthday; we went out for dinner and wondered what the next year had in store.

Despite this feeling of anti-climax, Candover were just as keen. Stephen Curran visited Manchester to look around a few shops and visit the office. He thought our buyout chances had increased and thought we could pay £37.5m. He also told me that Trevor Morgan gave a favourable report on the business, and, with Trevor's close connection to Michael Stoddart, a key Candover director, his opinion mattered.

During Stephen's visit, I received the first direct contact from Hanson – a telex telling us to cancel all capital expenditure. I also got a call from Richard Dyson of Ernst & Whinney to say he would arrive the following day to commence a detailed audit on behalf of Hanson.

I spoke to Stuart Lyons for the first time since the takeover – he felt

Hanson had handled him fairly but was bitter about Sir Robert Clark; "My family appointed Sir Robert as Chairman only to be betrayed".

Thursday 20th April was a critical day – Paul Orchard-Lisle was due to forecast the capital he felt he could raise. The telephone call was full of tension. With each figure, suspense mounted. Nearly 50 properties were involved, so I could only judge the full implications when all the rents and capital values had been added up. I needed to raise £32.5m, with a rent total no higher than £1.85m, otherwise, all bets were off.

In the excitement, my first calculation was wrong – an incredible £34.5m – eventually we got the sums to agree – Capital £32.5m – rental value £1.83m – just within our requirement.

The next step was to visit NatWest in Manchester. Peter Cookson, Roger Lane-Smith and myself met Alan Jones and his assistant, Rod Hudson. Our meeting went well; the idea of borrowing £7m wasn't out of the question. I was more concerned about meeting Trevor Morgan – the possible non-executive Chairman. We arranged to meet at our new home, Moss Farm, and Trevor was late.

I had known Trevor for several years through the Multiple Shoe Retailers' Association but this was our first one-to-one meeting. Trevor started with Saxone, who were acquired by Sears and became part of the British Shoe Corporation. After leaving British Shoe, he became Managing Director of Turner's Shoes, a multiple with about 150 shops owned by a family trust. In 1980, Trevor sold Turner's to Hepworths, then the UK's third-largest tailoring chain, and joined the Hepworth Board.

Two years later, Trevor acquired Kendalls Rainwear, a rundown chain of shops, and invited George Davies to join Hepworths to turn his acquisition into a new chain of shops called Next. Next was an immediate success and became the talk of the High Street.

We met in our recently converted barn, a quiet venue but cold; the heating wasn't working. Trevor's speciality was property and he was clearly unhappy that I had become so committed to Healey & Baker – he felt his expertise would have brought a better deal.

We dined at the Bridge Hotel in Prestbury, where Trevor said we had little chance of success. He didn't think we could fund our deal through sale and leasebacks. He thought Hanson would keep the properties or ask for a much higher price than we could afford. I was confused; by the time we finished dinner, he had destroyed my entire buyout plan.

I didn't agree with Trevor's analysis but felt he was ideally suited to be Chairman. I confirmed this to Stephen Curran, who, in turn, spoke to Trevor who was due to retire from his executive role at Hepworth.

We were in a similar situation to John Farmer, so I kept in regular contact with Patrick Farmer. We spoke after Tony Alexander visited the John Farmer office in Aldershot, when Patrick got the impression that Hanson wasn't keen on shoe retailing and didn't understand property – both bits of good news. Patrick told Tony Alexander he wanted to organise a buyout, but received little response – we all had to wait until Ernst & Whinney finished their report.

Despite these diversions, my main interest was our own buyout. Gradually, others in the business had to be told. I informed Charles Noakes, the Shoe Repairs Merchandising Director, so we could have a free discussion in our directors' dining room. The senior accountants were involved when we started to prepare a formal plan for Candover. I also told Mike Williams, our Property Manager. He talked to Healey & Baker in an attempt to improve their valuation.

Paul Orchard-Lisle stressed we had a special kind of deal. We were in a weak bargaining position – without the property sales, we couldn't fund the buyout. The need for confidentiality meant approaching a small number of property investors with plenty of money. The two selected, Commercial Union and Scottish Amicable, would be involved in considerable speculative work. Both asked for an outline of our Company Plan and wanted to meet me to see if I was, or appeared to be, an "honourable gentleman".

As Peter Cookson progressed our Company Plan, one big problem emerged – Capital Gains. Hanson could face a tax liability of at least

£7m if they sold the Timpson business. The tax problem was a decided setback, but Peter Cookson and Peat Marwick in Manchester thought there was a solution.

All my advice was on a "no deal no fee" basis but every advisor had the prospect of sharing in any successful outcome. This is part of Candover's normal risk, but Roger Lane-Smith went well beyond the normal amount of free speculative work. Roger has always had amazing determination – he was intent on building a leading law firm – not just in commercial law – and his client list included celebrities, but this was his biggest ever deal and he wouldn't receive a penny unless our deal went through.

Business continued to be good, so good that I had no need to worry about shoe shops and shoe repairs. The evening before the meeting with Tony Alexander was spent playing bowls for the local pub – The Moss Rose. The match that night was a disaster. I lacked concentration, played badly and lost. After the game, I went out with Alex to the local wine bar before a disturbed night. By then, I was having so many sleepless nights I slept in our converted barn so I did not disturb the rest of the family.

I rehearsed several ways of mentioning the management buyout but had no idea how the meeting would progress. It started well – Tony Alexander and I went to the same prep school (Wadham House in Hale) and had some mutual acquaintances, but he soon turned the conversation to business. He described the Hanson Trust philosophy which he summarized in five points:

1. The Hanson Head Office was as small as possible – the directors were proud that it contained less than 30 people.
2. Hanson Trust did not run the business; it controlled the managers who ran the business.
3. All results were measured by return on capital employed. Anything less than 20% was unacceptable.
4. If a poor return was caused by poor management, the management team was changed.

5. If the management was good but the return wasn't, they were in the wrong business and sold it.

Having listened to this description of Hanson, I declared that my preferred outcome was a management buyout.

Tony Alexander said everyone in UDS seemed to want to buy their business and expressed disbelief that anyone could raise enough cash or that a buyout could be financially viable.

I told him my approach was not half-baked. I said we could offer £35m, but he did not believe me. He asked how I could raise that kind of money. I said there would be an element of sale and leaseback and support from NatWest and Candover. He found it difficult to believe I could raise £35m but agreed to discuss the idea with his colleagues and also talk to Stephen Curran.

I had dinner with Michael McAvoy to discuss our strategy with Hanson. We decided I should demonstrate shoe retailing is a high-risk business and that Timpson was well run but very dependent on myself. We wanted Hanson to believe Timpson couldn't achieve their required return and should, therefore, be sold.

Charles Noakes
(TSR Merchandise Director)

Alan Chatterton
(The hyperactive engine room of TSR)

Mike Williams
(Property Director)

Martin Tragen
(Finance Director
1991–2003)

Patrick Farmer
(The perfect Non-Executive
Director)

Move from a big office and distribution centre to modest premises

Timpson House, Southmoor Road

Timpson House, Southmoor Road

New Timpson House, Claverton Road, 1987

New Timpson House 2021

Overwhelming shoe retail competition

The Buyout Board

Bill Dawes, Retails Director. Michael Frank, TSR Controller. Bert Brownhill, IT.
John Timpson, Managing Director. Peter Cookson, Finance Director.
Jim Taylor, Buying Director

Trevor Morgan
(Chairman)

Stephen Curran
(Non-Executive)

Roger Lane-Smith
(Non-Executive)

Partners in the UDS Group

Bernard Lyons
(Chairman)

Stuart Lyons
(Managing Director)

Marketing in the late 1970s

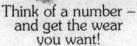

Think of a number – and get the wear you want!

The Timpson Shoe Code is designed to give you fair wear and a fair deal. The numbers (and their associated colours) tell you exactly what to expect from each of the 6 main classes of Timpson footwear.

1 Wet weather wear
Wellington boots, overshoes.

2 Specialist footwear
For climbing, long-distance walking, football, golf and other sporting activities.

3 Heavy duty
Industrial working boots and shoes – also warm-lined footwear.

4 Outdoor every day
Shoes to wear in and around town, suitable for the majority of normal business occasions.

5 Outdoor occasional
Fashion shoes for parties and smart occasions; also sandals, lightweight shoes and summer holiday wear.

6 Indoor
Slippers, dancing shoes, lightweight evening shoes.

Let the numbers help you to choose shoes wisely – and get the full benefits of the Timpson Promise.

The Timpson Promise
If you have a good reason to be dissatisfied with our shoes or our shoe repair service, we will give you your money back.

John Timpson

Footwear Care
Footnotes from

The Shoe People

at Timpson Shoe Repairs

Speaking for your shoes, may I offer a few tips on how to treat us? We'd appreciate your attention, and promise to repay it in even longer, trouble-free service to you and your feet.

£1 off all Timpson Loafers

£1 OFF Loafers

£8.99 £12.99
£13.99
£4.99 £8.99
£9.99
£12.99
£13.99
£15.99

Genuine reductions on our normal stock of loafers! We are altering nothing except the price! At £1 less than the usual Timpson prices, LOAFERS are even better value. Now you can afford casual comfort for the whole family. But hurry! This special offer is for a limited period only. Remember, if you have good reason to be dissatisfied with your shoes we will give you your money back.

It pays to come to

TIMPSON
The Shoe People

Fit for School

No need to pay more for correctly fitted children's shoes

Timpson is young but far-sighted right through those long classroom hours—and for a lifetime of healthy growth.

The right-fitting shoe calls for a half size or a special width. So we supply them in most extra sharp, from a range combining parent-pleasing prices with styles that youngsters like to wear. And, of course, there's no charge at all for the care and skill of our specially-trained children's shoe fitters. Remember, if you have good reason to be dissatisfied with your shoes we will give you your money back.

CUT PRICE VALUE!

Plimsolls	99p
Plimsolls	£1.50
Wellingtons	£1.50
Wellingtons	£1.50
Boys Football Boots	£3.50
Slippers	£1.50

It pays to come to

TIMPSON
The Shoe People

CHAPTER FORTY-TWO

NEGOTIATING

AFTER THE MEETING WITH Tony Alexander, I stayed in London for the rest of the week.

Each day started with a sightseeing jog from my hotel at Marble Arch. The tour included Park Lane, Hyde Park Corner, Buckingham Palace, Westminster, Trafalgar Square, Piccadilly Circus, Regent Street and Oxford Street. It took 40 minutes – a splendid start to the day.

I visited Richard Shops to discuss our concessions. They thought Hanson knew little about retailing and expected to be sold; Bassishaw was their favourite predator.

I had a longer meeting than usual with Paul Orchard-Lisle, who introduced me to Chris Kennedy from Commercial Union. I had also offered to meet Scottish Amicable but they only wished to see our Company Plan. It is amazing how many bankers and accountants put their faith in forecasts without meeting the people who make up the numbers.

Commercial Union, having surveyed a number of sites, were unhappy with the condition of some buildings – this did not surprise me, as UDS always pruned maintenance expenditure. At Hanley, Lincoln, Inverness and Falkirk, money would be retained from the price pending satisfactory repairs.

The property in Market Street, Manchester, had to be treated separately. Our shop was next to John Collier, with the two properties interlinked in a way that reduced the value. We went under their basement and they occupied all the second floor – a 'flying freehold' It would help to sell the Timpson and Collier shops as one freehold and share the proceeds.

The likely proceeds of properties offered to Commercial Union, Scottish Amicable and a third institution, New London Properties, looked like this:

C.U.	£19m
Scot Am	£11m
New London	£3m
Manchester	£1m
	————
Total	**£34m**

We would pay a total rent of £1.85m with reviews at 3, 5 or 7 years and sign a 25-year lease on each property.

All this seemed encouraging but they couldn't offer help with our Capital Gains Tax problem.

We got more good news. Roger contacted Sir Gordon White, who, like Tony Alexander, was waiting for the Ernst & Whinney report, but already knew UDS was a complicated business. He agreed to meet us for dinner during his visit to the UK in three weeks.

When Bill Dawes made his usual Saturday call, the sales were good but Bill was worried. He had heard about a visit by Hanson's Peter Turner to David Hall at Collier. David's car and chauffeur didn't fit the Hanson scale of perks and changes had to be made. Bill knew I was meeting Peter Turner the following week and suggested I gave both Ben Potts and my car a holiday.

Bill's concern prompted a chat with Alex. We discussed what would happen if Hanson decided not to sell Timpson. We agreed I wouldn't change the way the business was run. I would continue with my business lifestyle, including the same car and Ben Potts. I would give Hanson no more than two years but then would probably leave and completely change our approach to life. That conversation strengthened my negotiating position – I had no fear of losing my job or the impact on our family.

When Peter Turner came to visit the following week, instead of giving Ben Potts the day off, I sent him to meet the train.

Before Peter Turner arrived, I went through Ernst & Whinney's report with Richard Dyson. There were no problems, so he wished me success with the buyout plan mentioned by Roger.

Peter Turner arrived late. He left the train at Stockport, but we had arranged to meet him at Wilmslow. To demonstrate the risks of our business, we visited towns with lots of competition. I showed him the refitted store at Wigan and other shops which, in contrast, were in dire need of investment.

In five hours, we saw twelve shoe and shoe repair shops, toured the offices and visited the warehouse. The only executive he met was Jim Taylor, who showed the full range of footwear and demonstrated the complexity of our widespread market. I didn't let anyone else see him; I wanted to appear as the driving force with no strength of management in support.

During the day, he emphasised that we were not for sale, but from the questions he asked about the management team and our competitors, he knew we were a risky business.

While taking him back to Wilmslow Station, I asked how I could obtain investment capital from Hanson. He suggested I should make a video and send it to him in London.

He just caught his train. I found him very personable – and he never mentioned my car or Ben Potts.

While Hanson waited for Ernst & Whinney, everything was on hold. I was kept going by the prospect of meeting Sir Gordon White. Despite the uncertainty, I felt surprisingly happy and confident. This helped when

I met employees at Wythenshawe or in the shops. They were worried about their future and my cheerfulness (not something I am normally known for) may have given some hope.

Peter Turner's request for a video provided an excellent way to communicate. My film showed all the risks – high stocks, heavy competition, fast-changing fashion, and massive changes on the High Street. I hoped it would ensure my message was received and understood.

I also wrote a C.V. for Roger to include in a letter to Sir Gordon White. He felt my background and the circumstances that led to the UDS takeover would show we were the best buyers for Timpson.

Once that letter went to Sir Gordon White and the video was dispatched to Peter Turner, there was nothing else to do but wait.

I rang Peter Turner who hadn't shown the video to anyone because there was no capital available for refits. It was Spring Bank Holiday weekend, which I spent with Alex and our four children in my mother-in-law's Welsh cottage.

I left the family in Wales and returned to the office. On Wednesday, Tony Alexander rang to say he wanted to visit with the designated UDS Chairman, Peter Harper. Tony was keen to come as early as possible, so we arranged to meet the following day.

Father called at the office. He was even more disturbed about Mother whose dementia was worsening. We went to the Hale Conservative Club for two frames of snooker. The standard of play was awful, with Father worried about Mother and me thinking about Tony Alexander's visit.

I kept myself occupied until bedtime. After calling back at the office, I played squash, cooked a meal and went to "The Drum & Monkey" where I stayed until closing time.

I had a pint too many and felt slightly fragile as I waited for Tony Alexander and Peter Harper to come off the London Shuttle. Peter Harper had been brought back into Hanson Trust to run UDS, after three years with Laing Construction. He was a pleasant man but I have never met anyone less like a multiple retailer.

I never mentioned the buyout – nor did Tony Alexander. We spent the time discussing how to calculate our return on investment. They conceded that property assets needed a different accountancy treatment to the Hanson standard and we agreed Timpson would never clear the 20% Hanson hurdle. Peter Harper had clearly watched my video and received the risk message. They caught the shuttle to London having completed my programme, but I didn't know if I had persuaded them to sell Timpson. While I was in Italy, travelling from Rome to Venice, Sir Gordon White was due to visit London with Jim Taylor and Chris McLullich, looking at shoe shops as a guide to the following summer's styling. I was looking forward to the trip, especially as Alex was joining me for a few days in Venice.

By the time we got to Florence, Sir Gordon had arranged to meet us the following Wednesday. He said he had received several offers for our business, and the assets were valued at £52m. They would give the management first shout and preferred to sell to us.

Progress at last – our business was for sale and we had a meeting. The waiting was over and we could make the offer we had been planning for over a year.

CHAPTER FORTY-THREE

NEGOTIATING WITH HANSON TRUST

AS SOON AS I GOT TO VENICE, I made arrangements to fly to London the following Tuesday. Alex was joining us together with Gay, Jim Taylor's wife. We planned to spend two days in Venice and another two at a shoe fair by Lake Garda. I looked forward to a relaxing weekend.

On Saturday, Alex brought the daily papers with news of the Birthday Honours List. We were now negotiating with Lord Hanson.

I spent Sunday with Alex on the Lido, where I made notes for the meeting with Sir Gordon White. I felt we should offer a lump sum for the business and its properties, and that our offer must be under £40m – I tried to list reasons why that represented a fair price to Hanson. If they were looking for £52m, we had a difficult task.

I left Alex in Italy, dropped the car at Linate airport, and, after an uneventful flight, booked into the Inter-Continental Hotel in London.

I went to Michael McAvoy's office for lunch. He was insistent that no matter what I said to Sir Gordon White, I must include the phrase "This is the best thing for the business".

NEGOTIATING WITH HANSON TRUST

Later in the afternoon, we had a meeting at Candover with Roger, Peter Cookson and Stephen Curran. We went through the figures yet again. Assuming we could raise £34m from sale and leaseback, we could afford to pay a further £6m for the business and still provide an attractive return. Our calculations assumed a 5 1/2% rental on the leaseback and an average bank overdraft of £4m to fund the working capital – with peak bank borrowings of £7m. Stephen Curran felt confident that he could raise the £6m required from his institutions. Some properties were owned by William Timpson Limited; the remainder were on the books of UDS. We would incur Capital Gains Tax of £2½m on the William Timpson properties, and we assumed Hanson would pay any Capital Gains Tax on properties owned by UDS.

We agreed to offer £37½m or £40m if Hanson paid all our Capital Gains Tax. There was an inter-company balance of £2m that UDS owed to William Timpson, but there was no way we could expect to recover the money, so to enhance the price, we decided to offer a dividend of £2m to write it off.

I rang Trevor Morgan and he agreed to the terms and wished us luck for the next day.

Gordon White, a tall, bald, congenial man with a playboy reputation, was accompanied by Tony Alexander, who was more serious than I remembered him from our previous encounters.

We didn't waste much time. I thanked them for seeing us and explained why I thought a management buyout was the best thing for the business and outlined our offer of £37.5m. Tony Alexander responded immediately saying, "We are a long way apart; we have something worth £54 and you are offering less than £40m." However, he went on to give a bit of hope.

"The only way this is going to work is if you can help us with our tax problem. We face a £7.5m Capital Gains Tax bill. If you can find a bit more money and solve our tax issues, we might be talking."

After Roger jokingly suggested Hanson should roll over all the gains into a very expensive racehorse, he asked for permission to approach

Tax Counsel at Hanson's expense. That was agreed and our meeting was at an end.

There was not much more to be done that day. I went to Candover to report to Stephen Curran, who was mildly encouraged and rang Peter Cookson who started work on the tax problem.

Capital Gains Tax was included in our calculations but we assumed Hanson would have a way of mitigating their own liability. We never contemplated having to solve Hanson's problems as well as our own.

The following day, Peter Cookson was enthusiastic – he believed there was a solution. We spent the day with David Briggs from Peat Marwick, Manchester, discussing whether his idea worked. Although we offered a lump sum for the business including the property, at some stage we would have to split the price between the purchase of William Timpson Limited and the properties not owned by Timpson. We hoped to use that split to our advantage.

UDS bought William Timpson Ltd for £26.5m in 1972, so we proposed to buy the Company for £8m thus establishing a large capital loss that Hanson could set against the gain made on the properties – which we would purchase for £32m. The net gain would be £3m reducing their tax liability to less than £1m. At the same time, the gain we made on those William Timpson properties involved in the sale and leaseback could be rolled over into the other UDS properties. Our tax would be no more than £0.5m.

After discussing the scheme for most of the day, I was still doubtful we could come to terms with Hanson but at least there seemed more hope.

The week ended with everyone hopeful. The tax scheme seemed viable. Roger sent a letter to Tony Alexander confirming an increased offer of £40m for the business and its properties. At my insistence, he included a detailed property list.

As some were no longer trading as Timpson, it was important to clarify what we were offering to buy.

We met at Candover prior to seeing the Tax Counsel, Peter Whiteman, Q.C. While waiting outside the chambers, we talked to the Peat's team, who didn't feel our tax scheme had much chance of success. The conference was in stark contrast to their advice.

The favoured route was to pay £40m, split in the following way:

£8.35m for William Timpson Ltd
£25m for properties owned by UDS that we proposed to lease back
£6.65m for the other properties held by UDS.

This would give a tax liability of £540,000 for Timpson and £1.455m for Hanson Trust.

Peter Whiteman was personable, sympathetic and expressed himself very clearly – he thought the scheme should work.

We returned to the Candover office where the experts continued their intellectual tax discussion, and I rang Roger, who was on holiday in France – he was pleased with the news.

I should have been staying at the Howard Hotel, near to Candover's office but they rang to explain their air conditioning was not working. I readily accepted a transfer to the Savoy – not realising they had no air conditioning at all.

Before a very humid night, I met Stephen Curran for dinner. We began the evening talking about the following day's meeting with Tony Alexander, then the conversation strayed to other matters.

I started to discover the real Stephen Curran – a man who enjoyed the same strong rule from his wife, Ann, as I experienced from Alex, with business tugging in the other direction. Stephen explained how the tension of each deal was heightened by the knowledge that it was a major event in the personal lives of the managers he was representing.

We discussed the directors' percentage stake. I made it clear that I would expect a majority of the management shares.

For the first time, Stephen suggested the Company should take out an assurance policy on my life. It made me realise things were becoming serious.

CHAPTER FORTY-FOUR

SERIOUS
NEGOTIATIONS

I WENT TO BROMPTON ROAD by tube and caught the wrong train. Panic set in. When I found Hanson Trust at 9.58 am, I was sweating profusely and found Stephen Curran waiting anxiously at reception.

At precisely 10.00 am, we went into Tony Alexander's office – he was joined by fellow director, Tony Branson.

I outlined our tax scheme, which would reduce the Hanson tax charge to less than £1.5m.

Although Tony Branson said they expected us to suggest something similar, their mood was encouragingly enthusiastic. Our scheme saved us £2m in Capital Gains Tax which was why we revised our original offer to £40m.

Tony Alexander was obviously giving our deal serious thought. He gave us details of the freehold properties we shared with other UDS companies where we would be offered a 150-year lease at a peppercorn rent. During this conversation, I asked whether Oxford was involved in any special treatment. Oxford was worth £3¾m, and I wanted confirmation it was included in the deal. There appeared to be no problem.

We discussed pension schemes and the possible timing of a deal. In response to our offer of £40m, Tony Alexander promised to speak to Sir Gordon White and come back with their idea of price – Stephen agreed to put our offer in writing.

For the first time, we had a real chance of doing a deal – it was their move – they promised to come back within a week.

Suddenly, I felt anxious. For 12 months, I pursued the idea of a management buyout without much chance of success. I enjoyed the chase but never seriously thought we would be successful. Now, success became a possibility and I would be disappointed if we failed. I was subdued on the very day the adrenaline should have been running freely.

On the way to meet Trevor at the Royal Thames Yacht Club, I bought two suits from Marks & Spencer. Alex later persuaded me it would be bad luck to wear them while we were still negotiating with Hanson. I followed her advice.

Over lunch, Trevor said the properties were worth over £37m, at least £3m more than the Healey & Baker figure. We arrived late at Healey & Baker to meet Paul Orchard-Lisle because Trevor (a cost-conscious man) insisted we went by tube instead of by taxi. Within five minutes, I knew that Paul and Trevor would not get on. Paul was impetuous, Trevor was deliberate. Paul took a broad-brush approach, Trevor enjoyed detail – neither had respect for the other.

While events moved quickly at Timpson, there was also frantic action in the rest of UDS. I had no inside knowledge, but heard lots of rumours – 'John Collier have difficulty getting city backing for their buyout, but Hanson are considering giving them some financial support – Halpern is willing to pay the earth for Richard Shops – Ronson could sell his UDS shares'.

I was having a normal business meeting with Bill Dawes, my Sales Director, who had just returned from holiday, when Roger rang. He had heard from Tony Alexander who made the following points:

- "Our tax plan appeared to be workable"
- He was concerned we only had 80% of the finance available (we had made this point as a negotiating ploy).
- Our price is at the lower end of their range. If we could go up by £3m (to £43m) we will carry the day.
- So far, they have kept their word and not offered the business to anyone else".

The deal was coming to a vital stage. I arranged to meet at Candover the following morning.

Our ability to match the Hanson price depended on raising enough money from the properties. I rang Bryan Laxton at Healey & Baker to confirm a deal was in sight. He sounded much keener and estimated £34m could be raised with some higher-yielding properties worth £3½m left in reserve.

I spoke to Alan Jones at NatWest, who felt he could support an overdraft of £7m. I checked again with Trevor Morgan, who still thought we could raise £36m from the properties.

I was up at 6.00 am for a five-mile run before joining Peter Cookson and Roger on the early train to London. We discussed tactics on the way and agreed the best way to bridge the gap between £40m and £43m was by offering some form of deferred consideration. We felt it better to introduce a new element into the negotiation rather than simply increasing the price.

We waited all day before arranging to meet Tony Alexander at 5.45 pm. Stephen, Roger and myself, got to Brompton Road at 5.30 pm – Tony Alexander was joined by Alan Hadrup to start the meeting at 5.52. We started with concessions. We agreed to enter into a concession contract with Burton, Bassishaw or the Collier management. We talked about our flying freehold at Market Street, Manchester before moving on to the real deal.

Roger, acting as our spokesman, offered £40m plus £1.5m payable over 3 years. In addition, we offered to purchase £1m of tax losses by setting

£0.5m against the inter-company loan. We would also pay a dividend of approximately £2m to extinguish the inter-company loan account. We agreed an interest rate of 10% on the £1.5m deferred consideration.

They withdrew, and, on returning, asked for the £1.5m to be increased to £2m. We agreed. Alan Hadrup poured us all a stiff whisky while Tony Alexander rang Sir Gordon White.

Tony Alexander quickly returned and told us we had a deal.

There was goodwill on both sides; we all agreed it was a good deal for the business and good public relations for Hanson.

Before we left, Tony Alexander said he wanted a line to be drawn on the inter-company account at the end of that week, on June 30th.

We left elated at having a deal, but, in the taxi, Stephen felt we could have paid £0.5m less.

The taxi dropped us at the Cumberland Hotel where Peter was waiting to hear how we had done. Cruelly, I rang his room, said we were in reception and that the news wasn't bad. He looked concerned, but it was a pleasure to see his broad smile when we told him we had agreed a price.

We arranged to go out for dinner, but first I rang Alex. She was at a tennis club committee meeting – I left the message with our daughter Victoria that I had good news. Finally, I rang Michael McAvoy who was over the moon.

The evening finished with a memorable dinner for Roger, Peter, Stephen and myself. I will never be as excited. I couldn't believe the agreement to buy the business was a reality. I kept walking around the hotel bedroom saying, "We've done it! We've done it!"

But there was still plenty to do before contracts could be signed. Cash flow was vital, success still depended on the business being successful.

I went to bed at 2.30 am.

CHAPTER FORTY-FIVE

LICK OF THE SPOON

I WOKE UP AT 3.00, 4.00 AND 5.00 AM and, finally giving up any idea of sleep, went for a run around St James's Park at 5.45 am.

Before breakfast, I rang Alex who wasn't the slightest bit surprised – for months, she had been predicting success. I also contacted the other members of the buyout team, Jim Taylor, Mike Frank and Bill Dawes. Trevor Morgan saved the final telephone call by ringing me. Everyone gave the impression of strained excitement – as if I had told them we had won the pools but they were not sure I had posted the coupon.

My next call was to Paul Orchard-Lisle. He seemed worried, so I arranged to meet him at 9.00 am.

I had breakfast with Roger, two coffees, one tomato juice and two bread rolls – expensive at £9.90. We went to Healey & Baker and immediately came down to earth. Paul Orchard-Lisle said he could only speak for £28m – £6m short of our requirements. Roger sank into despondency.

The tension was real but short-lived – within 10 minutes, we had cleared up the misunderstanding. He had pledges for £28m, but with other properties available, would expect to raise a total of £34m – still leaving £3½m of secondary sites in the balance sheet.

I had done all the negotiations with Healey & Baker – my only previous property deals were those involving my three houses, 2 Priory Road, Merithorn and Moss Farm – a big jump from £95,000 to £34 million. It was a relief that the property information I had given Candover, Roger and Peter Cookson, proved to be substantially correct.

Despite Paul's assurance that he could raise the cash, Stephen Curran was still nervous. He was right; during the day, Paul rang twice more with changes to his forecast. Nearly all the funding for our buyout had to come from the sale and leasebacks. We depended on Healey & Baker's ability to raise the money.

Peter Cookson went to the UDS office to start discussing accountancy details with Harvey Lipsith. I saw Michael McAvoy before catching the train home.

Michael was concerned about a leak before any public announcement. I met Roger on the train – he was sat next to another solicitor, John Elliott, son-in-law of Geoffrey Noakes. When he saw us together, he shouted across the train, "Are you buying the family business back?" – It would be difficult to keep the deal a secret.

When I got home, Peter Cookson rang. "I have found a mistake with the figures!" My heart sank. "We are £4m better off than I anticipated – I will check them again tonight!"

There was nothing I could do until the morning, so I took Alex for a celebration dinner in Knutsford.

The difference in Peter Cookson's figures was due to intercompany balances. The Company forecasts, produced for Candover, were originally based on a proposed completion date in April. As the UDS and Hanson saga dragged on, the forecasts were never updated.

There had, in the meantime, been a massive change in the intercompany balance mainly due to our increase in stock – UDS paid a large number of major bills on Timpson's behalf. Tony Alexander, by insisting on a firm cut-off date, clarified our cash position, and, for us, the whole deal was £4m better than we expected.

The following day, Peter joined me in Roger's office to discuss the sudden improvement in our position. We agreed to tell no one until we were certain of the figures and had thought through the implications.

Although I spoke to Stephen Curran, who wanted us to deal with Peats in London rather than Manchester, and Trevor Morgan who visited Wythenshawe, I never mentioned our latest discovery.

I was starting to realise that the agreement with Hanson was just one of a whole series of deals to be negotiated. The list was a long one – property agents, property investors, Candover, the Institutions, and the lawyers – everyone wanted a lick of the spoon.

One property deal was progressing well; Paul confirmed an agreed figure of £16.9m from Commercial Union – over half our funds were in place.

Nat West offered an overdraft facility of £7m plus some bridging finance – in view of our improved cash position, we would need to talk some more.

I played 36 holes of golf on the Saturday, but before going home, I called at the office to see how Peter was progressing with the figures. We called our stroke of fortune Hanson's "own goal" – because their insistence on the cut-off created £4m. Peter confirmed the "own goal" was still in place.

That evening, I explained the "own goal" to Alex, who quickly grasped we were in a much stronger position. I spent most of the night working out how to take advantage.

Our offer to Hanson assumed £6m came from Candover, for which they would receive between 75% and 87.5% of the equity depending on performance. The "own goal" meant we only needed £2m which I thought would give Candover no more than 25% of the equity. By the time morning came, I had a clear objective – 80% for the management with over 50% for myself. Having witnessed the problems between my father and Geoffrey Noakes, a controlling stake had great appeal.

I woke at 5.00 am, trying to work out who we should tell about the "own goal" and in what order.

At the end of my morning run, the Sunday Telegraph headline was "Timpson Buyout Agreed By Hanson". It was a speculative piece, but throughout the UDS saga, The Telegraph had the most accurate rumours. Probably leaked by Hanson.

By 9.15 am, Patrick Farmer was on phone to check if the story was true. They were yet to make an offer but intended to make an approach the following day.

To avoid any more calls, especially from journalists, I spent the day out of the house. In the afternoon, I took my mother out from the Nursing Home then visited Peter at the office to check the "own goal" was still there and tell him my thoughts on share ownership.

Peter was upset when I said the main reason for wanting over 50% was that experience had taught me to trust no one. Perhaps it was insensitive, but I hadn't anticipated he would link my lack of trust with himself, but, in retrospect, I understand how he felt. He played a major part in negotiating the buyout and deserved a substantial lick of the spoon. But I was also looking at the stewardship that comes with owning a family business. I was determined to stick out for at least 50%.

That evening, Roger came to see me at Moss Farm to discuss tactics. We agreed our priority was to see Alan Jones of Nat West, but first, Roger should speak to Stephen Curran about the "own goal".

The following morning, before going to NatWest in Manchester, I briefed the Timpson directors and asked them to subscribe to the new holding company.

I didn't tell them about the 'own goal', sticking to the original Candover deal that gave us 12.5% rising to 25%. The split was to be 10% for each director and 60% for myself. They were putting up £20,000 each, while I was subscribing £120,000.

Before Peter and I left for the bank, David Briggs confirmed that the "own goal" had truly been scored. The figures were watertight.

Our meeting with Alan Jones at Nat West was brief and to the point. Having already studied the figures, he greeted me with "Fairy Tales seldom happen, but we seem to have one here". He said we didn't need a bank, but was very happy to support the deal.

We went to Roger's office; it was time to talk to Candover.

The "own goal" meant, theoretically, that we could have done the deal without Candover, just relying on bank borrowings. However, we did not want to exclude them. Any change at this stage could have alerted Hanson that we had a good deal, or undermined their confidence in our ability to raise the money. Continued Candover support gave us an insurance policy against things going wrong.

Before we rang Stephen, Trevor rang me. He was miffed, upset that he heard of the "own goal" from Stephen, not from me. He thought we were being too aggressive, and that Hanson may renegotiate the deal when they discovered how good it was. I could see no reason why Hanson should change their mind – the figures hadn't changed – we just understood them better. I told Trevor I wanted over 50% of the equity but still wanted him as Chairman.

Stephen then rang Roger; he was on a loudspeaker 'phone so Peter and I could hear.

"I can see the numbers have changed considerably," said Stephen. "I suggest we double the management percentage to 25% going up to 50% depending on performance."

"That's not the sort of arrangement we had in mind," replied Roger. "We are looking for management controlling the majority of the shares."

"How about 51% – 49%?" said Stephen.

"Our figures are 80% – 20%," stated Roger.

"We are not used to arranging mortgages," said Stephen.

"We could treat it as a banking deal," said Roger.

"I see where you are coming from," conceded Stephen.

The deal was struck; 80% for the management, 20% for Candover.

Peter was delighted. By then I was totally bewildered. I had hardly slept for five days and had spent the past 48 hours working out a deal that gave me the prospect of controlling the family business.

In the evening, we went to the Wine Bar in Alderley Edge, then Roger asked me round to his house. I met him at 10.00 pm.

He had spoken to Stephen and they wanted to talk about their "lick of the spoon". I was probably too soft, but needed their help and support – especially from Roger. That evening, I reduced my 60% to 54%, giving 2.5% to Roger, 2.5% to Candover and 1% to Trevor Morgan.

My next two days were dominated by changes to the shareholding.

I started by telling Roger that I agreed with all of the previous night's figures, except that part of the Candover shareholding should come from the Institutions' 20%.

Roger rang back to confirm the institutional holding would drop to 19% – putting my share back to 55%.

I then put my holding back to 54% by allocating 0.5% to Bert Brownhill and 0.5% to Charles Noakes – the two senior managers who were not directors of the buyout company.

Stephen then rang to say Candover would take a further 3% from the institutions' allocations, leaving 14% for other subscribers. I thought this a bit of a cheek as I'd just reduced my share to provide equity for Candover. Still, at least the subject of shareholding was now closed – 54% for myself, 5% for each of the other directors, Bill Dawes, Jim Taylor, Mike Frank, Peter Cookson, and 0.5% for Bert Brownhill and Charles Noakes, 5.5% for Candover, 2.5% for Roger and 16% for the institutions.

I finalised my slides for a presentation to Michael Stoddard of Electra, a Director of Candover and the biggest, most consistent investor in their schemes.

Trevor spoke of him in glowing terms, explaining how good he had been at Hepworths when he stepped in as Chairman to take over from Terence Conran. Trevor explained that Stoddard supported George Davies in building up Next, and had lots of connections in the city.

It was nearly a week since the deal had been done and I was starting to get a taste of the battles still to come. I had to keep alert. I wanted the deal to be completed as quickly as possible, certainly before a family holiday to the States that was booked for August 7th – one month to go. Alex also wished to see the deal finished, as did Ben Potts, who drove me to London to prepare to meet Michael Stoddard.

I was talking about the allocation of shares again when I met Michael McAvoy. He argued for a substantial block of employee shares being available to the employees, feeling that the Executive slice was too large. He also hinted he would like a small holding himself.

Perhaps I rushed into the shareholding issue too quickly, but a prolonged discussion would have caused more aggravation and more pleas for a "lick of the spoon."

I had considered the idea of employee shares carefully. It sounded right and would have created good public relations. But I could not see how it would work. We were about to encounter enough legal problems without making the deal more complicated.

I only made one further change to the shareholding, splitting 0.5% of my stake between Michael McAvoy and my sister, Janet. That was the way it ended but I was soon due to meet others wanting a "lick of the spoon"; the financiers, the auditors, the bankers, the actuaries, and, last but not least, the lawyers!

CHAPTER FORTY-SIX

RAISING THE
FUNDS

I TRAVELLED TO LONDON by car so I could take the heavy black projector holding my slide presentation for the benefit of Michael Stoddard at Electra.

I described the Company history, from its foundation by my great-grandfather and covered our customer care programme with the complaints policy and code of practice. I had pictures of our refit in Wigan, which was now performing well, and shoe concessions in John Collier and the Burton Group. I was able to show a considerable increase in market share over the past 18 months.

The shoe repair slides showed our acquisitions, Broughall's and Shoe Care, and pictures of our main competitors. I pictured TSR as a pedestrian but profitable business, before Peter Cookson went through the figures. Michael Stoddard gave us a hard time with searching questions, but I felt the meeting went well.

I was uneasy about the relationship between Stephen, Trevor and Michael Stoddard. It seemed like a mutual admiration society with Stoddard dominating the other two. Our 80% equity stake was an unwelcome departure from the normal buyout, and, as a result, I was viewed with suspicion. Despite my misgivings, we needed city backing and were committed to Candover.

Our dealings with the institutions, who we thought were on our side, were in stark contrast to the relationship with Hanson. Roger and I visited Tony Alexander to discuss the freehold in Manchester, the property that combined Timpson and John Collier shops. To obtain the full value, we needed Hanson's co-operation and Tony Alexander promised to help. He was clearly keen to get our deal done.

When we made our agreement with Hanson on June 28th, I naively thought the deal would be completed before my holiday on August 7th.

But the deal with Hanson was the easiest part of a complicated package – we now had to satisfy NatWest Bank, Candover, the Candover Investors, Peat Marwick, the actuaries, various property investors, Healey & Baker and the 16 law firms studying Scottish Law, English Law and legal quirks in the Isle of Man on behalf of all concerned.

Raising the money didn't seem too difficult – NatWest were very positive and Electra backed the deal – but this was only in principle – no one would give their full approval until we had settled the sale and leasebacks.

CHAPTER FORTY-SEVEN

PROPERTY PROBLEMS

FROM THE BEGINNING OF JULY, the property package changed nearly every day.

Healey & Baker, Commercial Union and Scottish Amicable studied the portfolio in detail and the more they looked, the more points emerged.

A long leasehold in Bolton was withdrawn by C.U. because of some terms in the lease. The freehold in Spalding was unacceptable because they did not like the sublease. We withdrew the Perth shop from the Scottish Amicable package. It was being demolished to make way for a new shopping centre – we would receive more money from the Compulsory Purchase.

As the package changed, Trevor Morgan hinted we could do a better deal with his favourite agent, Molyneaux Rose. At one stage, he suggested Electra should provide a bridging loan in place of the £12.5m Scottish Amicable offer. This created mistrust all round, especially with Paul Orchard-Lisle, who clearly found Trevor a difficult man.

In the middle of July, it still seemed likely we would raise £32.5m from three deals – Commercial Union £16.9m, Scottish Amicable £13.5m and London Shop Properties £2.4m.

On July 14th, London Shop Properties pulled out – with no reason given. Paul seemed unconcerned; he would approach another institution immediately. Trevor had other ideas – he thought Hanson would want clear evidence of our fundraising and Molyneaux Rose and Electra could help. We were back on course the following day when Paul said London Life had agreed in principle to take over the deal for £2.5m.

When the offer was made to Hanson, we provided a list of every property, which included some branches where we had ceased to trade. Our calculations assumed the deal included many sub-leases from adjoining shops or upstairs offices.

My main concern was 33/35 Queen Street, Oxford (bought by my grandfather in the 1930s for £40,000). The property was valued by Commercial Union at £3.7m. It included a Timpson shoe shop, a Jeans shop, extensive offices above and a restaurant. It was fundamental to our funding that Hanson sold me the whole of this property – not just the Timpson shop, which, on its own, was worth no more than £1m. Fortunately, no query was ever raised about Oxford.

As we reached the end of July and my family holiday got closer, the property situation continued to fluctuate.

London Life did not like the shop in Grainger Street, Newcastle – that took away £700,000 but by the end of July, we still had funding for £31.5m with a number of properties in hand.

From the time we discovered the deal was much better than we originally thought, I was regularly being told that Hanson would discover our good fortune and pull out.

Trevor expected Hanson to insist on evidence of our funding. Once they realised we could afford a higher price, they would ask for it.

On every deal, there is a shift in position from the original terms to the final contract. My advisors expected Hanson would use this 'deal creep' to their advantage. Hanson had many chances to exert that pressure. But it wasn't in Hanson's interest to be tough on our buyout. It was the first deal following the UDS acquisition, so Hanson could afford to be generous.

Although Michael Stoddard gave his blessing, we had to give our slide show to a wider group of Candover investors. They included Investors in Industry (3'is,) Murray Johnson, Robert Fleming, and the BP Pension Fund. We met in Candover's office – the potential shareholders sat around the board table looking at my black box projector. I felt confident, our presentation went well and the audience was enthusiastic, especially Ian Tullock from Murray Johnson.

Stephen had to produce a detailed report for his prospective investors. During its preparation, he had bombarded Peter and myself with queries, his temper getting shorter as the report got longer.

Stephen mellowed when the report had been issued to prospective investors. Robert Fleming was the first institution to invest in our buyout. This was only two days after my presentation and the day after Trevor told me Michael Stoddart was pouring cold water on our plan.

Eleven days later, we were oversubscribed. Of the eight units available, 3i's had three, Electra two, BP Pension Fund, Fleming and Murray Johnstone had one each. BP and Electra both wanted more. Stephen's report was a success.

I had to find £135,000 to pay for my own shareholding. I kept my father in touch with events and he lent me £20,000 interest-free. I visited his sister, Hester, and stepmother, Lillian, who also knew about my buyout plan. Lillian agreed to lend £10,000, as did Hester, who usually followed Lillian's advice. Father's eldest sister, Ruth, had already agreed a loan of £20,000.

I had £15,000 from the money I had received for my UDS shares but still needed to borrow £60,000. Alan Jones at NatWest in Manchester, who was decisive and helpful from the day he heard of our deal, agreed to a personal loan and arranged finance for the other directors.

CHAPTER FORTY-EIGHT

IN NEED OF A BREAK

THE KEY MEMBER OF OUR TEAM was Alex. When Roger first mentioned a buyout in 1982, she decided it was the right for the business, for me and the family. Early in 1983, she was convinced that we would be successful. Her intuition gave me lots of confidence. I also needed her tolerance during the bizarre timetable that left little time for home or family. When I was not away (usually in London), we went out nearly every night and talked over the latest twists and turns. We didn't just discuss the buyout; Alex had her own problems to share with me.

We had four children at home, including Oliver, who was spending his first year with the family. I did little to help Alex. Although I had almost given up playing golf, I still played squash and had just discovered the relaxing pageantry that surrounds crown green bowls. I became a regular member of the Moss Rose 2nd Team, playing in a local league that was serious enough without ruining the evening. Matches started at 6.30 or 7.00 pm and the rest of the team usually put me on first so I could get home in time to take Alex out to the Wine Bar.

The adrenaline brought by the deal meant I needed little sleep, often not going to bed before midnight and waking again at 5.00 am. I had usually completed a regular five-mile run by 6.00 am.

Both of us needed a break – a four-week holiday was booked for 7th August – in a motorhome with all four children in the USA driving coast to coast.

In March, when the holiday was booked, I was convinced the whole Hanson/UDS buyout situation would be settled one way or the other. When we agreed the heads of terms with Hanson on 28th June, I expected us to exchange contracts within five weeks – at the very worst, I could join Alex and the children a few days into the holiday.

I was still hoping to see contracts exchanged before our holiday when, on July 20th, Roger met Tony Alexander. It was a successful meeting in all but one respect – the date for exchange was delayed. It would now be late in August – during our holiday – a change in my travel arrangements seemed inevitable. Alex wasn't pleased. I planned to leave the family for a few days in Galveston Island, so that I could fly home, exchange contracts and return a few days later. A naive plan.

As the holiday got nearer, things went badly wrong, not helped by a drop in sales, but the big problems were over property. On August 1st, Paul Orchard-Lisle said the deal with London Life for £1.65m had fallen through.

The next day, it was all smiles again when Peter Cookson revealed the cash flow forecast was £2m better than budget. But there was another property worry – dilapidations – part of the purchase price retained against any maintenance expenditure – Commercial Union expected to hold back 5% of the total price – a staggering £770,000 cash that would be missing on completion.

Two days before my holiday, I heard about High Alumina Cement. Any property constructed with HAC was blighted – no institution would touch it. HAC had been found in our Wakefield shop, a long leasehold valued at £250,000. Then, Scottish Amicable indicated their dilapidations could be even greater than Commercial Union.

On my last day in the office, things got worse. Scottish Amicable lost interest in West Bromwich and wanted a £50,000 retention at Whitehaven and Bishop Auckland.

Then, Paul rang to say Commercial Union now estimated dilapidations at £827,000 and had dropped the valuation of Dundee by £66,000.

I finished my last day in the office £2m short of our cash requirement.

Although I had left the office, I had not left the country – we were due to leave on Sunday.

I spent much of Saturday away from the telephone. In the morning, I took James fishing at Lymm Dam with his school friend, Oliver Robinson. I had taken the boys on fishing trips before – I have never been a fisherman – neither will they be. I had never seen either of them catch a fish – this trip was no exception.

I also went to see my mother in the nursing home in Sale, I couldn't have gone away without saying goodbye. She had deteriorated alarmingly and was permanently agitated. She escaped several times, on one occasion being found wandering down a road over 3/4 of a mile away. She was beyond normal conversation when I visited every week.

Despite being out most of the day, I was still tracked down by Trevor Morgan, Stephen Curran and Roger. Both Trevor and Stephen said I needed a contingency plan to find the extra £2m and they proposed a form of bridging loan against further property sales.

My final conversation was with Roger. I trusted him more than anyone else to look after my interests. I made it clear he shouldn't allow anyone to talk about changing the equity percentages during my absence.

CHAPTER FORTY-NINE

KEEPING IN TOUCH

I RANG HOME NEARLY EVERY DAY, usually from spartan campsite phone boxes at 7.00 am – we were 6, 7 or 8 hours behind UK time. I spoke regularly to Peter, Mike Williams, Roger, Barbara, her deputy Doris Watts and my father. During our absence, Mother was finally diagnosed with dementia – with no prospect of returning to her former self.

Before I left on holiday, the battleground was clear. We were confident of completing with Hanson at the agreed price and sufficient finance could always be secured – the "Own Goal" had seen to that. The bother was over equity stakes – it was a tussle between the Candover consortium and myself. My opportunist move that secured 80% of the equity invited an aggressive reaction. The venture capitalists looked for a larger slice for them; our underfunding wasn't a threat but an opportunity.

The ground rules were clear. We needed to pay for the business on completion and continue to trade without breaching our borrowing limits. If we failed, the management forfeited some of the equity.

Of the £42m purchase price, £2m was deferred consideration to be paid to Hanson over the next two years. Our borrowing limit was set at 5m, the equity was £250,000 and the institutions put in £2.75m, so we needed a minimum of £32m from our sale and leaseback deals. There was, however, another source of funds – cash flow within the business. With Hanson setting a cut-off date for intercompany transactions at the end of June, any cash created from then on would contribute to the purchase price.

The Scottish Amicable and Commercial Union property packages produced a total of just over £30m but the retentions for dilapidations work and shops blighted by High Alumina Cement reduced cash on completion to under £29m.

The Manchester shop had a potential value of £750k, but as it was a joint freehold with John Collier, it had to be dealt with separately. The proceeds wouldn't arrive for several months, and couldn't help our cash on completion.

We needed a further property deal of around £3m – with the hope that nothing else went wrong.

I 'phoned each day to track the latest position. During the first week, I had a succession of good news – Hanson agreed to a deferred payment of up to £0.75 to compensate for retentions – Royal Insurance made a verbal offer of £2.85m for a batch of six properties – Commercial Union dropped their retentions by £200,000.

Everything seemed more optimistic. During this spate of good news, Candover suggested the institution equity stake would increase to 36% if we needed £3m more debt. The way things were going, we wouldn't need it.

The other main topic was the date when we would exchange contracts. By the time we reached Fort Worth, it was clear nothing would happen before September 7th.

There was no need to go home early, but we still intended to spend two nights at the hotel on Galveston Island. As we headed towards Houston, the weather changed. First black clouds, then heavy rain brought by a ferocious wind that became stronger.

We stopped for lunch at McDonald's in Madisonville where a fellow camper driver gave some firm advice; "Turn round and drive fast." We turned on the radio to discover we were heading towards Alicia, the first hurricane of the season and the worst in Texas for over ten years. The eye of the storm was 125 miles away, near Galveston Island, en route for Houston.

We kept driving for four hours, making slow progress in driving rain and unbelievable winds. When we reached Waco, the rain stopped, the wind was down to a strong breeze and Alex felt we were safe enough to hook up for the night. We found a spartan campsite, but who cared – it was our port in the storm. As soon as we arrived, so did the deluge. We were back in the driving rain and deafening wind we had driven so far to avoid. When we had registered and collected the restroom key, the receptionist forecast the hurricane would not get that far. "but it will blow a bit tonight". There was nothing else to do but huddle together in the camper and hope we survived until the morning.

In the middle of the night, I was desperate for a pee and headed for the restroom. It was like walking into a waterfall – as soon as I stepped outside the camper, I sank into six inches of mud – moving mud. Our camper was parked in the middle of a newly formed river. Even if I had remembered where the restroom was, I could never have got there – the wind would have blown me over. I peed against the camper wheels and climbed back to relative safety with my pyjamas soaked to the skin. Amazingly, Alex and the children were all asleep.

When I woke, it was still raining but the camper was upright. In daylight, you could see that our campsite had changed – trees uprooted, and the ground was under water, but none of the campers or caravans appeared to have suffered.

We couldn't get to Galveston Island – the hurricane had closed it down. A Police Marshall told us to "Turn round your rig and park someplace else!" We returned to Houston and found a very wet and sorry campsite.

On our way to Lafayette, Alex suddenly said I should go home early – for no particular reason, she just thought it was the right thing to do.

Her intuition had always been reliable, so I booked my return flight for August 28th, giving us a week to get to Miami, where I left the family in the Eden Roc Hotel.

CHAPTER FIFTY

GOING HOME

WHEN I RANG ROGER from the Lafayette campsite, the news wasn't good. The subscription agreement written by Candover's lawyer, Ashurst, Morris and Crisp, was conditional on us exchanging contracts with Royal Assurance before completion with Hanson, otherwise, management's share of the equity would drop. Roger was pleased I was returning home.

After announcing my early return, there was bad news nearly every day. Poor sales dented our cash flow by £175,000. Royal Insurance got board approval but wouldn't take Blackburn – £400,000 less than I expected. Scottish Amicable set their retention figure at £700,000 – £200,000 worse than the estimate. In four days, our cash forecast fell by £775,000 and the venture capitalists were hovering for a bigger lick of the spoon. However, with Roger confidently expecting to exchange contracts on September 14th, we still had time to improve the cash flow.

Lafayette was a staging post en route to New Orleans. We went on the scenic Route 90 – well worth the extra travelling time – and still arrived at our RV Park by mid-morning. Parc d'Orleans was the only campsite within the city boundary – we parked on exactly the same spot we had occupied in 1981.

New Orleans has charisma – a real buzz with unique character. It's
pleasant to find somewhere so un-American in the middle of a journey
across the U.S.A.

On every camper holiday, Alex had a day of panic, convinced I hadn't
left enough time to reach our destination. On Tuesday, 23rd August,
Alex decided we should get moving – we set off at 4.45 am! Driving in
turns, just stopping for a McDonald's breakfast and lunch at the Red
Lobster near Tallahassee, before we arrived at a K.O.A. (Kampgrounds
of America – pity the Yanks can't spell) at 7.15 pm.

The next day, although less intense, was still driven by Alex's sense
of urgency. We raced past Tampa and Clearwater, reaching a campsite at
Dunedin Beach for lunch. We had covered 475 miles in a day and a half.
We were back on schedule and spent the afternoon on the beach.

Not being genuine campers, the Timpson family prefer parking our
motor home outside a restaurant rather than messing with a barbecue
or campfire.

It took us some time to find our level from the range of restaurants
on offer. McDonald's hadn't come to Wilmslow in 1983, so Big Macs and
Chicken McNuggets had novelty appeal. We tested most options, Burger
King, Wendy's, Stuckey's, KFC, Long John Silver, but the children's favourite was unquestionably McDonald's. God knows why; some of their
restaurants looked unhygienic and were full of unsavoury customers. In
the end, Alex and I conceded that McDonald's was ok for breakfast but you
could hardly call it lunch or dinner. We found our feast when we moved
upmarket. Once we had discovered the multiple family restaurants like
Bennigans and the Red Lobster, we were, as they say in Winsford, "made
up". What attracted me was not the consistent standard of food or the
well-marketed menu; I was impressed with the customer service.

The last few days of a holiday go very quickly, and all too soon I
would be back on stage acting in the drama of my life.

Before reaching Miami, we were stopped by the police – we had driven
right across the States with an out-of-date number plate. No one spotted

our offence for 3000 miles and yet 15 miles after being apprehended, another State Trooper flagged us down – 20 minutes of paperwork on each occasion.

I threw everything into the last day – mini golf, waterslides, campsite by West Palm Beach – Bennigans for lunch and Red Lobster for dinner. Alex grew more tense by the hour and I tried to be the perfect father and husband – I was as unhappy as Alex leaving the whole family behind, but I had to go back and the Apex fare structure made any idea of the family coming with me far too expensive.

The rest of the family were looking forward to the week on Miami Beach until they saw the Eden Roc Hotel. As soon as we went to reception, I knew I had made a mistake. The Eden Roc was a good hotel once, but now it was faded, twenty years out of date. Cheap furniture, hard beds, no pictures on the wall – a depressing atmosphere. Alex and the children looked longingly at the hotel next door – I would have had a fonder farewell if I had booked The Fontainebleau.

My last few hours in Miami were short of conversation. I pointed out the excellent swimming pool but was wasting my breath; Alex was unhappy.

Just before we said goodbye, Alex abandoned her criticism and wished me success with the buyout – her change of mood made a big difference. Alex faced a difficult week with four children in an unfriendly hotel, but she knew I needed to get back to business.

Suddenly, I was alone, driving towards the airport, trying to find the American Land Cruiser depot from a sketchy map. But we had been to the same place two years before and I remembered the route.

The flight took off two hours late, delayed by a thunderstorm. There is something significant about the moment of take-off – the point when life moves on to a new stage. I was going back to the next chapter of our buyout – just a few weeks away from success or failure.

CHAPTER FIFTY-ONE

BACK HOME

AUGUST SALES WERE POOR; the hot weather was too late for sum-mer merchandise and delayed the 'Back to School' business; stock levels, on the other hand, were reducing.

My major worry was the property deals. There was no certainty that either Commercial Union or Scottish Amicable would produce the full amount required and the third smaller deal with Royal Assurance still needed their Board approval.

The cash position was so unsure that Stephen Curran insisted on an alternative plan. Any shortfall up to £2½m would be covered by extra venture capital, with a corresponding reduction in my personal share-holding. I was surprised and relieved to find their emergency plan would still leave me with 40%, which, together with the other management shares, would keep institutions in the minority.

I went through three briefcases full of paperwork – personal notes, minutes of meetings, reports and loads of figures – nothing of great inter-est but enough to fill my mind full of the business detail I went on holiday to avoid. I needed a big waste paper basket. It's amazing how little hap-pens during your absence and how much paper is produced to tell you about it.

The longer I am away, the more my priorities turn further and further away from business and family matters gain greater importance. That afternoon, I went to see my father whose news of Mother was not good – he had been told no treatment could reverse her dementia. The news had little effect on me – the mother I knew had died several months before when it was clear her mind had totally changed.

The day after a Bank Holiday is almost another holiday. People use phrases like "I am owed a day's holiday." – "Making it a long weekend," or it's always quiet after a Bank Holiday!" These arguments, which extended Christmas into a ten-day break, have made the last Tuesday in August very quiet at the office.

I visited some local branches with Jim Taylor to gauge the reaction to our autumn stock. For over 40 years, I have tried to spend at least one day a week meeting shop colleagues. Shop visits keep you in touch and are a source of inspiration – you don't get many ideas sitting behind a desk. After a long holiday, it's the best way to get back into the business – much better than pouring over paperwork.

The day told me our poor trading was caused by a prolonged heat-wave – our colleagues were confident about the new stock. A change in the weather would make a big difference. I was more concerned about shoe repairs which were well below last year. But shoe repairing never featured highly in our buyout discussions; any problem could be dealt with after the deal had been completed.

By Thursday, my normal business tempo had returned and I was back in London hearing about other deals within UDS.

Patrick Farmer had made a £5m offer for his 85 shops – an offer that was rejected. Patrick suffered from his own success. If his business had produced the more pedestrian level of Timpson's profit performance, he could have bought his business at a much lower price. Sometimes, it doesn't pay to be at the head of the pack.

I met Michael Wood at Burton, who thought they would buy John Collier and Richard Shops within two weeks. An hour later, David

Franks, Sales Director of Richard Shops, rang to ask if we would open 40 more concessions in their stores. David claimed he was close to clinching a buyout.

Just about everyone in UDS was involved in a deal of one sort or another, but for us, only one deal mattered.

I had gone to London to make a presentation to Royal Insurance, yet again, using the large, heavy black suitcase, with its built-in screen and projector, in another attempt to create confidence in our business plan. The meeting went well, finishing with a warm smile and a handshake.

Scottish Amicable were the most difficult of our potential property funders. They had question marks over significant properties at Dundee and Bristol, and now questioned the commercial viability of the Timpson buyout deal itself.

Roger Lane-Smith sent Scottish Amicable a long telex defending our covenant. If they pulled out it was difficult to see how we could get the deal with Hanson back on track. I rang Scottish Amicable the following day and one of their team, Chris Hainsworth, explained their problem – they had no difficulty with the properties or our business plan, their concern was timing; they felt they were being rushed.

I ended the week in confident mood – most problems had been solved and nothing seemed likely to put our buyout off course. I spent Friday in the North East of England where our shops were busy. We were clearly going to enjoy a busy 'Back to School' period.

The only worry was a request to meet Tony Alexander 'to iron out some problems.'

CHAPTER FIFTY-TWO

FIELDING THE WOBBLERS

ON MONDAY MORNING, after a short spell at the office where figures confirmed that 'Back to School' trading was excellent, I went to the airport to pick up Alex and our children. They went straight home to bed and I had to go back to the airport and catch the Shuttle to London for the meeting with Tony Alexander.

I need not have worried; he simply wanted to sort out the outstanding property problems. The 'flying freehold' in Market Street, Manchester had already created months of unresolved discussion and would take many more weeks to unravel.

To solve the immediate problem, Hanson kept the Manchester freehold and dropped the buyout price by £800,000, as long as we paid over that amount for the shop within 12 months.

Inter-Group properties were also on the agenda. UDS had transferred some freehold properties between different parts of the group. It worked well, but now the company was being carved up, we needed separate leases. We had sublets from John Collier, Richard Shops and John Farmer. In each case, Hanson gave us a 999-year lease at a peppercorn rent.

The meeting was friendly enough for us to enquire whether an agreement had been reached with Burtons – I sensed a tone of contempt and was told nothing had been agreed.

At the end of the meeting, we were told that an exchange of contracts should take place in a week's time on Tuesday, 13th September. I went to bed feeling the marathon was nearly over, but the following day brought me back to earth. I got further proof that the easiest part is the agreement between buyer and seller; it is the other people – bankers, lawyers, accountants and actuaries who cause the real anguish.

The meeting that morning at Ashhurst, Morris and Crisp, lawyers to Candover, is etched in my memory. Their three lawyers 'nit-picked' through every clause, while Roger and I got increasingly irritated. We were studying the subscription agreement, which looks after the interests of institutional investors. Stephen and Trevor argued against me throughout the discussion and I started to wonder whose side they were on.

That meeting showed how little I knew about law and finance – I felt like a novice being taken for a ride. Looking back, we probably did as well as most buyout teams but I still felt abused at the time.

Fourteen years later, I met Geoffrey Green, Candover's lead lawyer, in a convivial social environment and we discussed the meeting. It was a real pleasure to meet him and find he fully understood and had sympathy with my antagonism towards the company lawyer on the other side.

For some time, I'd had a running debate with Stephen Curran over his 'Plan B' and what cash shortfall would trigger it. The scheme was designed to ensure that if Royal Insurance didn't complete their property deal, I would lose 15% of the equity. I agreed to a broad cash criterion, arguing that it didn't matter how we kept the cash under control as long as we met the overall target. We spent several hours on the telephone arguing minute theoretical points surrounding 'Plan B'. In the end, I mostly got my way.

I sensed an increased sense of urgency, which caused the lawyers and accountants to work through the weekend. On the Sunday, I was at Lee Lane-Smith, Roger's office in Manchester, from 10.30 am to 8.30 pm.

During the line-by-line discussion of legal documents, I was a spare part, sat in the corner, only required to speak when spoken to. We covered every page of the acquisition and subscription agreements; a tedious day. I felt I was doing penance – everyone else was working for my benefit, so why should I escape ten boring hours in a stuffy office on Sunday in the middle of Manchester?

It was more fun back in the office on Monday facing a stream of last-minute wobblers and potential deal-breakers.

Inverness became a big property problem. The upper floors were owned by Coats Viyella, we could fall £300,000 short on the sale and leaseback price. Stephen was back on the telephone raising the threat of 'Plan B', still suggesting that more capital was needed and my shareholding should be reduced.

The deal-breaker of the day was the UDS agreement with Citibank over 'Vantage', the credit card, another UDS initiative that became a financial disaster.

For years, UDS Tailoring had sold made-to-measure suits on credit – the Vantage Card replaced that credit system and gave customers the chance to use the new credit card in all UDS shops. The scheme had a poor credit screening process and, before long, the unbanked population, particularly in the North East, seized the chance to buy goods on credit without the need to be creditworthy. The result was bad debts approaching £12m.

Tony Alexander discovered the size of this problem rather late in the day. He rang me to say Hanson had decided to divide the bad debt between the trading companies – on a turnover basis, our potential liability was over £2m. A real deal-breaker.

Over the next hour and three telephone calls, we discussed various ways of allocating the bad debt, and, in the end, agreed the fair method would be to allocate debt according to the number of accounts opened by each business. As Timpson opened only ten out of several thousand accounts, I avoided another potential wobbler.

Paul Orchard-Lisle indicated further problems with both Commercial Union, who were rejecting Inverness and Scottish Amicable who simply claimed they needed more time.

David Franks of Richards Shops rang to say he could not sign the concession agreement for three weeks. I spoke to Tony Alexander who simply told David Franks and David Simons of John Collier they had to sign a side letter committing them to our concessions. They both readily agreed.

Just after lunch, I got a worried call from Brian Laxton at Healey & Baker. Tony Alexander had rung him to say if they could not sign by tomorrow, the whole deal was off! Tony also rang Commercial Union saying, "If you can't make tomorrow, you might as well file your papers!"

An hour later, Paul Orchard-Lisle spoke to Scottish Amicable, who said, "It is not impossible."

Roger took this dramatic move from Hanson and the Scottish Amicable response as a sign of real progress. We caught the next train to London.

CHAPTER FIFTY-THREE

FAIR EXCHANGE

QUITE A LARGE TIMPSON TEAM booked into the White House Hotel near Euston Station. In addition to Roger, Peter Cookson and myself, we had Mike Williams and Roger's property lawyers, Jeremy Fieldhouse and Eric Quirk. Jeremy and Mike spent the evening at Gouldens, the Hanson lawyers, while the rest of us joined Stephen Curran for dinner.

Before I went to bed, there was a new property problem, this time at Mansfield, which joined Inverness in the unresolved category. If Hanson expected to exchange tomorrow, there was still much to be agreed.

At Candover, I met the usual daily ration of wobblers. The Scottish Amicable solicitors were being difficult – they demanded £13,500 fees and lots of information about our subscription agreement. Nothing had been resolved with Commercial Union regarding Inverness and Wakefield was still a problem.

Investors In Industry (3i's), our biggest institutional shareholders, led on behalf of the other investors. They felt the latest property problems should be matched by a £400,000 increase in our bank facility. I did not want to renegotiate with the bank at this late stage.

There was some good news amongst the doom and gloom – sales so far this week were 35% ahead of last year.

We moved from the Candover office to Gouldens to meet Alan Hadrup, who proved to be another helpful Hanson director.

Inverness was resolved by dropping the acquisition price by £300,000 and Hanson retaining the freehold. We agreed a further £300,000 reduction due to the property in Douglas, Isle of Man – the Isle of Man legal system made it impossible to complete that sale and leaseback in time.

For the first time, we signed something – The Acquisition Agreement – the deal between the Timpson team and Hanson had finally been agreed. But we had to sign all the other agreements for the money to be in place to complete the deal.

Everything seemed set for the exchange the following day, but Scottish Amicable and 3i's refused to sign the subscription agreement – they needed more time to think.

I had another sleepless night. Hanson made it clear that if the deal wasn't exchanged the following day, it would never happen.

Hanson needed exchange to take place before the Stock Exchange closed at 3.30 pm. This gave them enough time to circulate shareholders and complete the deal before the end of their half-year accounting period.

Deadlines have a strange effect on solicitors. They feel they have to take it to the wire. To sign too early would be wimpish and reduce fee-earning time. To miss the deadline could mean no fees at all. These solicitors produced superb brinkmanship, irritating as many people as possible by raising frivolous points up to the last minute.

3i's signed the subscription agreement at 1.00 pm – with two and a half hours left to spare.

Scottish Amicable got even closer to the deadline. In the hour before exchange, they argued about a connecting door in the basement of our shop in Walsall and refused to sign a Letter of Comfort in respect of the Isle of Man.

At 1.45 pm, thirty people gathered in a conference room at Marble

Arch House, the old UDS Head Office and Roger took charge of lawyers representing ourselves, Hanson, two property companies (one
for England, one for Scotland), Candover and NatWest. In total, the
professionals earned £1m in fees and had a mound of paper to justify
the cost.

Roger followed a detailed agenda which had almost been completed at 3.15 pm, when we had agreed to ring the property lawyers in
Scotland – all Scottish property transactions have to be physically signed
in Scotland.

At first, we could not reach the Scottish office switchboard. When we
eventually got through, the lawyer was in a meeting. When we insisted
on interrupting, he was on the telephone.

Twenty-nine pairs of eyes watched Roger anxiously as the clock went
past 3.25 pm. Suddenly, Roger's face changed; he was speaking to the
elusive lawyer who confirmed the last details of the deal had been done.
Exchange of contracts was completed at 3.28 pm.

I rang Alex who took the news very calmly; she always knew we
would succeed. It had, after all, been Alex and Roger who had pushed me
down the buyout path. Alex suffered nearly a year living with a husband
whose mind was thinking of something else, and yet, it was Alex who
gave me the determination to overcome obstacles that sometimes seemed
to make our mission impossible. She said, "Well done," but added, "Let's
hope we can have a proper weekend for once."

Having spent so long working in confidence, I looked forward to
breaking the news – I believed I was quite good at PR and here was a
wonderful opportunity.

In the event, the publicity following our buyout was an anti-climax.
Few turned up at the Press Conference near Fleet Street. I was interviewed by an FT journalist who gave the impression he covered stories
like mine five times a day. When my photograph was taken in Shoe Lane,
passers-by took no notice. The Timpson management buyout was hardly
headline news!

I stayed in London for a radio interview organised for the following morning at the BBC, where I was to be interviewed by my namesake, John Timpson, on the 'Today' programme.

I waited in an anti-room with another interviewee, Rodney Bickerstaff, a youthful Trades Union Leader. He was a pleasant companion whose personality took on a steely edge when he was in front of the microphone. I followed him into the studio for one of the worst interviews I have ever done.

I was very nervous and both John Timpson and Brian Redhead were edgy and bad-tempered; after all, they had been up since four in the morning. The interview was neither amusing nor informative. Nevertheless, a lot of people heard it, but most didn't realise it was about a management buyout.

I went to Heathrow via a photoshoot at our Hounslow branch for the Sunday Times. From Manchester Airport, I went straight to the office where I received a warm welcome. I did wonder whether the Timpson team would share my enthusiasm. I need not have worried. They had already been briefed by Mike Frank and Bill Dawes on the previous day within an hour of the deal being agreed. I simply shook a lot of hands and thanked my colleagues for their support. I felt a sense of relief – there had been a strong rumour going round the building that we would be bought by Burtons.

After touring our office and warehouse, I went into Manchester for more interviews and finally got home for a family weekend. The children were delighted to see our name on Teletext.

For two years, I had played squash at 8.00 am every Saturday, usually with the same opponent; an hour's squash was an excellent start to the weekend. That Saturday, I failed to turn up. I did not wake until 9.30 am – I had slept for 12 hours, double the sleep during any night for several months. The adrenaline had stopped flowing.

CHAPTER FIFTY-FOUR

COMPLETION

IT WAS A PROPER FAMILY WEEKEND. I took James to Stockport Grammar School for his rugby practice and nearly went back to sleep at Maine Road. I should have been wide awake as Manchester City won 6-0.

There was little in the papers about Hanson, UDS or our buyout, apart from a reasonable article about Timpson in the Sunday Times.

I spent most of Sunday at a mini rugby tournament near Bramhall. James was large and quick for his age, so his proud parents were able to see him score quite a few tries. At mini rugby, a try can be scored every 30 seconds!

Business continued to be excellent, but despite exchanging contracts, we still weren't in the clear. We had to avoid Stephen's 'Plan B.'

Royal Insurance looked 95% certain to complete their deal well on time, but more problems occurred when High Alumina Cement was suspected at Altrincham, Birkenhead and Aberdeen.

There was still a week to completion, a mixture of legal formalities, public relations and business as usual. One day, Roger arrived with a mountain of papers and a number of solicitors – we sat signing things for two hours. A journalist called John Rawlins came with a photographer and interviewed me for the Mail on Sunday – he was difficult to talk to – it would not be a great article.

I received loads of letters congratulating us on the deal, especially from Timpson colleagues. The mood at a day conference for Area Managers was excellent – business was good and they felt more secure about their future.

I travelled to London the day before our completion meeting. No news had emerged about other UDS deals, but the papers suggested the Richard management could not raise the money.

In London, Mike joined the property lawyers while I went out for dinner with Peter Cookson. At my invitation, we met Patrick and Tim Farmer at Rules Restaurant.

Patrick and Tim were pleased for us but despondent about the way things turned out for them. They ran an extremely good business but their high profits worked against them. Hanson was demanding a bigger price than they thought they could fund.

Following that dinner, I put Patrick and Tim in touch with Roger Lane-Smith, who did a splendid job but still failed to secure the buy-out they so desperately wanted. Their hopes were dashed by their own conservative accounting and an opportunistic offer from Philip Birch of Ward White.

In the end, Hanson sold their business to Clarks, and Patrick and Tim secured a modest management stake and played an important role in running several Clarks retail companies before Patrick became responsible for the Clarks retail businesses in Australia and the United States.

The papers were divided on Richard's Shops, some said their funding was in trouble, others thought the buyout would go ahead. We arrived at Marble Arch not realising the answer was still being resolved in the same building.

On the 4th floor, at a Hanson Extraordinary General Meeting, our buyout was approved with 170 million votes in favour and 68,000 against.

Stephen Curran was more relaxed than I had ever seen him. In an unguarded moment, he speculated that Candover's equity stake was already worth over £500,000.

Tony Alexander and Tony de Keyser told me that both the Richard Shops and John Collier deals would go through but they did not know in what form. They hinted the outcome would differ from anything suggested in the press.

Richards and Colliers were negotiating on the third floor of Marble Arch while Dixons were on the fifth completing a surprise deal to purchase the 12-shop Orbit chain of electrical shops recently developed by UDS.

We completed in time for me to take all the parties across the road for lunch at the Cumberland Hotel.

Thirty people went to the Carvery Restaurant; it was a great success. The lawyers and accountants, who had been scoring points off each other for weeks, became friends and appeared genuinely pleased our buyout had happened. There was jovial speculation about the outcome for John Collier and Richards.

It was a long journey home up the motorway, driven by Ben Potts who had shared my ups and downs over the past year. Ben Potts, a vital member of the buyout team, suffered early starts, late nights and a moody passenger. He was an admirable companion who put me to shame by finishing the Telegraph cryptic crossword more often than I did.

Back home, Teletext told me that the John Collier buyout had been completed but Terence Conran stepped in to take a majority stake in the Richard's deal.

So, at last, it was done – I had over 50% of the Timpson business, which could be valued at around £5m. I assumed everyone would be happy ever after.

On Sunday, the article appeared in the Mail on Sunday. It was even worse than I feared – a warning that things seldom go the way you wish.

PART THREE

CHAPTER FIFTY-FIVE

BACK TO BUSINESS

AFTER 9 MONTHS OF DEAL DRAMA, I wasn't expecting such a feeling of anti-climax. Although our buyout was reported in the business section of most national papers, the story was hidden on the inside pages. The focus was on Hanson creating cash by breaking up UDS and journalists were more interested in the Richard Shops and John Collier deals than Timpson.

There were a few good headlines – 'Timpson family in £40m shops buyout' and 'Timpson buys his shops back' but 'Hanson breaks up his high street chains' was more typical.

My colleagues in Wythenshawe were clearly pleased that we had secured independence. Many shook my hand, most were smiling, but the mood fell short of the enthusiastic joy I'd anticipated. You can't abandon the office, go to London and spend week after week buried in meetings without the organisation guessing what is going on. For nine months, I had focused on nothing but the buyout; the fairly muted response to the news was a sign that I needed to get back to the real world. For most of the year, I had been talking to Candover about our forward plan; the time had come to turn the forecasts into reality.

I thought the buyout strengthened the importance of being a family business and that giving great customer service gave us a key competitive advantage. So, I relaunched our service approach by producing a new training programme under the title 'Making Shopping a Pleasure', with detailed rules that required our shop assistants to provide a type of service that some considered old fashioned. The approach worked well when selling children's shoes, but I suspect many colleagues thought I was losing touch with the trend towards self-service already adopted by the majority of our competitors. In retrospect, I should have taken more notice of our colleagues' comments but it was another 10 years before I discovered the secret behind great customer service.

The expansion into John Collier always was chaotic. We took the easy route, put a rack full of basic men's footwear into 200 outlets and relied on John Collier staff to look after both sales and stock. After a few months, sales dwindled and we were left with plenty of uncared for, slow-selling, stock. To be successful, shoe concessions needed minimum sales of £1,000 per week, in a department run by our own staff.

Fortunately, the right decision was forced upon us when the Collier team succeeded in their bid for a buyout and gave us notice to exit all our concessions. (Within a year, the buyout ran into difficulty and John Collier was bought by Burtons). To fill the gap, we opened staffed concessions with Dorothy Perkins, Top Shop and Top Man. It was an easy way to grow, but, although more successful than units in John Collier, even these new concessions struggled to make money.

My main hope for growth was the Fitch refit. The scheme only achieved a modest growth in our first 5 refitted shops, but within a year, 43 shops were upgraded with plans to change half the shops by mid-1985.

Most new designs do well in the first few shops because enthusiastic executives ensure that the new look is supported with super sales staff and the best stock. The real test comes later. Like others before us, the more refits we did, the less benefit we saw, but we closed our eyes to the consequences. Fitch designed some attractive shops, but design on its own wasn't going to bring in extra sales. We needed the right stock with positive people serving the customers.

Immediately after the buyout, our business did well; sales up to Christmas were above expectations, despite a disappointing range of men's footwear (we misread the fashion and bought far too many fashion boots). Cracks started to appear the following spring when the sunny weather brought plenty of customers, but we misread the market. We tried to move upmarket, offering a wider range of better-quality shoes from £5.99, but customers wanted more cheap and cheerful styles under the Penny-Wise brand at £1.99. We ignored our core customer and forgot our heritage.

Despite weakening sales, we made a profit of £901k, enough to satisfy our shareholders and permit us to refinance the institutional debt on more favourable terms. My shareholders were happy, but I was starting to lose confidence and discovered that running a private business can be more difficult than controlling a subsidiary.

CHAPTER FIFTY-SIX

RE-SHUFFLING
THE TEAM

WE HAD BOTH FRIENDLY and business-like monthly Board Meetings. Stephen Curran, always charming, did his best to put me at ease, but I knew that any cash flow crisis would make us vulnerable. Stephen never gave a hint of disappointment; it was Trevor Morgan who made me nervous.

Trevor and I were complete opposites. Our common interest was the shoe trade, but Trevor concentrated on property and process, while I was fascinated by footwear fashion and innovation.

We got off to a bad start when Trevor told me he would have done a much better sale and leaseback deal. He wasn't going to do any more deals with Healey & Baker, so we switched to his favourite agent, Molineux Rose.

Trevor wanted to bring our stock control system up to date and replicate Next. When Next was founded, George Davies brought the fashion flair but Trevor took a close interest in merchandising. He thought his range planning and stock control methods would make a major difference to Timpson.

In 1960, our branch managers ordered whatever they wanted from the warehouse. Gradually, the office took control and started allocating stock. Once we installed a computer, the office was in charge and shops had to sell the stock they were sent. Trevor's system was far more sophisticated. To convert us to his world, Trevor recruited an ex-Turner's Shoe colleague, Gwynn Jones. With trade prospects looking pretty uncertain, I was keen to please Candover and clutch any new straw that came my way, so I readily agreed and Gwynn Jones started telling our buyers how many pairs to buy.

After the traumatic early 1970s, Timpson enjoyed nearly a decade of stability – same system, same culture, same boss, same people, but I'd failed to pay enough attention to succession planning. Several influential middle and senior managers retired over the next two years. Almost all handed over to people with no natural feel for our business and who lacked the big personality of their predecessors.

It is easy to take key people for granted – the colleagues whose instinct runs your day-to-day business. They don't need a culture manual; they just get it. It's only when new recruits turn up and make a few mistakes that you realise what you have lost. Long service and continuity can inhibit change, but stability and experience keep a company together.

Some of our most influential experts left within 18 months of each other – Tom Edwards, who established the original stock control system and ran it for 25 years, Tom Howell, who bought our children's shoes from the early 1960s and strengthened our reputation as a family shoe shop, Stan Jones, our most experienced field manager and Tom Hardman, a wily old bird with a wicked sense of humour, who bought basic shoes for women and, while patiently sharing an office, taught me how to buy using common sense.

These men were hard to replace, but we made life more difficult by a number of management changes. With Gwynn Jones taking a closer hold on the buying, Jim Taylor swapped from Buying to Marketing. No ladies' buyer had more than 5 years' experience of Timpson and I suspect none had visited more than 20 of our shops. Jim ceased to be a Group Board Director, as did Bill Dawes, who retired after 8 years running the Timpson shops. Less than 2 years after our buyout, things weren't going too well.

A major reshuffle was triggered by Trevor's decision to step down as Chairman. He said we needed a full-time Executive Chairman, although I suspect his main reason was to reduce his personal commitments. Whatever Trevor's reasons, we accepted his decision and started to search for a new Chairman. One candidate had dinner with Alex and myself. "You won't get on," said Alex. "He will make things worse, not better." I decided to do the job myself.

My life was a collection of difficult problems, which constantly filled my mind until I was so stressed, I couldn't continue with my day-to-day role as Managing Director. I became Group Chairman and Chief Executive, with Trevor, who sadly died a year later, becoming a non-executive director. Michael Frank stepped down from the Group Board to become Managing Director of Timpson Shoe Repairs. Mike Williams became Property Controller and we sought an outsider to be the Managing Director of Timpson Shops.

The two outstanding candidates were both from the Burton Group, Steve Cotter from Dorothy Perkins and Andrew Leslie from Top Man. It was a difficult decision; Steve had more sympathy with the Timpson culture but Andrew seemed to have the drive we needed – we picked Andrew. At a stroke, we put the future of our shoe shops into the hands of a total outsider.

I felt a sense of relief – someone else now had to find how to reverse our decline in sales and profit. However, handing over responsibility didn't halt my stress and depression. It was hardly surprising that I felt a massive failure. I'd been the recipient of an incredible piece of good fortune in buying the business back, only to gradually let it slip through my hands through a lack of good management.

CHAPTER FIFTY-SEVEN

THE WAY AHEAD

ANDREW LESLIE WAS DETERMINED to give Timpson the magic dust that worked so well for Burtons. There were no shortcuts; Andrew planned a comprehensive reorganisation and, like most imported managers, persuaded some of his previous colleagues to join him. His main appointment was Steve Knott, another Burton graduate, who became the Sales Director. There was no place in the team for Jim Taylor – Andrew would be finding his own marketing manager. So, I sadly had to tell Jim that, having dedicated over 25 years to the company, his Timpson days were over.

Many established long-service field executives failed to fit in with the Burton approach which meant several middle managers with Timpson knowledge were side-lined.

The new regime followed a familiar pattern. During the first six months, a new management team was put in place – more existing managers left or were demoted, and new faces appeared from elsewhere. The next nine months were spent getting to know the business with the help of marketing consultants and a bit of research. Sights were set on the launch of a new business (set for 6th March 1987) when all the ideas were due to come together.

The new team ceased trading in concessions, and, in doing so, simplified the business but eliminated 15% of the turnover. These shoe departments, mostly in Burton, Top Man, Top Shop and Dorothy Perkins, only made a marginal contribution to profits, but the change cost nearly £1m, mainly spent to clear redundant stock.

They abandoned my Fitch scheme and brought in a different design company, 'Design House', to produce another new look. This was stimulated by market research that characterised the two main Timpson markets using pictures of 'Susan' and 'Sharon' (Susan being fairly conventional and family-oriented, while Sharon, with a rebel streak, was seeking the latest fashion). The theory was that if we could capture the attention of Susan and Sharon, the rest of their families would shop with us as well. The target customers were described in detail – Susan was a 35-year-old mother of 0-2 children who reads a tabloid newspaper, watches Crossroads, Coronation Street, Dallas and Dynasty, drinks Vodka and lime, German wine and Cinzano, likes Barry Manilow and takes package holidays on the Costa Brava or Mallorca. Sharon was 28, lived with her boyfriend, and was the first member of her family to go to university. A series of meetings going into this sort of detail defined the future business and formed the basis of the new Timpson plan which was called 'The Way Ahead'.

By handing the job to Andrew Leslie, I became a spare part and found other things to do that didn't cramp his style. I opened a locksmith and alarm shop in Altrincham called Security Now, hoping it would be the first of many, but by the time the third branch opened, I knew it wasn't a money-spinner. I went to trade association meetings, did the long service lunch and visited plenty of shops, but had little or no influence on the overall business.

While visiting shops and walking around the warehouse, worried colleagues wanted to have a quiet word. The collective advice was, "We've lost the plot; the traditional bestselling parts of our offer have disappeared and lifetime customers feel abandoned; we are losing business to our competitors". But the new management team were fixed on their mission; Susan and Sharon were centre stage and my advice was of little consequence. Whenever I raised any concerns, the response was, "Once everything is in place, 'The Way Ahead' will transform the business".

I hoped Andrew Leslie would discover a new magic formula and the business would improve, but as the months went by, it became clear that my hopes were becoming unrealistic.

1983 was the last really good year for specialist shoe shops. The weather was perfect, sales were good and shoe multiples patted themselves on the back, facing the next few years full of confidence. But the severe winter of 1985/86 curtailed sales just when specialist shoe shops were feeling the effects of increased competition.

For years, there were too many shoe shops. The UK had over 70 shoe multiples of 10 shops or more with a large number of chains having over 150 branches – Timpson was competing with Stead & Simpson, Stylo, Barratt, Olivers, Turner's, Tylers, Easiephit, Greenlees, Frisbys, K, Clarks, Farmers and above all, the mighty British Shoe Corporation with an estimated 28% of the market. We all needed well-positioned expensive sites with lots of room to hold our stock at a time when retail rents were at an all-time high. Other shops developed a substantial shoe business – Marks & Spencer, British Home Stores and Littlewoods, the department stores and many of the clothing chains. Sports shops were the main beneficiaries of a massive boom in training shoes and the 'dressed down' look.

All specialist shoe shops were struggling, but, having sold and rented back over £30m or freeholds, Timpson was bound to suffer more than most. I had to sit and watch Andrew Leslie reorganise his team and promote his vision ('The Way Ahead') hoping he had found a route for success. I became more optimistic when ex-Clarks man, Robert Withers joined us as our Head of Buying. Robert was a shoe man who understood our market, a hard worker who we could have done with two years before, but by the time Robert arrived, 'The Way Ahead' had already been decided.

The first 'Design House' refit in Swansea made a reasonable difference, with sales up as much as 25%, but the second in Blackburn, didn't do as well. The refit at Swansea cost £170,000, a figure that put the future in perspective. The new look was critical to 'The Way Ahead' but we didn't have the money to fund it. It made me realise that we couldn't afford to open another shop. In retrospect, this was a blessing in disguise; we were probably the first to fully recognise the long-term problems facing specialist shoe shops. During 1986, there was no sign that 'The Way Ahead' was going to improve the Timpson shoe shops; every key figure – customer count, turnover and profit – was down on last year.

Peter Cookson and I reached the unpalatable conclusion that our way ahead was to sell the shoe shops, but it took some time to have the courage to start looking for a buyer.

CHAPTER FIFTY-EIGHT

TRICKY TIME FOR TSR

WITH THE SHOE SHOPS STRUGGLING, it would have helped if TSR had produced more profit, but they too were having a bad run. The fashion cycle had returned to slimmer toes, but, this time, the heels were not as slim as the stilettos in the 1960s. With more cheap imports at low retail tickets, fewer shoes were being repaired. Despite this fall in demand, lots of new independent cobblers entered the market and there was extra competition when Sketchley, the dry cleaners, introduced a shoe repair service into 120 branches. They wisely recruited experienced shoe repairers and key cutters as area managers, who knew the market, ran a good training scheme and poached some of our good branch managers.

TSR had the benefit of a strong and experienced management team – TSR Managing Director, Mike Frank and his loyal colleagues, Charles Noakes, Geoffrey Noakes' nephew, who was responsible for the merchandise and Alan Chatterton, a human dynamo, who looked after just about everything else.

Charles was a safe pair of hands who helped to build extra sales from hosiery, bags, shoe care accessories and a range of Christmas gifts. His gentle nature was appreciated by the counter girls who were responsible for display and stock control. Charles totally understood which items would sell in a shoe repair shop and found best sellers that included jewellery boxes, tote bags and Alibaba baskets.

Alan was a bundle of nervous energy who, apart from the hours he spent playing bowls in partnership with his wife Vera, thought about TSR twenty-four hours a day. He managed on the move, visiting shops and our suppliers – looking for new sites, approving refits and developing new machinery. Nothing was too much trouble to Alan – if asked to be in Plymouth at 8 am on a Monday morning, he would be there. Thanks to Alan, TSR was always ahead of the competition with more advanced machinery, better shops and the latest repair materials.

This was the team that had overseen the conversion of old-fashioned shoe repair shops into state-of-the-art heel bars, with all the repair machinery in the shop and cobblers helping to serve customers. Ever since 1967, it had been clear that the shops couldn't survive by simply repairing shoes. The key-cutting business increased every year and engraving produced useful but modest extra sales (almost entirely pet tags and badges for nurses) but the biggest turnover came from merchandise.

The customers' side of the counter was filled with shoe care, shopping baskets, leather goods, a staggering range of gifts and a wall full of ladies' tights – TSR was one of the top 10 retailers of hosiery in the UK. It was a mixture of services and merchandise put together due to necessity. Some of the shops looked like Aladdin's Cave but by bringing in extra sales, the shoe repair business survived.

I made a mistake by asking Fitch to design a new look shoe repair shop. My plan was to turn TSR into a franchise business. Having met the team from the franchised stationery supplier, Prontoprint, I was attracted by the way they could expand the number of shops without having to invest their own money. I didn't really think it through.

Fitch created a classy-looking shop which we called 'The Village Cobbler'. The design was put into King Street, Manchester where successful manager and quality craftsman, Steve Marsh was the perfect colleague to look after customers from professional offices nearby. The theory was great but the shop simply didn't work; it was closed within 12 months and I abandoned the franchising idea.

TSR had more success with concessions in ASDA, the company's first move into supermarkets, starting with heel bars inside the stores in Birkenhead, Coatbridge and Blantyre. The others that followed in Rotherham, Chapeltown and Merthyr Tydfil were all converted porta-cabins in the supermarket car parks – a very early version of the pods that we now have outside over 300 supermarkets.

In the middle of 1985, we made a somewhat limp attempt to make a major move. There was a rumour that our biggest competitor, the 550-shop Allied Shoe Repairs, was up for sale, so I arranged to have lunch with their Chairman, Fergus Watson. During a friendly conversation, I established that the rumour was indeed true, indicated our serious interest and, although I wasn't sure where the money was coming from, mentioned a figure of £10m. My offer arrived too late; three weeks later, Mister Minit announced that they had acquired Allied Shoe Repairs for about £10m.

It was a great deal for Mister Minit, who, despite having built a substantial 2,000-shop chain of heel and key-cutting bars throughout Europe, Japan and Australia, only had a modest presence in the UK (mainly inside Woolworths). Through one deal, they became our biggest competitor with over 600 shops. But they had a lot to learn; Allied ran fairly big units with a comprehensive range of leather goods – very different from the kiosks Mister Minit ran throughout the rest of the world.

Later that year, I was invited to a multiple shoe repairers' conference in Jersey as their keynote speaker. I described the decline of the shoe repair market since the increase of cheaper imports and non-leather shoes started in the mid-1960s. I used charts to illustrate my point, but they were based on pure guesswork. In the bottom right-hand corner of each slide was written 'Source – Imaginary Research Limited'.

A few weeks later, I received a call from a Financial Times journalist. "I understand you have statistics on the shoe repair market." "I have,"

I replied, "but I made them all up." My honesty wasn't enough to put him off. "They might not be true, but they are the only figures I can find, so I'm going to quote them."

With TSR having a tricky time, we asked former Timpson marketing manager, Kit Green, to join us for three months as a consultant. Since leaving Timpson in 1972, Kit had worked with Claude Gill Books, Royal Worcester and, most recently, with Sketchley, where he was a Regional Manager, responsible for running half their shops.

During his first spell with Timpson, Kit and his wife Di had become close friends of Alex and myself, a friendship that continued when they left Cheshire and moved to Buckinghamshire, their base for all Kit's jobs until he returned to Timpson. Kit had a relaxed, laid back management style, thinking deeply about strategy without getting too much into the detail. It was a good approach in the shoe repair market, which was going through a massive structural change.

Kit knew no more about shoe repairs and key-cutting than I did, but together, we produced an idea that changed the business. The profit on key-cutting was at least three times the merchandise margin, so we decided, as a trial, to throw bags and hosiery out of our repair shops in Leicester and Gloucester and replace them with a wall full of key blanks. It worked; within a year, key sales increased tenfold, transforming the branch profitability. It was one big bit of good news during a period full of problems.

Kit was asked to produce a five-year plan and recommended we should close 28 shops, which were making a loss or about to do so. Tired-looking branches, including Jarrow and Barrow, were part of a closure programme that was long overdue. We reduced the number of area managers from 12 to 8. The overhead saving made sure that TSR profits never fell below £375,000.

CHAPTER FIFTY-NINE

SHOE SHOP SALE

I FIRST SUFFERED FROM STRESS in the 1970s, but they were mild episodes of despair and bewilderment compared with 1984 to 1987. Stress sufferers are at their most vulnerable when life takes an unexpected and unwelcome turn. The buyout had been full of adrenaline, 9 months of late nights and early mornings, a constant saga of twists and turns. It was a fairy tale that had a happy ending, but 12 months later, I realised the story was far from over. Sales were slow, profits started to fall and I felt exposed as a failure. After all the excitement of doing the deal and the major miracle of buying back a majority stake in the family business, my dream started to turn into a nightmare. Slowly it dawned on me that the new Timpson wasn't a long-term formula for success.

With the whole multiple shoe market heading for a major upheaval, we faced an almost impossible task, but failure was unthinkable. The combination of circumstances brought back my stress, but this time it felt ten times worse. Alex was amazingly patient. I paid several visits to the doctor and popped plenty of pills, but, for much of 1985 and 1986, I was in a pessimistic daze.

I have written about stress before, but never revealed how it struck in the mid-1980s when I so desperately wanted to take full advantage of the events that started with my father being fired and gave me the chance, once again, to have a successful family business.

It is difficult for those whose life is stress-free, to understand what it feels like. It doesn't help to be told "Take a week off and you'll be fine" or, even worse, to "Snap out of it!".

Becoming Chairman and handing over the day-to-day management didn't stop me from worrying about everything, constantly thinking about every problem, big and small and praying we could find the magic answer. I felt guilty whenever I visited the shops, trying to smile, but knowing there was a big question mark hanging over their future.

I now know that almost every other shoe chain was heading for trouble. Cheaper shoes, higher rents, much higher wage rates, with most clothing shops and chain stores selling more shoes, produced a night-mare scenario. 90% of shoe shops would disappear from the high street over the next two decades. It could be said that we were lucky to be the first chain to see the warning signs because our buyout put us in a more perilous position than our competitors – we were highly geared and we were paying higher rents.

Peter Cookson became increasingly worried; less than three years after our management buyout, he could see we were heading for a loss. We discussed our problems at least once a week and eventually he per-suaded me that we had no alternative, we had to sell the business before it went bust.

Almost as soon as we starting working on a possible exit, I became less stressed and, at long last, started to think straight. After weeks of debate, we realised the significance of Timpson Shoe Repairs.

Our latest results showed sales of £56m (nearly £2m down from 1985 – due to closing concessions). Profit was down £322k at £1.488m. We were advised that plenty of buyers would want the shoe shops but few would be bothered about shoe repairs. One adviser expected offers of over £20m for our shoe shops, but despite dropping hints around the City, there was little interest.

Peter and I went to Next and met George Davies, who was expanding as fast as he could. However, value shoe shops didn't fit in with his plans. Our next discussion with Michael Ziff, of Stylo, led to another dead end. At our first meeting, Michael offered over £15m, but within days, chipped the price to under £12m and would probably have reduced his price many more times before doing a deal.

With shoe retailers having little interest in shoe repairs, we decided to split the business, so we could sell the shoe shops and keep TSR. We developed a neat proposal that gave a fair deal to everyone – a prospective purchaser, our fellow management shareholders, Candover investors and ourselves.

Our balance sheet had net assets of £15m, so we set that as the price, but the buyer would sell TSR to us for £3m, giving them the Timpson chain, with £50m turnover, for a net price of £12m – pretty cheap for a well-known brand with 250 shops.

The TSR price of £3m partly related to the £375k profit, but in splitting the company, we put all non-retail property assets into the TSR pot, including a few freeholds of the shoe shops that had been closed. Fortuitously, this gave the new TSR business an asset value of £3m.

It would be easy to think that the £15m we were asking for the Timpson Group meant selling the business at a substantial loss – after all, we paid Hanson Trust £42m. But all the Timpson shareholders were in line to make a handsome profit because we were selling the shares that, in total, had cost about £250k, a gain of around 6,000%. My fellow directors who invested £12,500 in 1983 would receive £750,000 before Capital Gains Tax. All we needed was a buyer.

The perfect purchaser appeared out of the blue when Peter Cookson heard a rumour that George Oliver Shoes were keen to expand. George Oliver, another family business, founded in the 1880s, expanded much quicker than Timpson in the early years. Founder George Oliver opened his first shop in Willenhall, Staffordshire, in 1860. By the time he died in 1896, there were over 100 Olivers shoe shops and a year later, with

253

140 shops, the company claimed to be the biggest shoe retailer in the world.

The Oliver chain stayed between 100 and 200 shops for the next 85 years. When it became a public company in 1954, they were down to 111 outlets. In the early 1980s, the company was headed by Ian Oliver but driven by General Manager Graham Taylor, who had joined from Sketchley. In 1981, Graham encouraged the family to buy Hilton Shoes, a chain of 185 shops which increased the Oliver chain to over 300 branches. Graham was ambitious and was on the hunt for another acquisition, and he could see how Timpson would transform the Oliver chain. By doubling the turnover but using the same head office, profitability should increase dramatically. The chains were an almost perfect geographical match; few shopping centres had both fascias. It was the perfect deal for Olivers.

Initial discussions went well, but we wanted to inject a sense of urgency; the longer we waited, the less our business was worth (in 1984, we could have got £25m). The need for speed increased while the deal was being negotiated. Our shoe shop sales fell by 6% in early February and 8% by the beginning of March, when the 'The Way Ahead' launch helped to put sales level with last year.

We had complied with all their disclosures but they missed a vital question. I dreaded being asked, "What were your sales like last week?" However, the question never came.

We were doing two deals. As well as selling the shoe shops, we were buying TSR through a new business. This time, there was no need for venture capital, with a strong cash flow and the purchase price matched by property assets, NatWest was happy to back the deal, but I never contemplated being the sole shareholder; it seemed right that the prime movers behind the deal should have equity in the new business.

The new buyout team included Mike Williams, who had a key part to play as our Property Director. He got 10% of the new company, Peter had 20%, Roger Lane-Smith, who masterminded the negotiations, got

5% and I had the remaining 65%. But our deal couldn't be done until we sold the shoe shops to Olivers.

Ian Oliver, Graham Taylor and the George Oliver legal team seemed to be as keen to do the deal as we were. Buying another 250 shops and more than doubling their turnover would create the UK's second-biggest shoe chain and do some short-term magic to their profits, especially if they could close our Wythenshawe warehouse and streamline the head office functions. Fortunately, when looking at our business, their team were looking for opportunities rather than problems.

As usual, the final session before completion went through the night, but very little changed. At 6.30 am, I somewhat sadly signed away the shoe chain founded by my great-grandfather 120 years earlier, giving little thought to the parallel purchase of TSR. In retrospect, it was probably the best deal I have ever done, but it didn't feel like a cause for celebration. I left the lawyers' office and headed for Heathrow. Before flying to Manchester, I told my father what I had done; thankfully he understood.

Back at Wythenshawe, I had to meet the Head Office employees to tell them I had sold their business. It was a long walk from my office to the dining room where everyone was waiting for me. I wrongly assumed that everyone had guessed what I was going to say, but most were taken by surprise. Many of them realised that sales were difficult and a few knew we were trading badly, but their top gossip topics didn't include me selling the business.

I listened to what I was saying and could hardly believe it myself. The impossible dream of buying back the family business had been broken in four years. Many of the people in the room knew my father and some had worked alongside my grandfather, who had presented them with their long service watches. I didn't talk for long; there was only so much I could say. Although I finished by thanking everyone for their personal support, I didn't feel they had anything to thank me for in return. More than ever, at that moment, I realised that the boss's main job is to support the colleagues who support the business, something I had failed to do.

I could sense the disappointment and despair, as most knew it would lead to redundancy. I walked out in silence before returning to my office to comply with one of the conditions of the contract. I had to tell Andrew Leslie he was losing his job.

I went home, found a babysitter and took Alex to the Wine Bar – she looked relieved and said, "At last, I've got you back again". It wasn't the way I wanted it to happen, but once more, after a long nightmare, I could relax. With 4 children and many more foster children to come, I had plenty to look forward to, but I didn't realise the future would also include a new love affair with our shoe repair business.

CHAPTER SIXTY

GETTING TO KNOW TSR

IT WAS NEVER MY PLAN to sell the shoe shops, but by doing so, I received £5m after tax, a life-changing amount. We moved away from Alderley Edge to a big house near Tarporley. Alex wanted to move from Cheshire's social bubble in Wilmslow and Alderley Edge and I was very happy to appoint her as our head of house-hunting. Roger was keen that I should invest a good slice of the money in a big house. We nearly missed it! Alex took me to view a house near Tarporley, but if we hadn't stopped a local farmer who knew where it was, we would never have found Sandymere, our home together for the next 29 years.

I made a conscious effort to work less, play more golf and tennis and take at least one day off each week to spend with Alex. There was plenty to do outside work, with three children still at school and a constant stream of foster children. My attitude to business was going to change; I intended to be a non-executive Chairman, not getting involved in day-to-day management.

I wasn't really suited to running a shoe repair business. My limited work experience, in the repair workshop in Sale between school and university, demonstrated my complete lack of practical skills. I have never been able to repair shoes or cut keys and yet I became the majority owner of a business that relied on skills I didn't possess.

I felt like an imposter and expected to be viewed with suspicion. Many colleagues thought their jobs were threatened; they had seen me sell the shoe shops and thought the same would happen to TSR. To get shop colleagues on my side, I went on a countrywide tour to meet every branch manager. I had a simple message – "TSR has been held back by our shoe shop problems, but now it is on its own, the business can reach its potential". I asked each group, "How can I improve the business and your bonus?"

At some meetings, my warm words got a frosty reception as they sensed my lack of technical expertise. I talked about the potential of key-cutting and the money available for refits and new shops, but my comments were greeted with a challenging silence which seemed to say 'I'll believe that when I see it'.

I met a particularly negative group in Kent, an area that never totally embraced Timpson ownership since the acquisition of Brian Smith's 'Shoe Care' chain in 1980. I was saved by Ray Jones, an outspoken eccentric from Maidstone. "Come on, lads," said Ray, "can't you see John's been through a bloody nightmare? We should be grateful he's come to talk, so let's give him our backing." Ray did my confidence the power of good.

The deal with Olivers gave us the right to use the warehouse and offices at Wythenshawe for six months, a tricky transformation period, while we decided where to go and who would be on the team. Those already working for TSR, in the office and warehouse, were assured of a job but we also needed support staff, especially from the Finance Department.

The Timpson HQ was put up for sale. It was uncomfortable working alongside loyal colleagues who were certain to lose their jobs and we were tempted to show our sympathy by transferring as many as possible to TSR. But Kit Green, who was to be Managing Director, wanted to keep overheads to a minimum. We picked star performers from the Finance Department, the two key computer managers and Rod Umpleby, the Development Manager, who all agreed to join us.

After six weeks, we confirmed who would be working for TSR. A week later, Olivers announced that the Timpson House office and warehouse were to be closed – a very small number of colleagues followed up the chance to move to Leicester, while over 200 took redundancy.

Within a few weeks, half the retail team had left, and every day there were more spaces in the car park. It was a constant reminder I had failed to find a long-term solution for our shoe shops.

It wasn't easy to find a new home for the central TSR team. We found what looked like ideal offices in the centre of Altrincham, but then realised that it might have looked ideal to us, but was far from convenient for many of our key colleagues. We had to find a new home in Wythenshawe so we could keep the core team together. We all moved on November 30th when our Claverton Road building opened. The only people left behind were the caretaker and three security guards.

Fortunately, I seldom had to drive past the old building, which was a constant reminder of my darkest hour. The office block became the home for several businesses, but the warehouse remained empty until it was demolished to make way for a Tesco Supermarket. Today, the office block has also gone and has been demolished to make way for Tesco rival, Aldi.

The TSR team remained the same, but there was a significant change in leadership. Mike Frank, the General Manager for nearly 20 years, decided to retire but continued in a non-executive role. Throughout his time in charge, Mike fiercely protected TSR's independence. While the company around him wrestled with a board room row, control from UDS and a management buyout, Mike and his tight-knit team stuck to their tried and trusted formula, based on the latest technology and the strict discipline laid down by the Standing Orders for Shoe Repair Factories. Thanks to Mike Frank, TSR had better shops than most of the competition.

Mike was succeeded by Kit Green who approached management with a much lighter touch, more interested in strategy than detail, giving managers the freedom to use their initiative. The technical expertise was still there – most area managers were in love with the machinery and senior managers Alan Chatterton, Charles Noakes and Bill Shore were fully briefed on technical developments. Kit had a marketing background so we started to talk more about customers. It was a subtle change that helped us to increase sales despite a continual drop in the demand for shoe repairs.

We decided to demonstrate our faith in the future by investing in more shops. The quick way was to make an acquisition, so I went on a fishing expedition, starting with Mike Strom at Automagic, with an impressive 110-shop portfolio. The company started in London, originally trading as Heelamat. Mike Strom brought in a partner called Lister, who helped the business grow. In the early 1980s, to fund a new head office in Harpenden, Automagic floated on the stock market and Lister sold his shares, leaving Mike Strom with just over 50% of the equity.

Mike Strom was happy to talk about a merger, but expected to be in control of the combined business. He was a buyer, not a seller. I got the same answer when I met Ted Adler, a wholesaler, who had recently bought Essex Shoe Repairs, with just over 20 shops.

It was third time lucky when I met the owners of Shoetech, Chris Fowler and John Stratford, who were based on the Channel Islands. They had developed 11 very successful shoe repair and key-cutting shops, nearly all in centres where we weren't represented – including Crawley, Reading, Worcester, Cardiff, Derby and Tonbridge. They were keen to sell but wanted a fancy price (talk of £1m). I had admired their shops for some time; most were in great sites and I felt we could learn from the way they did business, but we didn't have enough money, so I agreed to do something I will never do again – I gave the two owners a share in our business. We acquired Shoetech by giving Chris Fowler and John Stratford 18% of our equity – 9% each.

As part of the agreement, we were expected to float TSR within 5 years – a forecast flotation at £10m would give the Shoetech owners nearly £2m for their 11-shop business. We signed the deal three days before Alex and I left for a two-week motor home trip from Seattle to Los Angeles. While we were away, a hurricane hit the south of England and, only three days after we signed the Shoetech deal, the stock market fell by over 20% – good timing!

CHAPTER SIXTY-ONE

STARTING TO GROW AGAIN

WHILE AWAY, I SAW A NUMBER OF Can-Du service kiosks and a chain called Things Remembered, full of ideas that could help our engraving business.

I returned from California keen to develop engraving, by selling house nameplates, business signs, novelty pet tags, badges, trophies, tankards and memorial plaques. But I had to be careful; new ideas need to start slowly, building success one shop at a time. I was about to learn the importance of selling new ideas to colleagues before they become keen to sell them to customers.

To survive, cobblers needed to do something else. In the 1960s, TSR introduced a big range of merchandise, but despite more money going through the till, hosiery, straw shopping baskets, cuddly toys and cheap Christmas gifts failed to fit the service image and made miserable margins.

We needed to be a multi-service shop. Keys were our biggest opportunity; by giving each branch a big display of key blanks, key sales made up for the drop in shoe repairs sales. Engraving became our next priority.

During TSR's first 12 months of independence, sales rose over 10% and profits more than doubled to £900k. Most competitors had a good year but we did better than most thanks to a 25% increase in key sales, created by the big display of key blanks. This prompted me to find new ways to promote our services – I launched a 'New Deal for Shoe Repairs' with the blue spot heel, super-grip sole and top quality 'Benchgrade leather' all at premium prices. To increase skills, branches were encouraged to become 'Master Key Centres' (everyone went on a locksmith course) and a 'Qualified Engraving Specialist'.

The commitment to key-cutting solved our warehousing problem. We were rapidly running out of space because over half the storage was filled with merchandise, particularly bulky straw shopping bags and Ali Baba baskets. Wherever we installed a big keyboard, we stopped selling most of the merchandise. Within a year, our space problem disappeared.

Although these new initiatives improved profitability, my leadership didn't get the approval of the Shoetech shareholders. Chris Fowler and John Stratford had seats on our Board. At their second meeting, they launched into a well-rehearsed criticism of the Timpson profit performance. It was based on figures that showed 11 Shoetech branches making £150k compared with 155 Timpson branches making £750k. We caused the criticism by putting all the overheads against the Timpson shops so the figures weren't comparable, but the seeds were sown and our Shoetech directors continued to criticise my leadership.

Shoetech taught us how to encourage salesmanship. They were very successful at selling stick-a-soles to customers who just wanted a heeling job and the ace salesman was called Arthur Voller – he had the magic touch. We asked Arthur to give Timpson branches the secret of his success and he made a big difference. However, Chris Fowler and John Stratford kept complaining – I was never going to get off their naughty step.

Although Shoetech caused more trouble than I expected, I was still keen to expand. It was time to pursue an opportunity I had discussed in 1986, when I approached the British Shoe Corporation to see if they would sell their shoe repair outlets. The answer was "Yes, but not yet". Two years later, they were keen to talk.

British Shoe had a strange collection of shoe repair outlets, some inside shoe shops (Saxone, Lilley & Skinner, Curtess, Trueform, Freeman Hardy & Willis), and a few next door with a separate entrance. Two were in Cooperative department stores, three inside Lewis's stores (Liverpool, Manchester and Leicester) and the jewel in a crumbling crown was in the basement of Selfridges.

The man negotiating for British Shoe was Philip Hammersley, who I knew when he was at Clarks. It wasn't easy to see how a neglected group of workshops could be turned to our advantage. In some, the sales were under £350 a week. That pathetically low turnover gave me the idea for a deal. BSC were clearly losing money so any rent I paid would make them better off. My major cost was wages, so I suggested a commission of 20%, with the first £250 of weekly turnover rent-free – that paid for my wages. The deal meant we both won.

I was taking a problem off their hands and probably should have offered to buy the business for £1 but that thought never crossed my mind. My offer of £225k was accepted, but I added a condition. £50k of the consideration depended on whether we were still trading, on the same terms, in Selfridges three years later. By the time that deadline arrived, the BSC Management had all been replaced, so we never paid the extra £50k.

It was a good deal; in the first year, we made a contribution of nearly £300k and thirty years later, although the other 35 workshops are now closed, we still have a concession in Selfridges.

Investors fell in love with niche retailers. Body Shop, Tie Rack and Sock Shop had all wowed the market and floated at prices that were over 40 times earnings. We hoped to follow in their footsteps. We found an enthusiastic merchant bank and everything was going to plan until Alex walked into my study with a serious look on her face. "Are you still planning to float the company?" she asked and I nodded. "You're mad!" She continued, "You would never be able to live your life surrounded by institutional shareholders and stock market rules. After years of trauma, we now have a calm and secure future; why give that away for a sound bite of publicity and a modest amount of money?"

It was a compelling argument with a strong message – Alex was right. My fellow shareholders weren't happy; by abandoning the float, I denied them their big pay day.

Chris Fowler and John Stratford demanded to be bought out. We settled for £1m, the ambitious price they were seeking when we met in 1987 – an expensive deal at nearly £100k a shop. With no chance of a float, Peter Cookson and Mike Williams wanted a new shareholders' agreement and I happily agreed. At any time, I had to buy all, or part of, their shares at a price based on 10 times the previous year's profit. After 5 years, I could sell my shares on the same basis. With that settled, the Shoetech directors resigned from the Board and we got back to running the business. In between the golf, squash, tennis, foster children and holidays, I found the time to visit most shops every year, held the area conferences and long service lunches at our house, met every area manager for a detailed shop-by-shop review and attended at least 6 area dinners each year. My dream of being a part-time boss was falling apart; TSR was becoming a full-time hobby.

The sale to Olivers brought an unexpected bonus. As part of the agreement, we got a share of the Pension Fund. We suggested we were getting more than our fair share but their actuary insisted that his sums were correct. As a result, our new scheme was so well funded we enjoyed a 14-year contribution holiday, reduced the retirement age, improved the level of pension and returned funds to invest in the business. The actuary's error was very much in our favour.

With profits rapidly increasing, the company was full of confidence, and, despite paying out £1m for Shoetech, we still had the funds to open more shops. The hyperactive Alan Chatterton found plenty including an independent cobbler in York and Clatworthys, a busy competitor in Cirencester. We were opening 10 shops a year but still looking for the next acquisition.

In 1990, we bought a concession business from Ron Lillywhite. He was based in Yorkshire, but the 11 shops, inside Johnsons the Cleaners, were in Lancashire and North Wales, including branches in Bangor, Llandudno, Colwyn Bay, Rhyl and Mold where every manager was called Jones. They made a modest profit and led to more concessions with Johnsons.

I also took on four shoe repair units inside branches of Brooks, the dry cleaners, based in Bristol. It wasn't my best deal; the concessions in Egham, Chertsey, Ashford in Middlesex and Henley were taken on the understanding that we would acquire all their repair units, a promise that was never fulfilled.

Still keen to expand, we bought 12 shops in Kent, part of a chain run by Keith Dann, a tough and shrewd shoe repairer. They all made money, but Keith kept his best shops and continued to be a keen competitor.

The business had grown to 220 shops and we were keen to find more acquisitions. However, 1991 was tough on the high street; our spending spree came to an end and I was in for a shock.

CHAPTER SIXTY-TWO

100%
FAMILY BUSINESS

TSR'S FIRST THREE YEARS of independence gave us a false sense of security. Profits before tax increased from £450k to £1.6m (£1.m after tax) and we expected this success to continue, but trouble was just round the corner. The demand for shoe repairs continued to fall, our British Shoe acquisition was suffering from the decline of the host shoe shops, slim heels were out of fashion and a recession hit the high street. In 1991, we only made £1m and it seemed that 1992 would be even worse when, one Friday, Peter Cookson came into my office to make a heart-stopping statement. Using our shareholders' agreement, he required me to buy half his shareholding.

I did the sums while I drove home. According to the agreement, the company was valued at 10 times profit after tax, so, using the latest accounts (the record year), that made the company worth £10m – Peter had 20% of the equity, thus half his share would cost me £1m. I was wondering how to raise the cash when Alex produced one of her inspired ideas based on common sense. Within 10 seconds of telling her about my problem, she had the answer; "Don't just buy the shares on offer, buy the lot, all 35% you don't own".

267

If I had doubts, my mind was made up on Monday morning when Mike Williams made a similar proposal, but Mike wanted to sell all his shares, 10% of the equity, another £1m. Within a fortnight, the funding was in place, helped by a mortgage on our house for £1m. Six weeks later, I owned 100% of the equity. Peter left the business to pursue his interests in private equity (he was replaced by his deputy, Martin Tragen), while Mike continued as our Property Director for another 12 years.

Being the sole shareholder made a big difference. Four years earlier, I felt like an imposter, a shoe retailer gate-crashing the shoe repair world, but now I was on my home ground. Guided by Alex, with help from Kit Green and support from a team of experienced colleagues, I was able to put my own strategy into practice.

Our main mission was to create a multi-service shop. Keys and engraving gave us the best chance to grow but shoe repairing was still the biggest part of the business, so we continued to look for new ways to promote our core service. Still inspired by Shoetech's Arthur Voller, we monitored our stick-a sole sales. Following the ideas produced by John Higgs, our Cheadle manager, we encouraged every shop to have a display of finished repairs over the machinery and we kept looking for new and better soles and heels.

Key -cutting continued to be a growth business, but it was a challenge to maintain the 20% growth that had been the norm for 15 years. We got better at cutting car keys, put colleagues through a locksmith course to increase their expertise, and created a central 'Key Centre' which provided branch colleagues with a help line and supplied rare key blanks. Our key service was more advanced than any major competitor.

We put a lot of effort into developing the engraving service. Originally, we used a crude 'vibro' tool that scratched instead of engraving. This was replaced by a dentist's drill – the sort of kit used at the Open Golf Championship, but only suitable for a true expert. In the early 1970s, TSR made a major investment in pantograph engravers, a time-consuming but successful technique that many lifetime cobblers found tricky to learn. Today, the best engraving is produced by computer. Our first computer engravers were big beasts that we put into Selfridges, Solihull and Tonbridge. They did much more than pet tags and badges – big plaques, memorial signs and house nameplates became part of our range.

We made our fair share of mistakes, including a branch called 'Copy Shop' in the centre of Liverpool, offering a personalized printing service. It was a pet project of mine. I spent a lot of time designing the product range but the idea never worked. Another new concept, this time in Stevenage and Swindon, was a Timpson shop without shoe repairs, just offering key-cutting and engraving. It made money but not enough to encourage us to repeat the experiment.

Our most expensive mistake was a car key rescue service called 'Key Call'. The plan was, for a modest charge, to store customers' car key details on a central computer with the promise that if they lost their key or it was locked inside their car, we would cut a new key and a motorbike rider would get it to you within two hours. We spent months sourcing the technology, recruiting a nationwide motorbike courier, doing market research, writing the sales leaflets, doing a deal with a Call Centre and placing the adverts that launched our new product. We spent nearly £100,000 and only ever recruited 10 Key Call customers – one was an office colleague who was testing the system and another was my aunt, doing her best to support her nephew.

We made several unsuccessful attempts to find new ways to motivate the colleagues. The most ambitious was a branch profit bonus that gave managers a share of any increase in branch profit. It encouraged cost-saving – managers cleaned their own shop windows and thought twice before calling an engineer to repair a machine. It worked for a year, but after 12 months there were few further savings to be made.

The profit bonus didn't last long but the idea led to a franchise scheme. Like all multiple retailers, up to 80% of the profit came from about 20% of the shops; a lot of branches hovered around break even or made a modest loss. By franchising poorly performing shops to keen colleagues, we thought both the company and the new franchisee would make more money.

There was no shortage of applicants. It worked so well that 53 shops were franchised before the scheme started to unwind. With tough trading in all our shops, some franchisees lost money so we bought back their franchise to rescue the colleague and save the shop. Success also led to problems; franchisees who did well had ambitions of running a bigger shop or becoming an area manager. Although a third of the franchisees were happy to carry on, we bought all the shops back and the franchise scheme came to an end.

There was a limit to how much we could increase profits by improving the quality of our service. To grow, we needed to make more acquisitions. I had regular meetings with Terry Greer, chief executive of Johnsons the Cleaners, who had several concessions with Mister Minit and the photo retailer, Klick.

I also kept in touch with Sketchley whose shoe repair and key-cutting service was running into difficulty after their qualified area managers had been made redundant. We also got to know In-Time, a watch repair chain with concessions in department stores, mainly Debenhams.

But our number one target was always Automagic, whose well-sited shops were a perfect geographical fit. I had several unsatisfactory meetings with their Chief Executive, Mike Strom, but the only deal he would consider was if Automagic acquired Timpson. To take the initiative, Roger Lane-Smith suggested we should buy some Automagic shares. I followed his advice with unwise enthusiasm and paid £1m for 26% of the Automagic shares from an Edinburgh-based merchant banker. We hoped the share stake would lead to a successful bid, but Mike Strom retained his 47% holding and never spoke to me again. In 1992, The Automagic non-executive directors decided that the business was in a fatal decline so agreed to sell us 36 shops but Mike Strom blocked the deal.

In 1994, I invited Patrick Farmer to become a non-executive director. I knew Patrick well during my time with UDS and always regarded him as a top-class retailer with sound judgement and a caring personality. It was an excellent decision.

Our cluttered branches were a big contrast to the disciplined shoe shops Patrick used to run. He helped us improve the look of our shops but joined during a dire period of trading. We suffered during a heat wave in the summer of 1994, with shoe repair sales down 25% and total sales more than 10% below last year. For several weeks, we were making a loss.

However, our competitors were doing even worse. A very worried Automagic non-executive director wanted to talk about another deal. Mike Strom wouldn't meet me but his team were keen to sell 23 shops and we were close to agreement when I dropped our offer price and they pulled out.

The first half of 1995 was even worse. We were expecting profits to fall to £450k when Alex and I took some foster children for a week in North Wales. I had been there for 4 hours when Mike Williams told me that Barclays Bank had put Automagic into receivership. Our £1m shareholding was worthless; our ideal target seemed to be slipping through our fingers.

CHAPTER SIXTY-THREE

AUTOMAGIC

AT A STROKE, WE LOST THE advantage of our 26% stake and were on equal terms with 400 companies that responded when the Receiver put Automagic up for sale. We were told receivers sell most companies for a song, so we offered £1.8m. Our advice was incorrect. There was so much interest in Automagic that the Receiver asked for a serious offer so we tried £2.8m, but this still wasn't enough. We were told several bids had been made at around £3m and had 3 days to offer our best price.

We thought Automagic was worth £3.8m but NatWest wouldn't give us the backing we needed, even though I made a major sacrifice. It took three years to repay the £1m mortgage I took out in 1991, so I planned to reinstate it to give us a decent shot at buying Automagic.

It was a courageous decision because I didn't have Alex's support. I relied on her intuitive judgement and, on every occasion, she had proved to be right. For the first time, we disagreed. I was devastated but Alex refused to listen to my argument – I thought Automagic would totally transform the Timpson business, but Alex could only think of the mortgage. Without the mortgage, I would have had to give up some equity so I decided to go ahead without Alex's blessing.

Final bids were required by 5 pm on the middle Wednesday in September and with 3 hours to go, the bank still wouldn't back the £3.8m we wanted to offer, so we offered £3.35m and kept our fingers crossed. The Receiver promised to call early the following morning. I had a sleepless night and arrived in my office at 8 am to wait for the call.

It was good news and bad news. Our bid was pitched at the right level but two others had made a similar offer; one had to be our major competitor, Mister Minit. Knowing they had access to almost unlimited resources, I telephoned their chief executive, Kenn Begley, with a proposition.

I proposed a half, suggesting a joint bid, which, if successful, would lead to us tossing a coin. Whoever won the toss would pick the first shop and we would alternatively select the shop of our choice until all the Automagic branches had been split between us. Kenn Begley didn't give an answer; he needed to consult his Chairman.

Within 20 minutes, my offer was rejected as they were determined to acquire the whole of Automagic and, one day, buy our business as well. The offer of a half was our best chance of success; the next 24 hours would decide whether it was our last chance of doing a deal.

We were summoned to London. The Receiver had further information on the redundancy liability which would be available from midday so we could fix our final offer. Mister Minit had the money to outbid us, but perhaps we could force Mister Minit to overpay. I was likely to be a bad loser.

NatWest still hadn't formally agreed to support our latest offer, so Martin Tragen and I spoke to other sources of finance while Roger and Mike went on to London where Roger and the Receiver agreed there wouldn't be an auction; instead, the sale would be settled by sealed bids submitted at 7 pm.

By 6.30 pm, we were no nearer deciding on our offer. Although we didn't have the bank's support, we had to offer at least £3.8m. With 10 minutes to go, Martin surprised us all by going out on a limb. He felt we could fund a bid of £4m. Before we faxed our offer, I added £12,500. I knew Richard Branson added a bit extra to avoid being tied with another bidder on an exact amount. At precisely 7 pm, we faxed £4,012,500. Five minutes later, we learnt that ours was the highest bid.

We were asked to go to the Receiver's office immediately, to sign the paperwork, but Roger stalled. Our letter from NatWest wouldn't stand up to scrutiny. Roger found a range of reasons that bought us three hours to get better backing from the bank, but eventually, we submitted the original letter and got an ultimatum. If we couldn't produce stronger support before 10 am the following morning, we were out of the contest, because the other party was already in their office, ready to sign.

It was 10 pm before we sat down for a meal dominated by the mobile phone, making a series of desperate calls to find the extra £750,000 we needed. At midnight, we went to bed dreaming of how close we had got to the deal.

Back in Roger's office at 7.30 am, the clock ticked faster than normal as we approached 10 am.

The mood lifted slightly with 45 minutes to go when we got an encouraging call from Brian Ferguson at NatWest Stockport. By 9.45 am, we had his letter backing our offer. We rang the Receiver and were immediately called over to their office to complete the paperwork.

Roger stayed behind but 45 minutes later was on the telephone; "I've had a call from Mister Minit," he said. "I think that you ought to ring them and listen to what they have to say." I got through to Kenn Begley. "We seem to be in the middle of an auction," said Kenn. "Do you remember the deal you offered me yesterday? I think we should get together and talk about it." I told him I would think about it and ring back – but I never did.

For the next hour, we made rapid progress until being interrupted by a telephone call. The room cleared leaving the Timpson team behind to worry about this mystery caller. But this final Mister Minit intervention wasn't enough to sabotage our negotiations. The room refilled and two hours later I signed the deal with a nervous, squiggly signature.

CHAPTER SIXTY-FOUR

BIGGER BUSINESS

THE AUTOMAGIC DEAL WAS done on a Friday so we kept everything under wraps over the weekend. On Monday morning, Timpson
area managers started to visit all the branches and Patrick Farmer turned
up in Harpenden but was refused entry. The Receiver had told no one
about the deal, so Patrick waited in the car park for an hour before anyone
would talk to him. Within three weeks, we closed Harpenden and every
Automagic shop was serviced from Timpson House.

Two weeks after our acquisition, we discovered that Mister Minit
had written to the landlords of the most profitable shops, offering to take
on the leases at substantially increased rents. The implication hit me like
a thunderbolt. I thought the worst; if I lost all the best shops, I had no
chance of repaying my £1m mortgage and Alex would never forgive me.
Fortunately, I was being naive; it is an area of property law where common sense prevails and justice is seen to be done. We had the right to
renegotiate every lease and, in some cases, in a weak property market,
agreed lower rents.

It took six months to sell the Harpenden freehold for £400,000 (well
below our expectations) and even longer before we started to improve
the Automagic turnover. For the first 4 months, their sales were nearly

10% down at a time when Timpson was at least 3% up on last year. Acquisitions often do badly until the new owners gain the trust and confidence of their new colleagues.

Automagic colleagues were demoralised. Several years of ineffective management had made them suspicious. With no wage increases for three years, they took matters into their own hands. Housekeeping and customer service was poor; dishonesty was rife.

I asked their area managers to come to my office. I wanted to see if they had any good ideas we had missed – hidden gems that could increase sales or save money. I was in for a surprise. Most of them told me, in no uncertain terms, that we didn't know how to run a shoe repair business and the route to success was to run Timpson the same way as Automagic with computer stock control, smaller key displays and a wall full of shoe care products.

We ignored their advice and put big temporary key displays into every shop, backed by better machinery and some basic training. Key sales went up by 100% and total turnover increased 20%. Colleagues started to realise we knew what we were doing and the mood moved from highly negative to pretty positive. It got even better when we changed the fascias to the Timpson name using an updated design that we still use today.

Automagic was more successful than I ever imagined. In the second year, sales increased 23% and the branch contribution went up by 77%. It transformed our business, and, in three years, our total profit rose from £500k to £3m. To Alex's relief, I repaid the mortgage within 15 months.

The spectacular Automagic turnaround showed the strength of the TSR management team. Kit Green, who guided the day-to-day business from 1987 until 2002, had a very different management style to his predecessor, Mike Frank. Kit was more passive, doing a lot of thinking and plenty of delegating. The energy was supplied by our Development Director, Alan Chatterton, a coiled spring full of enthusiasm. Sadly, shortly after we acquired Automagic, we lost the other long-term member of the TSR team, my second cousin, Charles Noakes, the buyer and merchandiser, who died suddenly of a heart attack.

The purchase of Automagic persuaded my son, James, that it was time to join the business. James had been involved since he was 14, working during school holidays in our Northwich shop. During his gap year between school and University, James was taught how to repair shoes by Stan Knagg, expert cobbler and manager of Kirkby near Liverpool. When James got his degree, he wanted to gain experience working for someone else. However, this proved more difficult than he expected;1992 was a tough year to be joining the job market.

The problem was solved by mailing an advertisement, which offered James on a six-month free trial. The offer was taken up by Richard Zerny at Johnsons the Cleaners and James got a job on full pay, selling industrial cleaning to factories in Tyneside and Teeside for Harton Clean, a Johnsons subsidiary. It proved to be a great learning experience.

Eighteen months later, James took on a new challenge. He helped Morning Foods, a breakfast food manufacturer based in Crewe, to open a pet food supermarket in Congleton. Both bits of work experience were ideal preparation for James's career at Timpson.

James spent his first year back at Timpson using his sales experience to promote Automagic's specialist branded shoe repair service to the retailers of Timberland, Caterpillar, R M Williams and Henri Lloyd, from a charmless factory in Luton. But his next role, in central London, was more dramatic.

A few weeks before Automagic went into receivership, I was on Cannon Street at 6 pm on a Thursday and noticed a meeting taking place in the Automagic shop. A few months later, I discovered the purpose of their get-together. The area manager wasn't there; the discussion only involved all the managers in central London, who were deciding how much cash to steal from the company during the next few weeks.

Nearly everyone was taking cash from the till – they probably took 20% of turnover. Those colleagues who stayed totally honest were targeted by the rest of the gang. Threatening messages were delivered by anonymous phone calls, tyres were slashed and shop doors secured with superglue. It was pretty unpleasant and there was even a suggestion that, at one time, an area manager got a percentage of the ill-gotten gains.

We beat the rogues by targeting one shop at a time. Without warning, colleagues in the targeted branch were transferred elsewhere and replaced by the hit team – Don Randall, who later became an area manager, assisted by Huey – two honest guys who gave great customer service and knew how to create turnover. They stayed for three weeks and usually put sales up by over 40%. Then, the resident team were expected to match the hit team's figures. Some simply handed in their notice, a few started putting the money in the till but most were dismissed for gross misconduct.

The hit idea was such a success that a second team was set up and James spent several months working in London – they were less likely to steal under the nose of the boss's son.

Within a year, sales in the London shops had doubled and James discovered first hand the value of a great branch manager having the freedom to run the shop the way they knew best.

CHAPTER SIXTY-FIVE

NEW LOOK ON THE HIGH STREETS

A YEAR BEFORE AUTOMAGIC went into receivership, we decided to change the look of our shops. The move was prompted by a visit to Redhill by Patrick Farmer. The branch had just opened and I wanted to show off our latest layout. Patrick was far from impressed, describing the shop as a hotchpotch without any discipline. I was shamed into doing something.

Rod Umpleby, our resourceful and droll development manager, proposed renaming the shops 'Quick' or using my signature as the fascia. Neither worked, so we hired a consultant to take Timpson into the Millennium.

I spent two days with the consultant visiting a selection of shops. Three weeks later, they returned with some initial sketches. The narrative repeated what I had told them and their big design idea was to give each of our services a different colour. With so little to show for four weeks' work, I paid them off, deciding we could do better without them.

The next week, I visited Bath to look at an independent we were keen on buying. Bath was full of new retailers so I spent the morning photographing their shop fronts. Back in the office, we pinned the pictures on a wall and picked the letter style and colour scheme that worked best for Timpson. We called ourselves 'TIMPSON the quality service people' and added 'Est. 1903' (the date was pure fiction but 2003 would be the perfect year to celebrate our centenary).

The first shop to get the new treatment was Automagic in Fleet Street. Within 12 months, all Automagic shops had the new look, and, two years later, every Timpson branch got a makeover and key-cutting overtook shoe repairs to become the biggest part of our business.

The new-look shops had a traditional treatment of shoe repairs (unashamedly copied from a shop in Chesterfield owned by our competitor, Peter Bullock) with a display of finished repairs above the machinery – designed by John Higgs, our manager in Cheadle.

Every shop had an enormous key display; some key boards were over 20 feet long. Whenever we changed their colour, sales increased (probably due to what industrial psychologists called 'The Hawthorne Effect'). It worked so well that the boards were changed at least every 5 years.

It was important to be able to cut every type of key – not just the simple Yale or mortice lock for your garden shed – we needed to cut keys for cars, motor bikes, boats, aeroplanes, security locks, lockers and safes.

This commitment to cut 'every key every time' meant a big investment in key-cutting machinery, a vast range of key blanks and a comprehensive training programme. We created a specialist key centre at Timpson House, originally run by Ian Oakes, a key enthusiast, from the shop in Northwich, who provided instant solutions to help branch colleagues facing a key problem.

Our approach flew in the face of the classic 80/20 problem. When visiting the Mister Minit warehouse in Sheffield, their MD, Kenn Begley, proudly explained how they had reduced their range to the 75 key blanks that cut over 90% keys in current use. I was delighted; they had failed to realise that shops with a big range of blanks get many more of the popular 1A Yale keys than competitors with a limited selection.

I was so keen for the shops to never turn key customers away, that we employed mystery shoppers with tricky keys to check our colleagues were up to the challenge. Once, I spread a false rumour that Which? magazine was investigating key-cutting and a team of twenty researchers were covering the country. Which? never carried out the survey but while our colleagues were expecting them to call, our key-cutting turnover increased by 5%.

These moves built a £60m a year key business but one simple idea has been the biggest money-maker – "The second key is always half price". Ever since we introduced the deal in the 1970s, it has been an irresistible offer; over half our key customers take the second key. In the mid-1990s, we were visited by a Canadian repair chain called Moneysworth & Best. We told them about the second key deal, but, when James and I went to Toronto three months later, we were surprised they weren't promoting the extra key. "Didn't it work?" we asked. "It was great!" they replied. "We ran the deal for the whole of August." We have now been running it for over 40 years!

Key-cutting was so important that we appointed one of our Area Managers, Jim Jardine, as our Key-Cutting Product Manager and added a Key Development Manager to every area team. With nearly 350 shops, Kit Green split the country into two regions. Perry Watkins and Brian Elliot were our first Regional Managers, each responsible for 7 area managers. The business was now too big to hold our area managers' conference in my dining room at Sandymere.

We also invested in the engraving service by putting computers into 200 shops and opening a central engraving centre above our shop in St Helens. Our house sign business grew so quickly that we had to move to a workshop at Baxter's Lane, an industrial estate near St Helens.

The business was outgrowing the warehouse attached to Timpson House. We added a mezzanine floor but that wasn't big enough, so, in 2002, we acquired another building on the same estate and the original warehouse provided enough extra office space to satisfy our needs for the next 16 years.

After we bought Automagic, we spent 8 years creating a truly people-based service business. The principles that now define our culture were developed in the late 1990s, when, with no major acquisitions, we could work out how to run a multi-service retailer.

CHAPTER SIXTY-SIX

WATCH REPAIRS

THE AUTOMAGIC ACQUISITION encouraged us to take a serious look at watch repairs. Our main competitor, Mister Minit, had offered this service for some time, but our spies told us the turnover was seldom more than £20 per branch, per week. Before going into receivership, Automagic started working with John Lyons, an expert watch repairer, who rented space next to their shop in Stevenage.

Despite this initiative, I wouldn't have been interested in watch repairs if I hadn't visited the Automagic kiosk in West Bromwich. The branch manager, Glenn Edwards, was nervous and started to apologise; "I hope you don't mind, but I take in a few watch repairs, something I did before I joined Automagic." "How much money does it bring in?" I asked. "About £100; more in a good week," replied Glenn – that was good enough for me, so I had a coffee with John Lyons.

We started offering a modest service (watch straps and batteries) in four shops – Crawley, Fish Street Hill, Yeovil and Salisbury – they took an average of £90 a week, sufficient to spread the experiment but hardly enough to suggest watch repairs could become a major Timpson service. That changed after a visit from H Samuels.

We met to discuss how Timpson could provide an engraving

service to H Samuel shops. Before discussing any detail, the Samuels Sales Manager produced a stumbling block. "We won't do a deal if you continue as a direct competitor."

I assumed that he meant our range of tankards and christening gifts, but that wasn't his problem. "I was in Yeovil last week and noticed you are offering watch repairs – for us, it's a £13.5m business. If you want to develop an engraving service, you must stop repairing watches."

That told us all we needed to know. We abandoned any ambition to provide an engraving service for H Samuels and decided to accelerate the development of watch repairs. It was the first task taken on by James after he moved to Manchester as our Marketing Director.

We made plenty of mistakes. The new service was at the back of the shop so few customers knew what was on offer. We charged £3.50 for every battery, regardless of the watch's value. Some colleagues attacked a Rolex with enthusiasm, scratching the back of the watch and prevented it from being waterproof. You have to sell a lot of £3.50 batteries to pay the compensation on one ruined Rolex.

We employed some highly qualified watch repairers, but most were hopeless at serving customers. Our breakthrough came when James discovered the National Horology Centre at Upton, near Newark, where our colleagues could learn lots of basic skills in under a week. We block-booked the centre for four months and sent a colleague from every shop to gain their basic watch repair diploma. Some shops started taking £200 a week.

It took time to work out how watch repairs fitted into our shop lay-out. To attract attention, the new service needed to be at the front of the branch, but that was the prime location for promoting key-cutting, the most profitable service. The problem was solved by a new service counter on the opposite wall. The breakthrough came with a big watch repair area at the front of our Eastbourne branch, where sales shot up to £1,000 a week. We were on the way to achieving H Samuel's level of business.

Glenn Edwards, the man who started it all, transformed Timpson from a basic straps and battery service into a proper watch repairer. He created a central watch repair workshop above our shop in Wolverhampton, giving us the ability to service complicated mechanical watches. Within a year, Glenn built up a team of experienced watch repairers giving him the time to train branch colleagues – they started learning to pressure-test waterproof watches and tackle more complicated repair jobs. As part of the advanced course, small parties of Timpson colleagues visited Switzerland to spend a week with top quality watchmakers.

When we started doing watch repairs, I doubted whether customers would trust a cobbler to tinker with their precious watch and whether cobblers would be willing to repair watches. I was wrong. Our branch colleagues were keen to take on a new skill. They even invented our lifetime guarantee, which has helped to build a business that, at £45m a year, is now bigger than shoe repairs.

CHAPTER SIXTY-SEVEN

CHASING SHADOWS

THE LACK OF ANY MAJOR acquisition in the late 1990s wasn't for lack of trying. My major target was Mister Minit UK.

Mister Minit was founded by Don Hillsdon Ryan, an American living in Switzerland. He started with a heel bar in Brussels, a format he repeated around the world, building an international chain of about 3,500 outlets. When he bought the UK-based Allied Shoe Repair shops, they posed a different challenge – they were shops rather than kiosks selling a wide range of merchandise, including suitcases and leather goods. Run from Sheffield, they were rebranded 'Mister Minit', 'Gullivers' or 'Saddlers'. The business, run by Minit appointee, David Short, was profitable, but with almost twice as many shops, fell short of Timpson profits. It was a massive opportunity. I approached Hillsdon Ryan on two occasions; first in Geneva, the second time in London. Both times he seemed bewildered that I would want to, and could, buy part of his business. The deal never got off the ground.

I was taken by surprise in June 1997, when the whole of Mister Minit, worldwide, was acquired by UBS, the Swiss bank. This was my chance. Smart Swiss bankers were bound to realise that Mister Minit UK was underperforming and would see the sense of doing a deal with us.

Martin Tragen and I arranged to see the banker in charge, Ian Siddall, in London. We waited in the reception for 15 minutes, before being put in a meeting room, where we got tea. It was another 20 minutes before we saw Ian Siddall, whose arrogant manner matched his punctuality.

Ian Siddall described his glittering career which led to the leadership of Mister Minit, the world's leading retail service provider. Then he paused to ask why I wanted the meeting. I said that I wanted to buy Minit UK and he laughed. "I thought you were a seller, not a buyer." Then he continued, "Let me explain; we are experts at buying family businesses and putting in professional management. You are on my list so keep close to your phone. I will soon make you an offer."

Three minutes later, Martin and I were at a café outside UBS HQ, wondering how to compete with a cash-rich and pompous competitor.

With the Minit opportunity firmly closed, I looked elsewhere, starting with Sketchley, the company that once got close to dominating the UK dry cleaning market. In 1985, Sketchley claimed to be the market leader with 600 outlets and nearly bought rival Johnsons the Cleaners following a hostile takeover bid.

When the deal to buy Johnsons fell through, Sketchley diversified into other services. They bought SupaSnaps from Dixons. SupaSnaps, with over 400 shops, was a major photo retailer with branches that sent analogue rolls of film overnight to a central processing plant. The SupaSnaps chief executive took over the day-to-day running of Sketchley and photos played a big part in Sketchley's future plans. To save property costs, several SupaSnaps branches were moved into the front of nearby Sketchley units, but with dry cleaning in decline and photo competitors providing a 20-minute service, Sketchley profits came under pressure.

To provide a good news story for the stock exchange, Sketchley opened concessions inside Sainsbury supermarkets. However, the deal was somewhat one-sided. Sainsbury chose the stores and the location – often by the checkout furthest away from the entrance. Sketchley Chairman, John Jackson, was keen to sell the business so I was given a two-day tour of Sketchley and SupaSnap shops, a visit to the Maidenhead Head Office and access to their detailed trading information.

Although I spent three weeks visiting Sketchley and SupaSnap branches and had a couple of meetings with venture capitalists, it was a futile fishing expedition. As racing tipsters sometimes comment about a no-hoper, the Sketchley business was 'best watched'!

Throughout the 1990s, I paid regular visits to Johnson the Cleaners' Head Office in Bootle to touch base with their senior team, Terry Greer, Richard Zerny and David Bryant. My aim was to add more concessions to those we bought from Ron Lilleywhite in 1990. Most Johnson's concessions were operated by Mister Minit and I failed to make inroads until 2001 when Minit closed a few Johnson concessions.

I thought I'd found the perfect deal when I started talking to 'In Time', a chain of 50 watch repair kiosks, mainly inside Debenhams. The business was founded by Scotsman, John Mathieson, who ran the units from a central workshop in Southport. We were just starting to develop a meaningful watch repair service, so it seemed like a good move. 'In Time' units were producing far bigger watch repair sales than Timpson, and, with a profit of £450k a year, we were prepared to pay a fancy price.

The day-to-day business was being run by John's son, Angus, who was delegated to negotiate the deal, which included the promise of a role for Angus and continuity for the team at Southport. This limited our scope for overhead savings, but, with no other deals around, I bought Angus lunch at The Dysart Arms in Bunbury and agreed to pay £3.5m.

Luckily, Angus's father had second thoughts and the deal didn't happen. I now know it is unwise to buy a business that is trading well – you are forced to pay a full price and have to find ways to increase an already good performance to get a decent payback. It is so much better to buy a badly run business for next to nothing – as long as you have a plan to make things better.

The Mathieson change of heart means we hardly have any concessions in department stores, just Selfridges, Fenwicks in Newcastle and Bentalls in Kingston.

My only regret is being booted from Harrods – twice. The first time was when we ran a temporary engraving service (our tenure ended shortly after we engraved a trophy for Mohammed al Fayed's daughter and spelt her name wrong) Our second appearance in Harrods was as a traditional Timpson shop, which did well until our department was redeveloped and we were never asked to return.

We were always looking for more services to make up for the drop in shoe repairs. Spectacle repairs didn't produce enough turnover to be worthwhile, and we couldn't get customers to use our jewellery repair service. We had several other ill-considered trials that included buying gold, recycling mobile phones and even one product that was dangerously close to a payday loan. We never thought it right to open body piercing and tattoo parlours but James boldly provided an internet service called 'city.cobbler.com'.

The idea was that city traders would contact our website and, within minutes, a man would arrive on a motorbike with a pair of slippers for the customer to wear while their shoes were repaired at a nearby shop. We got 3 customers on the first day and five on the second. On the third day, the service was tested by a journalist from the Evening Standard, who, sadly, got no response – Keith, our courier, had fallen off his motorbike the night before and 'city.cobbler.com' came to an early end.

We learnt a lot during the late 1990s, mostly about what not to do.

CHAPTER SIXTY-EIGHT

UPSIDE-DOWN MANAGEMENT

TWO MEETINGS IN 1996 AND 1997 made a major difference to the way we did business. In March 1996, I met with our shoe repair product manager, Mike Donaghue. I revealed my ignorance by asking, "How do we train our colleagues?" "By working alongside an expert craftsman," said Mike. "We don't expect perfection, just a good commercial job." "Sounds a bit vague to me," I replied, "but I've got an idea; I'll be back in 15 minutes".

At the local garden centre, I bought a book by D.G. Hessayon with gardening tips in pictures and very few words. "That's what we should do," I told Mike. "Produce a manual that uses pictures to show how to repair shoes."

Over the Easter Bank Holiday, it poured with rain for four days, so, with nothing else to do, I wrote the first draft of our shoe repair manual. The fact that I can't repair a shoe was a distinct advantage – I used simple terms that didn't take anything for granted. Later that year, I wrote a Guide to Key-Cutting and in 1997, John Tucker, a Timpson colleague based in South Wales, produced Guides to Engraving and Watch Repairs.

These guides now help new recruits become qualified branch managers within 12 months, with rigorous tests for every skill. At first, colleagues got a reward every time they passed a test, but then we had a better idea. We updated the branch bonus scheme to include a colleague's skill rating.

Our bonus scheme puts a buzz into the branches. The elegant formula keeps wage costs down, puts sales up and encourages colleagues to learn new skills. The calculation is the same in every shop – the total wages paid out in the week are multiplied by 4.5 to set the target for that week; colleagues receive 15% of all sales over target, the bonus pot being split according to the colleagues' number of skill points. There is no limit to the bonus a colleague can earn.

The other meeting that changed our thinking was the short encounter with Ian Siddall at UBS. The realization that we faced such a well-funded competitor made us think. Mister Minit could afford to undercut our prices, poach our best colleagues and open next to our most profitable shops. The only way to compete was by giving customers a superior experience. It was then that we discovered the secret behind great customer service – the secret is simple and should have been obvious (I read all about it three years earlier in a book about Nordstrom the American chain of department stores).

You can't create great service by issuing a set of rules or running training courses that teach colleagues to look customers in the eye and ask open questions. It doesn't do much good having notices in the staff room saying 'Smile – You're on Stage'. The secret is to trust branch colleagues with the freedom to look after customers in the way they know best.

In the middle of the Nordstrom book, there is a management chart that is upside-down – shop colleagues are at the top with the authority to make decisions, and everyone else, right down to the Chief Executive, is there to support the colleagues who make the money. For over 20 years, we have been running our business using 'Upside-down Management'.

It took 5 years to make our 'Upside-down Management' work. Initially, I put a notice in every shop explaining that colleagues are trusted with the freedom to serve every customer in the way they know best and I threw away our rulebook replacing it with just 2 rules. Rule 1 – Look the part. Rule 2 – Put the money in the till. But branch colleagues were frightened to use any initiative; they knew their area manager would still tell them what to do. Middle managers were the big stumbling block. They didn't see how they could be held responsible for results if they couldn't tell team members what to do.

It helped when we gave everyone the authority to hand out up to £500 to settle a complaint without consulting anyone else and to give customers a discount if they thought it was the right thing to do. But the new ideas weren't popular with our area managers who claimed, "How can we be responsible for the performance of a group of shops if we can't tell anyone what to do?"

We redefined day-to-day management. No manager was allowed to issue orders; instead, we persuaded them to do their job by helping every team member to be the best they could possibly be. Their new role involved providing training and support and making sure that obstacles didn't get in their way of their colleagues. We recognised that colleagues in the shops provided our service and asked managers to focus on their people. Managers stopped telling the team what to do and started to concentrate on providing help and support. In the process, they became mentors and social workers, supporting team members through personal and family problems as well as solving work-related issues.

For Upside-down Management to work, we needed to change the role of 'Head Office'. Like most businesses, everyone assumed that Head Office ran the business and told everyone else what to do. We wanted something completely different. The culture and strategy would continue to be set and communicated by myself and Kit Green, but the departments were there to support people in our shops and make their job as easy as possible. To make the point, we scrapped the term 'Head Office' and started calling the central support team at Wythenshawe 'Timpson House'.

To emphasise that colleagues at Timpson House were there to provide support, we scrapped the automatic phone answering system (nearly all the calls came from shop colleagues who needed an immediate answer) and required everyone to work a day in a branch to qualify for their annual bonus.

It wasn't long before we realised 'Upside-down Management' only works if you have the right people. For years, we recruited shoe repairers and key cutters when we should have been looking for people with personality. You can teach lively characters to cut keys, but you can't put personality into a grumpy cobbler.

Our Mr Men interview assessment form helps interviewers to look for personality. The form pictures 24 different characters including Mr Happy, Mrs Keen, Miss Punctual, Mr Grumpy, Miss Scruffy and Mr Dull. Under each cartoon is an empty box, the interviewer ticks the boxes that fit the person in front of them. It works – we are not bothered about qualifications or what candidates write on their application form and we never use psychometric testing. We simply ask candidates who tick the right boxes to work in a shop for half a day alongside someone who 'gets it' and that tells us all we need to know.

Filling Timpson full of people who rate 9 or 10 out of 10 and letting them have the freedom to do their job the way they want has been a major factor in transforming our business.

This very informal management style would have seemed strange to my great-grandfather, and indeed, to my father who died suddenly in 1997 just a few months after my mother, who was mercifully released after suffering 14 years of dementia.

CHAPTER SIXTY-NINE

ALEX

APART FROM A SHORT SPELL as a shop assistant just before we got married, my late wife, Alex, never worked for Timpson, but her experiences as a foster carer helped to give us a social conscience. She never talked about turnover or profit; instead, it was always about people. She taught us the importance of kindness, passionately claiming that a company can be kind and make plenty of money at the same time.

I met Alex at a Hale Tennis Club social evening. I had been dancing with long-time acquaintance Wendy Marshall, who, clearly not being as keen on me as I was on her, introduced me briefly to Alex, who, in turn, seemed to show the same level of indifference.

The pair left the party but Wendy's Austin 7 wouldn't start and her disgruntled father arrived in his Bentley. I heard him say, "I suppose you expect me to drive Alex all the way home to Lymm," at which point, Alex claims, I jumped from behind a bush and announced, "I'll take her, Sir". We got married 18 months later.

Alex was a qualified nursery nurse. When we met, she was employed as a nanny in Baker Street, London, but soon found a new job nearer home with a family in Middlewich. In 1977, Edward, the youngest of our three children, went to school and Alex, who was never a lady who lunched, looked around for something else to do. She spotted an advert asking for foster carers. We were interviewed three times by Morven Sowerbutts, a social worker, before being approved by the local fostering and adoption panel. Six months later, I returned from work on a Friday night to find two extra children at home.

During the next 31 years, we fostered 90 children and adopted two more. We were short-term foster carers, which meant no more than six months. That limit was rigidly applied to the first couple, Simon and Shaun, who were taken away 10 days before Christmas. Alex was told they had gone to another family, but quickly discovered they were in Kilrie, a children's' home in Knutsford. She spent hours by the fence trying to spot the boys in the playground. By the time we finished fostering in 2009, short-term foster children often stayed much longer than six months – our last placement, a sister and two brothers, were with us for nearly three years. Our long-term foster child, David, stayed for 10 years and is still part of our family.

Alex loved the challenge, caring for a number of particularly troubled children. She looked after two babies born with a heroin addiction and several children with signs of physical abuse, including scars and cigarette burns. One boy was so aggressive that he killed one of our cats. The youngest arrived at our house when he was only two hours old (born to a mum with a history of child neglect). I was the speaker at a Pattenmakers' dinner in London that night – just before the coffee, I turned to the Master and asked "Do you mind if I pop out to make a phone call? My wife is expecting a baby."

The most memorable children include four-month-old triplets, who, thankfully, only stayed for seven weeks, and a 6-year-old boy who relieved his frustration by taking a sledgehammer to 110 panes of glass in my greenhouse.

Alex never stuck to the rules. Foster carers weren't expected to keep in touch with the children and their families after the fostering stint was over, but Alex did. She was a birthing partner on three occasions, organised a wedding for an ex-foster child, acted as a guarantor to help another find a home and supplied several cars to teenage ex-foster children and a couple of mums. Alex believed that one of the best ways to help someone find their way in life was to give them wheels. When she died, I inherited 10 extra cars, together with their tax and insurance. Alex explained, "If you live in a privileged position, that's what you do."

When we finished fostering, Alex became a Home-Start volunteer, helping families to keep their children out of the care system. The role gave Alex more rules to break – guaranteeing more rental accommodation, finding and funding lawyers to unravel unfair divorce settlements and doing a bit of shopping. Alex's hobby was helping other people.

We were lucky that a couple, Janet and Eric Done, gave us the chance to have plenty of proper breaks. Eric had worked for the previous owners of our house, Sandymere, and Janet became our regular babysitter. Janet and Eric bravely qualified as foster carers. Thanks to them, Alex and I got regular holidays including trips to Mustique, where Alex often talked about the children we had left behind.

As soon as Alex returned home, she would take her place at the head of our kitchen table with a pad on one side, telephone on the other, running her support and advice service for people facing life's problems. They became some of her closest friends.

I was the person who benefitted most from Alex's advice – without looking at a balance sheet or attending a Board meeting, Alex spotted the right answer by using common sense. She made me battle on after the Board Room bust-up in 1972 and, 10 years later, gave her wholehearted backing to our management buyout. Crucially, Alex stopped me from floating the business in 1989 and was happy for us to take out a £1m mortgage in 1991 so we could own 100% of the equity.

It isn't surprising that one of her best bits of advice was about people. In 2003, we were looking for a new Finance Director and the interviews took place at Sandymere. Each candidate was greeted by Alex before being interviewed by James and myself. The third and final interviewee,

Paresh Majithia, turned up late and was greeted over-enthusiastically by one of our dogs, while Alex put Paresh at ease.

James and I had a detailed discussion before making our choice, but before making our decision, Alex offered her opinion. As soon as Paresh left, Alex announced, "He's the one!" For 15 years, Paresh has played a pivotal role in transforming our business.

CHAPTER SEVENTY

CHARITIES

IN 1998, ALEX AND I were invited by The Duke of Westminster to a small dinner at Eaton Hall, held to launch the NSPCC Full Stop Campaign. When driving home, Alex said, "You haven't handed over a penny or pledged a donation – what are you going to do?"

The following morning, I told Alex the answer; "Little stitching jobs and holes in belts. Instead of doing little jobs for free, we will ask customers to 'Put a £1 in the Charity Box". Over the next 2 years, we raised nearly £400,000 for the NSPCC. Then, our colleagues picked ChildLine and we raised even more money. I became a ChildLine Trustee for 6 years until we persuaded Esther Rantzen to make ChildLine part of the NSPCC. For two more years, we raised an average of £265,000 for ChildLine and I kept in touch with both charities through regular meetings with Esther and NSPCC Chairman, Chris Kelly.

Alex and I thought that fostering was going to be pretty straightforward but were in for a bit of a shock. Most looked-after children come with a few complications and we didn't know why until Alex spent half a day at a training meeting. The speaker was Dan Hughes and for the first time, Alex learnt about Attachment Theory.

Most kids are lucky; they are brought up by loving carers (usually their parents) who give them the confidence and trust that lasts a life-time. But others, particularly looked-after children, don't get the cuddles and can grow up lacking in confidence. They don't trust the world and the people around them and constantly test to see if others really care. That testing can take the form of irritating, unacceptable and sometimes criminal behaviour.

A lack of attachment can cause children to perform poorly at school, be more likely to be unemployed and form a significant proportion of the prison population. Our adopted son, Ollie, was a classic victim. He joined us from that same children's home, Kilrie, at the age of six and his lack of attachment caused him to run away from home, caused consternation to teachers at 5 different schools, and despite having a magnificent treble voice, he was thrown out of Chester Cathedral Choir.

Knowing about Attachment Theory made a massive difference. At last, we started to understand Ollie and saw his difficult behaviour as a form of communication. Alex vowed that, whenever we got the chance, we would help others understand the importance of Attachment Theory. We got that chance when we met Lynn Charlton, Chief Executive of After Adoption, who developed a support package for adoptive parents called Safe Base.

In six years, the free jobs raised just short of £2m for After Adoption, which, by offering 50/50 funding, was used to persuade local authorities to offer Safe Base to adoptive parents. To help get the message across, I wrote two simple-to-read, illustrated books that explain attachment to carers and teenagers

Many of our foster children went to our local school, Delamere Primary, where Alex became a Governor, but it had problems and, in 2007, was threatened with closure. True to form, Alex told me, "You will have to do something about it!" My response was to offer a Bursary of £150,000 over 5 years to pay for extra-curricular activities that Alex said would 'open the children's eyes to the world of possibility'. I chaired the governors for a year and discovered the school only had 42 pupils – if the local authority didn't shut it, it was in danger of shutting itself.

I introduced some upside-down management when I told Steve Docking, the Head, "We have nothing to lose! Ignore all the policies, guidelines and directives. Just concentrate, in your own way, on giving the kids a great education that helps them make the most of the rest of their lives."

Steve went on the Timpson Leadership Course, Safe Base ran courses on Attachment and, within three years, the school was full – 168 children, 24 in each class. We now sponsor the North West Academy Trust with 8 schools under Steve as Chief Executive, several helped by Timpson Bursaries. Alex believed that our first duty was to look after Timpson colleagues, then the priority of our charitable support should always be children and young people.

Just after Alex died, I wrote a book for schools – 'How to Look After Looked-After Children" and since 2017, our shops have been raising money for the Alex Timpson Trust, with the main aim of encouraging schools to become 'Attachment Aware'.

CHAPTER SEVENTY-ONE

HOW COBBLERS BECAME PUBLICANS

IN 2003, ALEX PERSUADED ME TO buy a holiday cottage at Rhoscolyn on Anglesey. You could only get there by driving across the beach at low tide, but that wasn't a problem. Alex never liked cooking and her difficulty was that there were no good restaurants nearby. Alex's answer was to buy the local pub, The White Eagle, at the top of the road that led to our beach. In 2005, the owner planned to close the pub and turn it into flats, but there was a local outcry which led to a public meeting. Three days later, I agreed to buy The White Eagle for £375,000. We both took the licensee's course and appeared at Court in Llangefni so that our names could be above the entrance, proving it was our pub.

We were lucky to find our managers, Stuart and Kirsty, but they threatened to resign on the first day. The White Eagle needed a very deep spring clean and the only food in the kitchen was three fish fingers and a limp lettuce. Takings in the first week were just over £1,000, not enough to pay the wages.

We did a lot of research which mostly meant going round other pubs. The best ideas came from The Olive Branch at Clipsham and The

Grosvenor Arms at Aldford, where landlord, Garry Kidd was massively helpful.

Stuart and Kirsty started to turn things around. A lick of paint, a shelf full of children's games and colouring books and a more ambitious menu made a difference and the number of customers tripled from a trickle to a steady flow that created a buzz. All went well until Stuart and Kirsty handed in their notice and were replaced by a nightmare couple who were offhand to us as well as the customers.

We pleaded with Stuart and Kirsty, so they came back in time to push the August takings beyond £30,000 a week. Anglesey was starting to discover our revamped child and dog-friendly pub with proper food. Despite a succession of disgruntled head chefs who picked up a handsome pay packet, the business grew and made money.

However, Alex then announced, "I want to make it a great pub". It was closed for 9 months and almost completely rebuilt, while we went on more pub crawls in search of perfection. The White Eagle reopened during the spring bank holiday weekend and took £35,000 in three days; Alex had the great pub she wanted.

The White Eagle got an unexpected boost when Prince William and Kate Middleton took a cottage nearby when William was based at RAF Valley. I was in the Romford Tesco car park when our manager, Adrienne, rang with an urgent question. "I've got five journalists here asking 'where do they sit?', 'what do they eat?', 'how often do they come?' I suggested she should let them buy a meal but make it clear 'we never talk about our customers'. On the day of William and Kate's wedding, an Australian TV station anchored their coverage from The White Eagle.

Two years after The White Eagle was rebuilt, we got involved in another pub. It was the rundown Maelog Lake Hotel, in 70 acres of common land adjoining Rhosneigr beach, a major centre for kite-surfing. We had some extra cash so bought the pub then wondered what to do next. As with The White Eagle, the answer was to knock it down. As part of the rebuild, Alex and James wanted to establish a chefs' academy for young Anglesey residents with multiple barriers to employment.

Alex picked an architect with an ambitious plan. James and I were worried the final bill would be way over budget. So, much against Alex's wishes, we opted for a Huf Haus construction that still, ultimately, cost over £3m. The pub was renamed 'The Oyster Catcher'.

We recruited the first cadets for our Chef's Academy following a two-day outward-bound exercise that revealed the candidates' true character. The academy was a two-year course – the first mainly based at Coleg Menai, the second in the Oyster Catcher kitchen, overseen by head chef, Roger Gorman. Every two months, the cadets went on an adventure, including a cooking challenge in London, climbing Snowdon and an activity day at our home, Sandymere.

Gradually, the number of cadets dwindled, but each year, at least 6 out of the original 14 finished the course and were joined by their families at our graduation ceremony before getting jobs in the hospitality industry.

Alex's adventure was a great success but we were devoting as much time to 2 pubs as we spent on 1,000 shops. When Alex was diagnosed with cancer, we had to find an easier way. We kept the freeholds but linked up with 16 Hospitality, which ran our two pubs alongside The Swan in Tarporley and The Partridge at Stretton near Warrington. Cutting keys is considerably easier than catering.

CHAPTER SEVENTY-TWO

PROBLEMS OF PROFESSIONAL MANAGEMENT

WE TRADED PRETTY WELL around the millennium because our main competitor, Mister Minit, was doing badly. Ian Siddall, the expert at buying family businesses, failed to deliver his boast.

He used the UK part of Minit to develop a concept that could be spread throughout Minit worldwide. He wanted to create a multiservice, one-stop shop. With this in mind, UBS Capital completed the two acquisitions I dabbled in – Sketchley and In-Time. They matched the Matheson's asking price for In-Time at just under £4m, but it would prove difficult to integrate into their future vision.

Sketchley, which included Jeeves, the London-based dry cleaners, and SupaSnaps, cost UBS Capital £1.23m and came with a lot of baggage. The 120 Sainsbury concessions were poorly sited and lost money. SupaSnaps faced strong competition from Max Spielmann, Klick, Kodak, Boots, Asda and Tesco and Sketchley itself suffered from years of under-investment. The 600 branches trading in 1985 had ended as

300 dreary shops and 150 empty properties on which rent was still being paid.

Despite all these difficulties, Gavin Chittick, Minit UK's Finance Director, promised to transform Sketchley into a services supermarket by training staff to offer shoe and watch repairs, key-cutting, photo and dry cleaning under one roof. In addition to paying £1.23m for Sketchley, UBS Capital guaranteed the rent (including the closed shops) until the end of every lease – a potential liability of £50m.

Minit saw this as a quick way to build a multi-service business. He was in a hurry and pushed through some major changes inspired by professional management.

Minit UK traded under three retail brands; Mister Minit (the heel bars), Gulliver's (shops with a range of travel goods) and Saddlers (concentrating on quality shoe repairs). The new team of professional managers, following market research and advice from consultants, came up with a fourth fascia which defined their shop of the future – 'Minit Solutions'.

The overall idea was good, but a combination of management arrogance and market ignorance set Siddall on the road to disaster. The team was in a hurry, pushed through major changes inspired by professional management and made some fundamental mistakes.

1. The design consultants wouldn't allow dirty shoe repairing to be done next to finished dry cleaning. The shoe repairers were banished to a back room, often out of sight. I had seen the benefit in the late 1960s of putting shoe repairs front of house and getting cobblers to talk to customers. The Minit Solutions layout was certain to damage their shoe repair sales.

2. They believed shops should be managed by people with good 'A' Levels and, if possible, a degree. Existing colleagues, with a lifetime's experience, were demoted, handing over control to clever but inexperienced managers who couldn't cut the simplest key.

3. The area managers had worked their way up from the shop floor but UBS thought they had been promoted far too far – amateur managers in a world that needed professionals. They were replaced with area managers from elsewhere – Lunn Poly, Granada Rentals, Somerfield and Dorothy Perkins. Streetwise cobblers who spotted trouble by instinct made way for naive professionals trained by a business school to follow best practice

'Minit Solutions' never worked. Their conversion of a busy shop in Stratford upon Avon from Gulliver's to Minit Solutions produced a 50% sales increase in our shop round the corner. A quick look revealed all you needed to know. Four young bright but bewildered new recruits tried to handle key-cutting, engraving, watch repairs, photo processing and dry cleaning while the two experienced staff members were banished to the back of the shop to repair shoes.

In Minit Solutions inside Sainsbury Basingstoke, I asked a girl to cut a couple of keys. "Sorry," she said "I can't do keys. But come back next week and I will be fine – I'm doing the key-cutting course next Tuesday."

Minit management never saw what I was seeing. They still believed in their business plan and the power of professional management. No one dared suggest they were wrong; new recruits admired 'The Emperor's New Clothes' while old stagers kept quiet, knowing no one would listen.

Annual losses approached £40m before the axe fell and Ian Siddall was replaced by 'company doctor' Howard Dyer, hired to stem the losses and draw a line under an embarrassing experience.

At the beginning of 2001, James and I visited the Minit HQ at Sheffield on a fishing expedition. We met Martin Healey, the professional manager who succeeded Kenn Begley as Operations Director. Martin, an Irish professional manager, started by telling us he had played hockey 'to a very high level' then continued with an upbeat account of Minit's prospects. He believed they were on track to become a global brand.

But we knew how bad business was at Mister Minit. Every week, their branch managers called a special number to get the results. Through a mole, James obtained the telephone numbers and every Monday, he listened to their latest sales – they weren't good.

I started talking to Howard Dyer at the end of 2001. He suggested that I should speak to Ernie Gilbert who had succeeded Martin Healey. Ernie, a more realistic manager, was quite frank. He admitted the wheels had fallen off Minit Solutions and hinted that they might sell some shops in the North of England. When the list actually arrived, I visited most of them before going with Alex to Antigua. I knew those shops wouldn't make us much money but could lead to a bid for the whole business. While I was away, Minit changed their minds and the deal disappeared.

By the middle of 2002, my cryptic conversations with Howard Dyer were getting more serious. It was like a bullfight, a lot of teasing and innuendo, but I wasn't sure who was the bull and who was the matador. Once, I invited Jonathan Bowie of Bowie Castlebank to join us. He had recently bought Max Spielmann, a 250-photo-shop business based on the Wirral, so I thought he might take SupaSnaps so we could concentrate on Mister Minit. With a similar thought in mind, I spoke to David Bryant at Johnsons, but he wasn't interested in Sketchley. He was handing over to his successor, Stuart Graham, so his mind was fixed on retirement. I subsequently discovered Stuart Graham paid UBS a very full price of £4.5m to buy Jeeves of Belgravia, probably twice what it was worth.

The first hint of a deal came when we signed a confidentiality agreement, but the information we got from Howard was almost useless – total sales without any breakdown and estimated EBITDAR (Earnings before interest, tax depreciation, amortisation and rent costs.)

It was rumoured Minit UK was losing £20m a year, but that rumour was well wide of the mark. One year, Minit losses reached £40m and in 5 years, Minit Solutions lost £120m! No wonder Howard Dyer was economical with the truth.

For weeks, Howard tried to get an indicative offer and we attempted to get some detailed information. Then, suddenly, an e-mail revealed all the detail we needed to know for every branch. Someone had made a mistake; within an hour, we received another e-mail; 'The message was sent in error, please destroy the information and confirm you have done so'. It was their mistake, not ours, so we didn't reply.

We were dealing with a complicated business. The misdirected e-mail listed 127 Sainsbury concessions, 114 stand-alone SupaSnaps shops, 122 Sketchley branches (some with SupaSnaps concessions) and 426 Minit outlets (the business we really wanted to buy). The total of 789 didn't include In-Time or Jeeves of Belgravia, which were not part of the package, and 224 closed shops where rent was still being paid. In addition, the portfolio carried a huge liability for dilapidations. Anyone with any sense would have run away but instinct told us to keep going.

Howard Dyer never got flustered. Perhaps, like a swan, he anxiously paddled fast underwater, but he never seemed bothered – nor was John Edwards, his meticulous number-cruncher, who became 'my new best friend' but was, firmly, on Howard's side. Howard and John Edwards made a formidable team.

It was easy to fix the price; we were going to pay £1. Our negotiations concentrated on how to make £1 a reasonable deal. Howard threw in a few freeholds and included Minit Ireland, but there wasn't much else he could give us for our £1. They had to reduce our liabilities – particularly redundancies, and pensions.

To save money, Mike Williams proposed that we shouldn't take on Tricia Davis, manager of the Minit property department at Gilmorton. James and I met Tricia and thought Mike was wrong. Subsequently, we transferred all our property to Gilmorton and Mike took early retirement leaving Tricia and her team overseeing all our property work.

Minit paid the potential HQ redundancy costs but the pension deficit was a sticking point until we discovered hardly any of the colleagues moving to Timpson were in the pension fund. Their proportion of the deficit was a very small number – problem solved.

We agreed heads of terms and handed over to the lawyers, who started their battle based on warranties and indemnities. With a rundown chain of shops, full of fifty-year-old machines using dangerous chemicals, we expected generous cover against the potential risks.

We were represented by Roger whose growing law firm had changed its name to DLA. Minit used Slaughter and May. Their London office had a sense of humour failure on the day the two sides met. As it was April 1st, the security guard floated a rubber duck on their ostentatious ornamental pool in the foyer. I thought it funny but HR didn't; the security guard was dismissed for gross misconduct.

The lawyers justified their fees by finding plenty of issues to argue about, while James, Martin and I spent days in a soulless meeting room waiting for things to happen. Most evenings, James and I dined at The Bluebird, on the King's Road boosting our confidence with Barolo.

After days playing tit for tat with warranties and indemnities, we paused for breath before concentrating on one outstanding issue – a guarantee, demanded by UBS Capital, assuring that we didn't plan to put Minit into receivership and would pay the rent as due. Our accountants were adamant that I couldn't sign.

It was the deal's big moment. UBS made their assurance when they bought Sketchley. If I refused to sign the guarantee, there was a strong chance UBS would pull out of the deal.

I gathered our team in a small office and told them how I felt. "I've been trying to buy Minit for over 9 years. It is the ultimate piece of our jigsaw. And," I continued, starting to raise my voice, "I'm not going to throw away the opportunity of a lifetime because prudent advice prevents me from signing a piece of paper. We don't know what we will find until we open the books, but, right now, I have no plans to sink this business – if any of you aren't happy, you can resign from the team." My words were directed at Mike and Martin.

Nothing else was said and no one resigned. I signed a letter that satisfied both UBS and myself and we move on rapidly towards completion, helped by clearance from the regulator who discussed the monopoly implications at a 'fireside chat' which included mention of the industry statistics that I obtained from 'Imaginary Research Ltd' in 1985.

We agreed a communication plan at a strange meeting opened by someone senior from UBS who we never seen before and never saw again. She started by saying "Welcome to London!" as if we were amateur country bumpkins who had exchanged cobblers' aprons for a suit to make our first-ever trip to the capital.

Howard agreed to announce the deal to the Minit management at Maidenhead where Patrick Farmer and James would be present, ready to take control, together with Martin Tragen. Gouy Hamilton-Fisher met the team in Sheffield, Timpson field managers visited every branch and I was allocated the Property Department at Gilmorton (where my cousin, Stephen Timpson, was a surveyor).

Lawyers love last-minute drama and deals done in the middle of the night. They kept our communication network waiting for 36 hours before we were good to go. I was parked by a field near Gilmorton when the deal was confirmed. Five minutes later, I met the Minit property team and realised our business was a whole lot bigger.

Development of Anglesey

The holiday home – Wits End

The White Eagle   Maelog Lake Hotel

The Oyster Catcher

Perry Watkins
(Timpson General
Manager)

Sue Burden
(Max Spielmann
General Manager)

David Edwards
(Founder, Max Spielmann)

Ann Simpson
(Snappy Snaps General
Manager)

Ivan Sestan
(Photo Technical Director)

Andy Pringle
(Financial Superstar)

Gouy Hamilton-Fisher
(Colleague Support
Director)

Brent Sabey
(MOJO General Manager)

Martin Byrne
(Head of Logistics)

Johnsons the Cleaners acquired in 2017

Jeeves specialist part of Johnsons

Thorn Cross prison where our prison recruitment program started

ISnaps—the kiosk that made it easy to print pictures from a phone

Our photo booth that replace Photo-Me in many supermarkets

Max Spielmann inside Asda and Tesco

Brooklands, Tesco

Bridge of Dee, Asda

Some acquisitions

Broughall – 1980

Shoetech – 1987

*British Shoe Corporation
Repair Division – 1989*

Automagic – 1995

Mister Minit – 2003

Sketchley – part of Mister Minit

*SupaSnaps—part
of Mister Minit*

Max Spielmann – 2008

Snappy Snaps – 2012

Timpson in supermarkets

Morrisons Dry Cleaning concessions acquired in 2015

Timpson in Sainsbury—first concessions bought as part of Mister Minit in 2003

The Persil concessions were purchased in 2008

This pod in Wythenshawe opened in 2013 and was our 1000th shop

Development of watch repairs

*Original display in
first four watch repair
shops in 1997*

Typical display 2019

*The first big watch
repair display in
Eastbourne, 2001,
immediately created
sales of £1000 a week*

The local primary school that introduced upside down management

The book that talks about attachment awareness in schools

Important features of upside down management

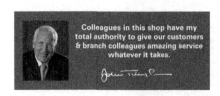

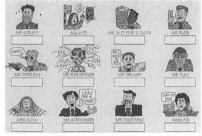

Sir John Timpson CBE
(Chairman)

James Timpson OBE
(Chief Executive)

Sarah Dunning
(Non-Executive Director)

Paresh Majithia
(Finance Director)

Stephen Robertson
(Non-Executive Director)

*Alex at the end of the kitchen table from
where she ran the world*

Oliver, James, Victoria, Edward and Henry in 1989

CHAPTER SEVENTY-THREE

MINIT SOLUTIONS

WHAT SURPRISED ME MOST were the postage stamps. Minit was dominated by cost-cutters based in Head Office. Branch managers couldn't buy postage stamps – they had to mail Head Office who sent the stamps in the post. Shop staff had to clean their own windows, but most didn't bother, not so bad for shoe repair shops, but you don't want dry cleaning shops with dirty windows.

UBS put the shops into three categories – current, closed and 'run off'. 'Run off' shops (a third of the total) only traded until the end of the lease, so a big slice of the business got no love and no investment. The Sketchley in London Road, Brighton hadn't been decorated for 25 years. The manager was so ashamed that she, along with her husband, painted the shop over a weekend. We had bought a broken business; it was difficult to know where to start.

This was James' first challenge as Managing Director and he hit the ground running by putting a new team in place. Existing Sketchley/ Supasnaps regional managers, Ann Howell and Graham Faint reported to our most experienced field manager, Perry Watkins. Mister Minit branches became part of an enlarged Timpson area structure headed by Bill Taylor who had been a Regional Manager alongside Perry. The offices and warehouses at Sheffield and Maidenhead were closed, with very few people moving to Wythenshawe. Fortunately, we had opened a new warehouse at Wythenshawe, which was able to cope with the bigger business, but we had to add 50 colleagues at Timpson House, particularly in finance, personnel and the warehouse.

It didn't take long to work out what to do with Mister Minit. We only had one major decision. Minit had a big merchandise business, selling lots of leather goods, which, in some shops, brought in half the turnover. But the merchandise margin was much lower than services. Our inclination was to abandon the luggage, but we needed to be sure we would make more money.

Livingston near Edinburgh provided us with the perfect test. The shop sold more merchandise than anywhere else, taking £4,000 a week on luggage, but we boldly replaced the stock with an enormous key board and a big watch counter. It worked; sales stayed about the same and we swapped low margin luggage for lucrative services – the profit shot up, and today, it is one of our most profitable shops. That told us all we needed to know, but we also needed some answers for Sketchley and SupaSnaps.

Sketchley and Supasnaps were a continual drain on the cash flow. It wasn't just the portfolio of closed shops (which would become less of a problem as leases came to an end), but the hefty contracts with suppliers, particularly SupaSnaps' 10-year contract with Agfa, which was going to cost £14m for kit that processed analogue spools of film (when the market was going digital).

Our problem was partly solved by Brian Green, restructuring partner at KPMG, who had developed the concept of a Company Voluntary Arrangement (CVA) to get landlords and creditors to accept part payment to allow a company to continue in business. Brian looked at Minit and produced a plan that, at a cost of about £2.5m, would release potential liabilities of at least £24m.

Brian was way ahead of the game. In 2003, few, if any, people had heard of a CVA and even fewer knew how it worked. Today, CVAs make a regular appearance, but often, Brian Green is still the expert who makes them work. The Minit CVA was agreed at a meeting of fewer than 10 people at a hotel near Heathrow. That deal improved our cash flow, but we still had to turn trading at Sketchley and SupaSnaps from loss to profit.

Towards the end of 2003, there was a significant change to our Board. Once the Timpson property function had moved to Gilmorton, Mike Williams retired. At the same time, Martin Tragen decided to move on. In December, Paresh Majithia became our new Finance Director and formed an immediate bond with James, Alex and myself.

The Mister Minit refit programme was an unqualified success, but all attempts at improving SupaSnaps and Sketchley failed to hit the spot. At least we could do something about the 115 Sainsbury concessions. It was a mixed bag – some units, including Aberdeen, Gloucester, Leamington Spa and Hedge End did really well, but others lost money, particularly those near checkout 35 (near the Tu clothing which doesn't attract as many customers as baked beans). Sainsbury gave us notice to leave some of the better locations, and, when we offered to build a unit in the car park, they refused.

We could close the loss-making Sainsbury concessions at a price – at about £20,000 a time, it was well worth it. Luckily, when we were evicted from Leicester, we received £100,000 compensation. Sainsbury handed the unit over to Persil Services, who were developing dry cleaning and photo shops using the Persil and Fuji brands. Their Chief Executive, Darcy Wilson-Rymer was keen to expand so we sold him 30 units. We closed 65 but kept the best 16 which all made money.

Every weekday, I receive a report showing our bank balance compared with the same day last year and the previous day's forecast. The report takes the temperature of our business and helps me sleep soundly almost every night. But I got a nasty surprise in January 2004, just before my plane took off from Gatwick towards the Caribbean. I expected the overdraft to be £3m, but instead, it was £4.8m. In his first month, Paresh found a few problems – Sketchley and SupaSnaps were leaking cash at over £40,000 a week. Sitting in the sun on Mustique, I prayed that we could find a buyer.

I thought our prayers were answered when Jessops, a 200 photographic shop chain, approached us with an interest in buying SupaSnaps. Jessops, the UK's leading camera retailer, was growing rapidly. ABN Amro bought Jessops from Bridgepoint for £116m and hoped to float within 2 years; acquiring SupaSnaps could strengthen their growth story. After two positive conversations at Jessop's Leicester office and Uttoxeter Racecourse, they offered £7m. Then, we heard nothing; we never even agreed heads of terms.

With Jessops out of the running, we renewed talks with Jonathan Bowie of Bowie Castlebank, where profits rose to over £10m after buying Max Spielmann for £25m in 2001. We thought Jonathan would be tempted to add more shops and another brand to his chain.

Then, another deal appeared possible; this time we were talking about Sketchley. The only possible buyer was Johnsons the Cleaners but their Operations Director, David Bryant wasn't interested. Then we had a big stroke of luck. Stuart Graham, who became Johnson's chief executive in 2001, wanted to do lots of deals. He failed to persuade Morrisons to sell their dry-cleaning business so the offer of Sketchley came at the perfect time.

Stuart Graham introduced us to David Walker, his bean-counter. They used a dashboard with traffic lights – red, amber and green – they would buy Sketchley if the forecasts were green. David Walker got lots of sales figures and a breakdown of costs but we left him to work out the margin for himself, so he never had enough information to paint the deal red.

Their opening offer of £7m remained through six weeks of discussion. David Walker worked a 14-hour day, contacting Paresh and James as late as 3 am with questions to control the traffic lights. However, neither Stuart Graham nor David Walker visited many Sketchley shops to see what they were like.

It was a rare deal – one side desperate to sell, the other desperate to buy, with both trying hard not to appear bothered about the outcome.

Twelve hours before finalising the deal on Sketchley, we sold Supasnaps to Johnathan Bowie for £100,000 – to seal the deal, we promised to take back any shop they didn't want after twelve months, a small concession because most leases only had two years to go.

By midnight, Stuart Graham, using plenty of bluff and bravado, brought his original £7m offer down, in stages, to £1, which, after a diplomatic pause, we accepted (my rock bottom figure was minus £6m).

In less than 24 hours, we had solved our two big problems, but there was more to do before life returned to normal. James had the unenviable task of telling Sketchley and SupaSnaps' colleagues we had sold their businesses. After 12 months of trying to prove we were a great employer, we put their futures at risk. It was particularly difficult to say goodbye to those extra colleagues recruited at Timpson House to run the bigger business.

We bought Minit UK for £1 but it cost at least £6m to end up with the Mister Minit shops we wanted and 16 Sainsbury concessions that made a decent profit. Today, those shops bring in a sizable profit every year.

CHAPTER SEVENTY-FOUR

NEW MANAGING
DIRECTOR

LOTS OF FATHER/SON BUSINESS partnerships don't work, often because Dad won't take a back seat or the son lacks the necessary talent. I have yet to see the same problem when a daughter takes over. Perhaps families are more demanding before sisters or daughters are put in charge.

James and I are lucky; we have always worked well together. In his early twenties, I knew James would do a much better job than me. My strengths are probably strategy and communication, but in addition, James has a real talent for getting things done. Putting James in charge was a brilliant move; his energy turned my vision into reality, with James adding significant twists along the way.

Patrick Farmer played a vital part in planning James's career. Patrick helped to overcome the doubts of those executives, who thought James, at 31, was too young to become Managing Director (I had taken on the role at 32).

James was keen to make his own mark. It wasn't going to be 'John and James', it would be 'James and John'. I was concerned when James visited the USA to see examples of excellence including Southwest Airlines and

Ritz Carlton. I thought James would come back full of ideas that would make me 'yesterday's man'. But I needn't have worried; James returned to say, "Nearly everything they do, we do already, but they are better at talking about them – we must strengthen our company culture and the way it is communicated".

We organised two-day leadership courses to explain how we wanted senior and middle management to run the business. To emphasise our message, we delivered the course ourselves. We also brought all our new recruits to Wythenshawe for a 24-hour introduction to the Timpson culture, a practice that has been so successful we have now welcomed over 100 groups of new starters to Wythenshawe.

'Upside-down Management' gave Timpson a distinctive culture, recognised by third place in the first Sunday Times list of Best Companies. However, James wanted to go further. He was impressed by Julian Richer's book, 'The Richer Way', which is full of bold ideas putting customers and colleagues at the centre of his business.

James was keen to copy Julian Richer's Rolls Royce – a car driven by their colleague of the week. We had a lively discussion at James's first Board Meeting, but fellow directors vetoed the idea. They were concerned the car could spend the week on a council estate in Droylesden – this was exactly the sort of place where James hoped it would be parked.

When James became Managing Director, he started to put Julian Richer's ideas into practice. Our first holiday home, where colleagues stay for free, was bought from Richer Sounds – we now have 20 holiday homes. James also copied Julian by inviting young managers to have dinner at his house and go for a hike the following morning, finishing at a local pub. And, 20 years after being thwarted by the Board, James bought a car (a Cadillac not a Rolls Royce) for colleagues to take home for the weekend.

James has always been tougher than his father. He is pretty ruthless in ensuring that he had the best senior team he could find – he has no time for company politicians or colleagues who constantly find reasons why things can't be done.

In the early 1990s, our area managers had their conferences around my dining room table, and during the day, they shot clays, did paint-balling or tackled an assault course in my garden. Now, with over 50 area managers, we are running a much bigger company, but we still like it to feel like a small business.

Our conferences have become an adventure – often abroad, full of fun activities with few formal sessions – the biggest benefit comes from the camaraderie. Recent events have been in Lisbon, Iceland, Dachau, Dublin and Majorca.

Celebrating success normally means a big marquee, originally at my house but now, James and Roisin host most of the events. It's easy to find an excuse for a party – The Millennium, the Timpson Centenary and my 50th year in the business. These weren't stuffy, formal dinners, they included our version of Stars in Your Eyes, Timpson's Got Talent and a Legends' Lunch. Our most ambitious celebration was in 2016, when we took 150 front line colleagues for an action-packed five days in Malta to celebrate our 150th Anniversary. Spending almost a week with 150 colleagues who all rated 10/10 was a clear demonstration of how our colleagues create our culture.

Until the lockdown in 2020, we both visited about 800 branches every year. For a short while, James had £50 notes in his pocket. If he spotted someone doing something special, he would hand over £50. It had a big impact which showed that that surprise awards really work but scared our Finance Department to bits. We spotted something more appropriate at Asda – in-house scratch cards that give an instant award including £10, £50, a meal out on James and the completely random 'the next sale is yours!'.

We do most things other companies do, like long service awards and a gift for special birthdays. We also give everyone an extra paid holiday on their birthday and a week off if they get married plus £100 for the flow-ers and the option of using our car as a wedding car, driven by Martin, our driver. If a valued colleague gets into debt, they can borrow from our hardship fund and every month, we make a colleague's dream come true. We spend over £500k a year paying for the dreams of a lifetime – often a flight to meet relatives on the other side of the world – trips to Vegas – IVF Treatments and a car that can carry a disabled relative. Every colleagues' name badge states 'Part of the Family Since . . .' stating the year they joined us. We want them all to have that family feeling.

Our most important job is to develop the culture. We use graphics in our shops to explain how we run the business. We are transforming our training centre into the Timpson University where colleagues can take a degree in Upside-down Management and become Bachelors of Service. These words appear on a wall in Timpson House.

'We prefer initiative to process and shop visits to meetings. We like working hard and having fun; we don't like secrets and don't do politics. We like lots of ideas and very low overheads. We keep it simple and do it straight away.'

CHAPTER SEVENTY-FIVE

RECRUITING FROM PRISON

JAMES GAINED A LOT from his membership of the Young Presidents' Organisation (YPO). The chance to talk in confidence with intelligent, experienced and personable entrepreneurs has been invaluable. This YPO connection helped James develop some of his most outstanding initiatives.

In 2001, the YPO held a meeting inside Thorn Cross, a prison near Warrington. Matt, the inmate who showed James around, impressed him so much that he gave him his card, saying, "When you get out, get in touch and I will give you a job." Matt still works for us as do 600 other colleagues we recruited straight from prison.

We learnt that over 60% of prison leavers re-offend within 2 years – the figure drops below 20% for ex-offenders with a job. We also discovered there were 85,000 people in prison but no business was actively recruiting ex-offenders.

In the early days, James did all the interviewing. He regularly visited prisons, talking to inmates on the wings, in the gym and in the workshops. He was looking for people with personality, who showed the spark of future ambition. The more prisoners he met, the more he was inspired to make prisons a significant source of recruitment.

James was on a mission. Dennis Phillips, from our colleague support team, was given the task of finding more people like Matt. Dennis was an ideal choice; a burly amateur football referee who was also a prison visitor. James joined Dennis on many prison visits, interviewing inmates approaching their release. They discovered plenty of the prison population are too naughty to fit into the world of work. Many have mental health and drug issues that we aren't equipped to deal with. However, lots of people in prison have the potential to be great colleagues.

At Liverpool prison, James met the Governor, Alan Brown, who showed James the workshops. They were dreary rooms full of workers in prison uniform, without a smile to be seen. James offered to set up a Timpson workshop as long as he could bring the Timpson culture into prison. Alan Brown agreed and the Timpson workshop opened a year later.

It was run by Wayne Pheasant, previously a manager at Knutsford and Northwich, with support from Timpson trainers and prison officers. The prisoners changed out of prison clothes into the Timpson uniform, the walls were filled with our culture graphics and curtains made sure you couldn't see the prison. The inmates followed our training scheme and were expected to pass the skill tests, but we weren't permitted to teach them to cut keys.

Further workshops were set up in Wandsworth, Blantyre House in Kent (opened by Justice Secretary, Ken Clarke), Forest Bank, a privately run prison near Salford, and two women's prisons – New Hall close to Wakefield and Downview in Surrey.

I was worried about the reaction from colleagues and customers. We kept quiet about the scheme, only telling colleagues who worked alongside ex-offenders. But that changed when the Sun newspaper told the world under a bold headline 'CONS TAUGHT TO CUT KEYS'. A few months later, the Belfast Telegraph ran the even more dramatic headline

– KILLER COBBLER CUTS KEYS. We announced what we were doing in the Timpson weekly newsletter – our headline was 'THE SUN WON'T STOP US'.

I couldn't have been more wrong. Our colleagues made the scheme a massive success by giving their wholehearted backing through skill training and personal support, and many customers now come to Timpson because of what we do for ex-offenders.

When the number of ex-offenders on our payroll reached 100, James and his wife Roisin (who became involved with prisons as a member of the Hardman Trust) held a special lunch at their home, for foundation colleagues and their guests. The unique significance of the Timpson Foundation was marked by speeches which were introduced on film by Prime Minister, David Cameron.

James broke new ground; no other business has attempted such a comprehensive prison recruitment programme, so we were bound to make a few mistakes. Eventually, we realised that in Wandsworth we had made the wrong choice and Liverpool became less suitable. We realised that we would do more good in open prisons like Blantyre House, where prisoners were approaching their release date. We also recognised the importance of recruiting for personality. The crime wasn't important (but we don't employ anyone guilty of arson and, because we provide a personal service, never recruit sex offenders) we simply look for positive characters who will fit into the Timpson culture.

Within a year of release, some prisoners can leave prison to work in one of our shops, returning to prison each night. Some become branch managers before leaving prison. Ex-offenders who start working on the outside while still serving their sentence are very likely to make Timpson their long-term career.

Ex-offenders often find it tough getting their lives back on track. For many, the sentence really starts when they leave prison and face a life full of problems – no home, a broken marriage, no bank account, banned from foreign travel accompanied with stress and depression. Against this background, I'm regularly inspired by the Foundation colleagues I meet. Other people ask how many let us down (less than 2% re-offend), but the better question is how many succeed. Someone joining from prison is likely to be more loyal and successful than colleagues recruited through the usual route.

Darren Burns is a great example. I first met Darren in 2012, at our Tesco concession in St Helens. He had joined us from Shrewsbury prison and was quickly achieving some record turnovers. James was so impressed that he selected Darren to work with and then succeed Dennis Phillips to run the Timpson Foundation, which he has been doing since 2013 – recruiting prison leavers and military veterans, helping with personal problems and advising other businesses how to follow in our footsteps. Darren has played a major part in making our recruitment of ex-offenders a great success.

Over 10% of our current colleagues joined us straight from prison, numbering over 400, with one or two joining us every week. James hopes to encourage other companies to copy what we do. Several, like Greggs and Halfords, have taken up the challenge, following James's leadership, which he now uses to improve the prison system as Chair of the Prison Reform Trust.

CHAPTER SEVENTY-SIX

MAX SPIELMANN

ON DECEMBER 3RD 2008, despite the banking crisis causing concern for much of the economy, we were enjoying a period of relative prosperity. Sketchley and Supasnaps were a distant memory, and, with all the Mister Minit shops converted, we produced record profits of £15m. I was enjoying a quiet break at Wits End with Alex when I got the e-mail – Bowie Castlebank had gone into administration.

Bowie Castlebank, based in Glasgow, had the UK's biggest chain of photo shops. Set up as Munro, a dry-cleaning business, they developed photo under the brand Klick before buying Foto-Processing, based in Leeds, and paying £25m to acquire Max Spielmann, with 160 shops and a processing centre near Birkenhead.

The business wasn't founded by Max Spielmann; the name was invented by entrepreneurs, David Edwards and Ian Graham who processed spools of film in a laboratory on the Wirral. Initially, sales were driven by press adverts and envelopes at airports, picked up by returning holiday-makers. When they opened retail outlets, they needed a name. Max Spielmann was chosen over a pint of beer to give the feeling of German expertise. Although Max didn't exist, many customers around Merseyside knew him well and claimed they were entitled to a discount.

In 1999, Ian Graham, visiting a trade exhibition, spotted a digital camera and immediately called David Edwards. "It's time to go," said Ian. "The party is over – let's sell the business." In 2001, Bowie Castlebank bought Max Spielmann for £25m and their profits rose to £11m. By 2005, customers were rapidly switching to digital cameras and their profit of £5.2m became a loss of £5.1m. A year later, losses reached £13.1m.

David Edwards parted company with Bowie Castlebank and Max Spielmann but stayed in touch with James, regularly swapping stories of the High Street in general and photo processing in particular.

In 2007, I met Jonathan Bowie's father at their Head Office on Byers Road in Glasgow. We talked about us buying some of their southern stores but negotiations fizzled out and I forgot about Bowie Castlebank until getting that e-mail at Wits End.

We didn't know much about photo and had had that bruising experience with Supasnaps but there was a chance that a few sites could be converted to the Timpson format. So, James and I looked at some branches, starting at Ellesmere Port. By the time we reached Kirkby, it was clear that the Timpson package wouldn't work. We needed to talk to someone who understood the business and contacted David Edwards, who ran Max Spielmann before it was sold to Bowie Castlebank. That afternoon, we got together with David who agreed to help and put us in contact with the management team. Two days later, we met General Manager, Jackie Dale-Jones and technical guru, Ivan Sestan, at a 'Little Chef' outside Chester and started to see a possible deal.

Before meeting David Edwards, we visited Chestergates, the office and warehouse near Ellesmere Port, run by Dave Whittle, who showed us around a soulless building that felt like a ghost town. Lots of colleagues had been made redundant and all deliveries were suspended, including special orders for specific customers.

The Administrator's team showed bewildering retail incompetence. Three weeks before Christmas, they cut every cost they could find. The maintenance team was laid off, so, if a machine broke down, customers were turned away. In most shops, staffing was cut to one person. In Commercial Street, Leeds, Michelle Dodd was on her own, running a two-floor shop taking £5,000 a week. Total company sales were 50% below last year.

When buying a business out of administration, you can pick and choose. We picked the 179 shops (out of a total of 374) that were each making over £20,000 a year. The buyer must honour contractual commitments to colleagues but agreements with suppliers, lease companies and landlords come to an end. The dire economic background of Christmas 2008 created the weakest property market for years; we expected some rent reductions and better deals on the equipment leased to Max Spielmann.

Other buyers were interested in bits of the business but the administrator wanted to do one big deal. We agreed to pay £1.3m. James went to Glasgow with Paresh and finance guru, Karina Pickering, who had supported every deal since our management buyout, and the deal was signed on December 19th, 17 days after the company went into administration.

The administrator had done a lot of damage. The shops were short of stock and disgruntled customers never received personalised orders in time for Christmas. Sales were 20% down throughout the spring, but that was more than matched by lower rents. In a weak market, we renegotiated almost every lease, dropping rents by an average of 20% and getting the first 6 months rent-free. For next to nothing, we also bought all the stock held in those shops that we didn't buy. Sales were poor but the margin was excellent. With no rent to pay, we got back the £1.3m purchase price in 9 weeks.

This was already a very good deal, but it was difficult to see a long-term future. David Edwards was a marketeer who created sales through TV advertising and piles of photo frames in every shop. We followed his techniques but the market had moved on. Much of the merchandise turnover came from cameras, which lost money. We had several break-ins every week, always targeting the cameras. With a pathetic markup, we needed to sell three more cameras to pay for each camera that got stolen. We stopped selling cameras.

Led by Sue Burden, the ebullient Sales Director, Max area managers started recruiting the Timpson way, picking personalities. Max was changing into a people business, when most competitors, particularly Boots, Asda and Tesco, were relying on more self-service. We rebranding those shops called Klick, added 12 Scottish shops that weren't in the initial 179 shop package and changed every fascia to 'Max Spielmann – The Photo Expert'.

With less reliance on merchandise (with no more cameras or media cards and fewer albums), we put our effort behind higher-margin services. The demand for passport photos (already 25% of total sales) was growing at an annual rate of 15%. Following a promotion spotted by Ivan Sestan in the USA, '10-Portrait package for $5', we launched a portrait service that got colleagues out from behind the counters to help customers. This hands-on service paid dividends when Ivan and his team invented iSnaps, a replacement for the dated KPMs (Kodak Picture Makers) and we were able to offer a while-you-wait service on canvas prints and personalized mugs. The iSnap kiosks use Bluetooth to download images and print pictures from a mobile phone.

After two years, Max shops looked totally different. All the big analogue processors had disappeared and been replaced by a bank of self-service iSnaps kiosks, but our colleagues were always there to help. While Max shops started to look more appealing, Sue Burden, the Operations Director, quickly understood the wisdom of upside-down management and raised the overall standards of our colleagues by finding lots of superstars and letting weak performers leave to find their happiness elsewhere. Her lively team of area managers, helped by Regional Managers, Lisa Kennedy and Rachel Myers, lifted morale and Max profits increased to £2.6m.

We were also approached by Snappy Snaps, a London-based franchise business, with over 120 photo shops. I had admired their business

KEEP IT IN THE FAMILY

ever since I saw their first store with its conveyor belt parading finished prints in the window, on the corner of Bond Street.

The business was founded by Don Kennedy and Tim MacAndrews in 1983 with the first franchises established in 1987. Snappy Snaps became the best-known photo brand in London and got nationwide publicity in 2010 when the singer, George Michael crashed his car into their Hampstead shop window and 'Wham' was written in graffiti on the shop window.

We were interested in Snappy Snaps, but didn't have enough cash in the bank and hadn't much appetite for franchising. Things were different in 2011 when Don Kennedy met James at The Goring to say they had agreed to sell the business, but the deal (it turned out to be with WHSmith) was proving difficult to complete. If we could exchange contracts within 6 days, we could have the business. We did just that, paying £4.5m.

We had a lot to learn about franchising and passport photos which made up over 33% of the total turnover. It took time to win the respect of the suspicious franchise partners, who lacked trust in their new franchisor. They thought we wanted to end their franchises and own each shop ourselves. Members of their lobby group (the Flic Committee) were especially critical and spread unrest throughout the franchise network. It took us three years to win their respect. Those who kept close ties to Don Kennedy were the hardest to please and some who never made us welcome eventually moved on. However, Ann Simpson, the Snappy Snaps Operations Director, supported by April Rowley, who is responsible for branch standards, along with four area managers helped both ourselves and most franchisees make more money and our photo business has become even bigger than key-cutting.

We introduced a much-needed store makeover into Snappy Snaps, in which the majority of franchise partners have invested. We quickly recognised that most of our partners ran an extremely good business, but it took some time to gain their trust. It is easy for conflicts to exist between a franchisee and franchisor, but Snappy Snaps colleagues became firm members of the Timpson family when our support helped them to make more money.

Snappy Snaps joined our Photo Board and shared experiences with Max Spielmann. We held regular Snappy Snaps conferences and several franchise partners joined other Timpson colleagues for our special celebration on Malta. Recently, some of our best franchise partners have expanded their business by acquiring more stores and at least 3 new shops have opened each year.

With both Max Spielmann and Snappy Snaps being part of the Timpson Group, we had the two best photo retailers in the UK. We were helped by the decline of our main competitors. Jessops concentrated on selling cameras and accessories, Boots starting shifting towards self-service, while both Tesco and Asda had failed to update their old-fashioned analogue processing departments.

The Max Spielmann acquisition included a large warehouse on a short lease – Chestergates, near Cheshire Oaks outside Chester. With photo expanding inside Timpson as well as Max and Snappy Snaps, we needed to provide a significant level of support through both warehousing and specialist photo gift production.

James boldly acquired two buildings near Port Sunlight on The Wirral – a leasehold warehouse that we called The Quad and a Freehold production unit that James named the ICE Building (ICE standing for Imaging Centre of Excellence). They have played a major part in the development of our photo business over the last few years.

Yet again, we were proving the benefits of being the leading player in a declining market.

CHAPTER SEVENTY-SEVEN

TESCO TRIAL

IN 2009, WE WERE ASKED TO pitch against Johnsons the Cleaners to be Tesco's preferred dry cleaning supplier. Tesco's research suggested that the dry cleaning offer was critical to their customers but our wider offer, particularly the comprehensive key-cutting service, brought most of the turnover in our 10 trial stores and won us the contract.

We were running out of new places to trade on the high street, so it was the perfect time to expand out of town. In 2008, we established a stronger presence in Sainsbury, when Persil Services (which included 30 branches we sold to them in 2003) went into administration and we bought 48 branches in a pre-pack deal.

Persil Services had been poorly managed, with too many colleagues and a lack of expertise. It took us two years to make a proper profit and we were thwarted by regular Sainsbury requests to close our unit due to a store refit. These refits became such a regular feature that James proposed a way to re-site our concessions in the car park. James and Toni Horsfield designed a special pod that accommodated our full range of services and fitted neatly into the equivalent of two parking spaces. However, despite incorporating some innovative eco-friendly features, the Sainsbury team weren't interested, so James suggested the pod idea to Tesco.

Our trial units in Tesco were very small with only two near the store entrance but they made money. A Tesco market survey gave us high marks and James got on well with Tesco's Board and Michael Fletcher, their head of revenue generation, who lived near Chester. They met on the touchline while watching their sons play rugby.

James showed Michael Fletcher the pod design that was rejected by Sainsbury, and he was keen to have a go. To avoid Tesco politics, the first pod was put in the car park Tesco share with Warrington Wolves. James put in a top manager, Neil Klemp, who took £1,800 in the first week, a figure that quickly grew to £3,000.

The second pod, outside a store near Romford, quickly ran into trouble. Kevin Grice, a Tesco director, ordered it to be removed. One of the best retailing ideas of the decade was in danger of being killed off within a month of being born. Thankfully, we won the battle and now have over 200 pods in Tesco car parks, and all the other main supermarkets, seeing the Tesco experience, also have our pods outside their stores.

Helped by the supermarkets, our business had found a way to grow rapidly. In 2013, the 1,000th shop was opened outside the Tesco in Wythenshawe, on the site of the old Timpson shoe warehouse, which I sold to George Olivers in 1987. Once supermarket executives had become accustomed to pods appearing in their car parks, they rapidly became a popular part of supermarket shopping. As long as we could get planning permission to put a pod near the entrance to a store which was taking over £700k a week, the footfall created enough customers for us to do good business.

Other retailers were building an online business to make up for sales lost on declining high streets, but our services are almost impossible to sell online. However, supermarket pods have provided us with our new source of business. Over half our shops are now out of town.

CHAPTER SEVENTY-EIGHT

PHOTO
CONCESSIONS

IT IS SURPRISING THAT IT took so long for service concessions to become a major part of the retail landscape. Most department stores, although filling every floor with concessions, failed to develop a shoe repair business because the only space we were offered was often on the top floor or in the basement. We have done well with Selfridges, Fenwick's and Bentall's but our units in the Coop, UDS Stores, House of Fraser and Debenhams all ended in disappointment.

Early success with Asda in the 1970s should have led to a big business, especially when we developed converted portacabins in the car park, but we didn't have a strong relationship with their senior management and our negotiations never got off the ground.

Our deal with British Shoe showed how concessions provide a profitable answer to businesses that struggle to manage an in-house service. At a stroke, British Shoe converted a loss-making activity that required investment and gave a lot of hassle, into a guaranteed income, while we dealt with all the problems.

In 2012, James spotted a similar opportunity with Tesco's photo business. A quick look at their photo counter was enough to tell us they had a problem. Outdated equipment, languid displays and disinterested colleagues were signs they that had lost their way. We had the answer – let Max Spielmann run your photo shops, save the headaches and get a guaranteed cash flow.

Fortunately, Tesco had some enlightened executives who visited some Max Spielmann outlets and saw the difference. We never paid anything for Tesco Photo. We covered any redundancy cost, which turned out to be modest, got a lot of stock for free and inherited some great sites. At a stroke, Tesco turned a problem into a permanent profit-producer for themselves, and we found a new way to grow our business.

Sue Burden and her team had plenty of work to do. The photo shops were run by part-timers, who were expected to help on the checkouts and sell lottery tickets. One branch, with sales of less than £1,000 a week, had 13 colleagues, all part-timers for whom the photo business was well down their list of priorities. Two years later, 80% of the original colleagues worked back in Tesco or found a new job elsewhere. Sue found lots of new colleagues, bubbling with personality. Max Spielmann made a massive difference – sales more than doubled and some shops now take five times the turnover.

In addition, we took on the £5m-a-year Tesco On-Line and self-service kiosks in 265 Tesco stores that didn't offer a full photo service. Twelve mobile technicians look after these self-service units, forming a new profit centre that James calls 'Jura' after his favourite malt whisky. Initially, we thought that the Tesco Photo website would give us a valuable introduction to a substantial online business, but our service provider ran into a data breach problem, the Tesco photo site was suspended, and instead of producing an online boost, we had to fight claims for £1m compensation.

Moving Max Spielmann into Tesco increased our turnover by £30m and gave Tesco an income stream of at least £4m a year. A great deal for both sides.

Following the success of Max in Tesco, James approached Asda with a very similar proposition. In the days of analogue spools of film, Asda found photo was a big money-spinner, but, when digital came along, Asda failed to keep up.

Asda photo staff stayed behind a counter with a massive £100k photo lab that processed fewer and fewer films, while most customers used the digital self-service kiosks.

James proposed a Tesco-type deal to the Asda team, who instantly fell in love with the idea, so much so, they started talking about us taking on their florist business and opening a trial barber's pod in the car park. James had over 20 meetings with the Asda team and talked about the Timpson culture at Asda's annual strategy conference. It was all going well until Asda's parent company, Walmart insisted on a formal procurement process. Paresh dealt with Raj Varma, who, following the orders of Asda accountants, provided limited digital information through a data room.

The lawyers didn't understand the logic of our offer.

In most acquisitions, we look for a solution that works well for both sides. Once this deal became a process, it became confrontational. We were starved of information, and, at one point, an Asda accountant claimed that the photo business was running at a profit (we reckoned they were losing at least £4m).

Through a mole, we knew there was a rival bidder – Photo-Me International, the passport booth business based in Surrey. Photo-Me hoped to protect the existing vending business, having seen a sales decline in their Tesco booths after we acquired Tesco photo. James pointed out that Photo-Me had no experience of personal service, but the Asda team had forgotten about our culture and were purely driven by numbers, like Johnson's traffic light system of decision-making.

At the beginning of November 2016, we received an ultimatum; 'you must bid within the next two days. To beat your rival, you need to offer over £4m.' We decided not to bid and withdrew from the process.

Photo-Me struggled to come to terms with the world of service retailing. Perhaps their plan was to replace the staff with self-service kiosks, but they certainly never recreated what we had done in Tesco. At one point, Serge Crasnianski, their CEO, came to Timpson House with a proposal, suggesting that we might run their Asda concessions, merge them with Tesco photo and share the profit – a great deal for him but nothing in it for us.

At least we got a bonus – Photo-Me ran the Asda units so badly that many more customers came to nearby Max units.

Despite our disappointment, James didn't ignore Asda. Instead, he continued to promote the idea of Timpson pods and kept in touch with senior Asda managers in Leeds. I joined him on a regular visit in June 2017 when we got a big surprise; Photo-Me were about to terminate their photo contract only 8 months after it was signed – could we help?!

By December 2017, most Asda photo concessions had ceased trading, so we moved in after Christmas. Even before the units were refitted, turnover jumped well beyond the Photo-Me figures. Sue Burden, who worked miracles, had a big advantage – Photo-Me made everyone redundant so Sue could recruit 10/10 personalities from day one.

With a satisfactory deal on rent, stock and machinery, the 110 Asda photo shops made money as soon as they reopened. It got better; suddenly, we were in Asda's good books and got the chance to open a number of successful Timpson pods.

CHAPTER SEVENTY-NINE

NETWORKING

JAMES WAS NETWORKING BEFORE he could talk. When wheeled out in a pram, he smiled and passers-by stopped to make faces and silly sounds. Once he could talk, James never found conversation difficult. It was a natural skill that helped him serve his first customers in Northwich, at the age of 14, and, 9 years later, persuade hardnosed manufacturers in Sunderland and North Shields to buy Johnson's textile rental service in the middle of a recession.

This determined charm helped James establish a good relationship with many of the decision-makers at Tesco, Sainsbury, Asda and Morrisons. His mission was to gain their trust and eliminate any obstacles in the way of building a big business, while realizing that we had to provide a great service.

James used the same patient technique to build bridges with our competitors in a search to expand our business. What appeared to the outside world, and our own colleagues, as deals out of the blue, were often due to many years of contact. James regularly popped in to see Ted Adler at Essex Shoe Repair over a period of 10 years before Ted agreed to sell. Chris Wilson at Charles Birch met James nearly as often, as did Brian McEwen from Uppermost with 16 shops in Scotland. Although the deal with Brian was finally agreed when I had dinner with Brian in St Andrews, James did all the groundwork.

The Minit acquisition and James's relentless networking helped us to grow from 350 to over 2,000 in less than 15 years – but this bold expansion programme wouldn't have worked without a comprehensive branch support network.

'Upside-down Management' abolished the term 'Head Office'. It is now called Timpson House and its role is to support customer-facing colleagues. Branch colleagues get the starring role but support teams play a vital part. We have a specialist workshop for each service. Watch experts are in Wolverhampton, Engraving in St Helens, Photo Imaging on the Wirral and Shoe Repairs inside Thorn Cross prison.

At Wythenshawe, each department is a helpline covering Key-Cutting, Finance, Buying, Warehouse, Payroll, Training Customer Support, Machinery and Branch Development. Our aim is to leave branch colleagues free to look after their customers.

Much depends on our area teams who recruit the branch colleagues and giving them day-to-day support. Mister Minit and Automagic had an area manager for every 30 shops, which they had to run on their own. We used to do exactly the same but now area managers have a team to help.

Field management can be a lonely job; you need someone to help you talk through the problems. Also, a field manager has to multitask. In a single day, one of our area managers is expected to be a trainer, to issue praise and corrects faults, to calm complaining customers, rearrange the rota to cope with sickness and be on call for 24 hours as a social worker.

We now know that to make it work, each area needs three area assistants (covering Training, Branch Standards and the Colleague Rota). To be effective, every area team member usually joins us as an apprentice. We never recruit area team members from outside the company.

Having a strong support structure through Timpson House, the Excellence Centres and our Area Teams have given us the chance to add 1,700 branches in 15 years.

CHAPTER EIGHTY

DRY CLEANING

WE GOT INTO THE DRY-CLEANING business by circumstance rather than intent when we bought the Automagic chain in 1995. Some of their London shops offered dry cleaning which was serviced by an independent dry cleaner who provided a 24-hour service. Despite only earning a modest margin, we enjoyed some extremely worthwhile turnover in the City shops, particularly Cannon Street, Fish Street Hill and Cheapside, but the business wasn't strong enough to encourage us to introduce dry cleaning into our original Timpson branches.

Eight years later, we suddenly acquired a more significant percentage of the dry-cleaning market when we bought Minit UK, which included Sketchley and over 100 multi-service concessions in Sainsbury. Sketchley was a neglected business that struggled to make any money and looked fated to get worse. Most of the Sainsbury concessions were poorly positioned inside the store although 16 made good money.

We were lucky to sell 30 of the Sainsbury concessions to Persil Services, a Venture Capital Company which planned to build a nationwide dry cleaning and photo business using the Persil and Fuji brands. We closed most of the others and just kept the 16 solid profit-makers. We were even luckier to sell Sketchley to Johnsons, although the price was bargained down to only £1. Johnsons' chief executive, Stuart Graham, who was keen to expand the business through acquisition, had just failed to acquire the Safeway dry cleaning business that had become part of Morrisons, so Sketchley was a bit of a consolation prize. We kept our Sainsbury concessions to maintain a meaningful presence in both supermarkets and dry cleaning.

Over the next few years, we were in close contact with Darcy Willson-Rymer, the chief executive of Persil Ventures, whose ambitious plans to grow the business included an unsuccessful attempt to buy Johnsons the cleaners (at a price approaching £100m).

Our 16 Sainsbury units continued to trade well and in 2008, when we heard that Persil Services were about to go into administration, we arranged to take on 40 of their units in a pre-pack deal that, after James patiently went through some painstaking discussions, had the blessing of Sainsbury. The deal was completed on the day my son Edward became an MP by winning a by-election in Crewe and Nantwich.

It took two years to get the Persil units converted to the Timpson brand and match our existing Sainsbury concessions. By then, the new concessions we were opening with Tesco had to include dry cleaning – it was part of the deal. All our dry cleaning, apart from the London shops, was being done in Sainsbury units, but we couldn't clean clothes at Sainsbury that customers had taken to Tesco. The Tesco concessions were too small to have dry cleaning done on the premises so we had to find independent dry cleaners who could offer a pick-up-and-deliver service.

As the Tesco business grew, we started opening our own dry-cleaning hubs on industrial estates. It worked well; we discovered that 3/4 colleagues in a hub with 2/3 delivery drivers could provide a 24 or 48-hour service to up to 35 shops from bright-looking premises with new machinery (a much better environment than most high street dry cleaners).

Although our dry-cleaning business was growing, we still only had a small share of the market. The Sainsbury concessions were averaging £1,500 a week but most Tesco concessions produced less than £300.

At least 70% of the trade was done by good independent dry cleaners, who, in contrast to independent cobblers, were still able to make good money. The only major players were Johnsons the Cleaners and Morrisons who inherited a strong in-house dry-cleaning business when they acquired Safeway.

Having achieved success with the acquisition of Tesco Photo, James talked to David Potts, CEO for Morrisons, about doing a similar deal on their dry-cleaning concessions. This was never going to be an easy win because Morrisons had built significant dry-cleaning sales by charging rock bottom prices. The margin was so low that it was difficult to see how they made money. When we looked more closely, the high wage bill meant that many branches made a loss.

We hoped to make money by introducing the usual Timpson services and bringing the staffing levels into line with the turnover, and, to some extent, that is what we did but not until we had won over the colleagues by buying every branch a kettle. Their biggest complaint was that Morrisons didn't allow them to have a cup of tea in their workroom – the kettles solved the problem.

The Morrison units became part of the Timpson area structure, which ensured that wherever shoe repairs, key-cutting and watch repairs were added, we achieved some significant extra turnover, but it took some time to get the original Safeway and Morrisons colleagues to get used to upside-down management.

In 2014, Chris Sander, who ran Apparelmaster, the workwear part of Johnsons, was appointed as Group chief executive, and, within a year, put Johnson the Cleaners, the retail division, up for sale. James had already started to have regular conversations with Chris Sander, and, in December 2016, they agreed a deal. In January 2017, Johnsons and Jeeves joined Timpson, making us the biggest dry cleaner in the UK. Johnsons joined our Morrison concessions in a separate retail division called MOJO, with a dedicated field team overseen by general manager, Brent Sabey, who had previously been a Timpson Regional Manager.

Jeeves, with its Royal Warrant, was kept as a distinct identity under the guidance of Will Lankston, who was also responsible for the specialist dry cleaning workshop in Tottenham and Jeeves International (a franchise business with about 25 branches around the world).

We quickly discovered that Chris Sander had been wise to sell the shops. Demand for dry cleaning was declining in a similar way to shoe repairs, but whereas Timpson was rescued by key-cutting, Johnsons never developed a second service of their own; even the repairs and alteration service was relatively unsuccessful.

Brent Sabey and his team worked hard to introduce upside-down management and welcome Morrison and Timpson colleagues into the Timpson family. The shops all got a refit, and, although we failed to stop the decline in sales, better cost control kept the businesses profitable until 2020, when Covid 19 caused so many people to work from home and stop socialising. The massive change in behaviour halved the demand for dry cleaning.

CHAPTER EIGHTY-ONE

KEEP IT SIMPLE

SINCE JAMES BECAME OUR Chief Executive in 2002/2003, the business has been through two decades of continual change. We aren't just cobblers (shoe repairing now only produces 6% of our sales); we have become a collection of many different businesses. Timpson has become a complicated business and outsiders may wonder how James is able to keep in touch with all the moving parts of such a diverse organisation.

Most weeks, James visits some shops in our four retail chains (Timpson, Max Spielmann, MOJO and Snappy Snaps) and their day-to-day support is provided by area teams who follow the principles of upside-down management, but there is more to shopkeeping than just serving customers.

We have a buying department, warehouses and a development team that organises maintenance and shopfitting. Our colleague support team, led by Gouy Hamilton-Fisher, helps with personnel problems, deals with payroll, takes a special interest in colleagues who join from prison and oversees training and health and safety. We have a customer support department that handles queries from clients. The finance team are involved in management accounts, auditions, acquisitions, paying bills and keeping the books.

Our property department, run by Tricia Davis, has been based in Leicestershire since we acquired Mr Minit in 2003. They keep track of all our leases and the modest number of freeholds, negotiating acquisitions, lease renewals and branch closures. James takes a close interest in all property deals and carries out an individual property review every six months. He will always have visited a site before deciding to open or close a shop. Over the last twenty years, we have built a tidy freehold portfolio, acquiring most of our office and warehouse buildings as well as buying the freehold interest of a few shops which were previously leased.

Our IT Department has made a major contribution over the last few years by focusing on the needs of front-line colleagues. While most other companies are driven by data and the needs of Head Office, our team has looked at life through the eyes of our customer-facing colleagues. Instead of using point of sale data to inform central decision-makers, our IT team gives the facts and figures to people working in a shop.

Armed with more information, while talking to a customer, our branch colleagues can take the initiative. Instead of analyzing data at Head Office and telling these troops what to do, we find that it is much better to give the data to our experts who talk to customers.

Despite selling services that are seldom bought on-line, we have our own websites which give information about our business (our culture, the range of services, shop locations and opening hours, etc.,) and also do about £6m business a year, mainly on photo products from our workshop or Click and Collect.

Occasionally, we are tempted to venture away from our comfort zone and invest in a new business that we don't fully understand. It happened when we bought our house sign supplier, The HouseNameplate Company, a specialist manufacturer based near Wrexham. We were in an unfamiliar world when we decided to develop an offsite locksmith service and we were way off-piste when we bought a lighting and sound events business called Out There Events. To a lesser extent, we ventured into unfamiliar territory when buying Johnsons the Cleaners, especially when it came to understanding dry cleaning machinery and the individual nature of the service Johnsons had agreed to supply to Waitrose.

Our boldest and most challenging venture was when Alex persuaded us to buy The White Eagle and get into the pub trade. Luckily, Alex's instinctive grasp of the ideal family pub and our grounding in customer service created a very successful formula, but after a time, we realised that it was taking us as much senior management time to run two pubs (The White Eagle and The Oyster Catcher) as it did to run over 1,000 shops. Whenever we need to learn new tricks, James has to get involved and devote a disproportionate amount of his time to a small part of the group that may make little or no profit.

James keeps in touch with the detail through upside-down leadership. He trusts every member of the management team to use their initiative and run their team the way they know best – as long as they give the same freedom to each member of their team. This upside-down management style is very different from most other businesses. The emphasis is on getting things done – less time is spent in meetings, we have no standing committees, there is no need to produce policies and processes, we don't have a formal appraisal system and, refreshingly, we seldom experience internal politics. In ticking all the professional managers' boxes, other companies fill a lot of time that should be used to get things done.

James's management style works because he is happy to delegate and has picked people who he can trust. Upside-down management only works with the right people – you need like-minded characters who 'get it' and thoroughly understand the culture.

Most of James's team have been promoted from within the company, but whenever we recruit outsiders (usually into Finance, IT and Colleague Support), they also must have the right personality and get the culture.

Although James has an Operating Board that meets at least 6 times a year, most management is done through constant one-to-one dialogue. The business is like a continual soap opera and James keeps up with the plot through regular conversations with members of the cast.

However, James doesn't delegate the pursuit of new shops and acquisitions. He visits every proposed new site at least once before giving approval. That includes supermarket concessions, where the shops in car parks are literally like peas in a pod, but success depends on the position of the pod – we need sufficient footfall near our entrance. You get a good idea from a drawing and google maps, but the best way to gauge the potential is to go there.

Our supermarket business also depends on our relationship with key members of the supermarket teams, especially the Chief Executive and the Concessions Director. James sees this as his job; our supermarket hosts expect a direct line to the boss.

The golden rule of a good acquisition is to make sure, as a buyer, that you know more about the business than the person who is selling it. Between 2016 and 2018, James spent a fair amount of time in China, the USA and Europe. He saw our attempts at developing a Master Timpson Franchise in China, explored the possibility of Timpson concessions in Walmart and made five visits to the Continent to evaluate the purchase of Mister Minit Europe. None of these deals got off the ground but only after James was able to gather the facts for himself.

James couldn't do his job without the talented team of executives who he trusts to run the business. He is undoubtedly the conductor of the orchestra but it is his colleagues who play our tune.

CHAPTER EIGHTY-TWO

A BIT OF PUBLIC RELATIONS

I SPENT THE FIRST THIRD of this book as a narrator. In 1960, after I joined the business, I started writing in the first person – Anthony Timpson became 'my father' and what is essentially a history book became a bit autobiographical. For the last few chapters, I have been a bit of both – talking about James and his team, while sitting in the background – but still with a small part to play.

Being no longer being involved in day-to-day management gives me the chance to reflect on how much the business has changed. At a time when most other organisations became overwhelmed by process, compliance and best practice, we went in the opposite direction. The Upside-down Management approach and our emphasis on trusting great people with the freedom to use their initiative has created a strong company culture.

Upside-down Management makes it much easier to run the business. There is no need to devise detailed plans so we can tell colleagues what to do; they simply need to know what we want them to achieve. Compared with many other organisations, we save a lot by not advertising or commissioning market research. We don't waste much time on budgets and we abandoned our last staff appraisal system 34 years ago.

Our Group Board Meetings concentrate on new ideas and our future strategy. We don't dissect the Management Accounts – that is done by James and his operational directors. Our prime concern is the cash flow. In the 1980s, it was considered almost immoral to have cash; responsible companies borrowed to the hilt so that they could invest more in the business. Today, we value the security that comes from having a pile of cash – happiness is no borrowings, no outside shareholders and cash in the bank.

This may all sound far too 'maverick' to be sensible, but by ignoring dashboards, research projects and annual budget bids, we can clear our minds and find the time to use our initiative to think about the future.

Every three years, I exercise my imagination by writing a Chairman's Statement that I forecast will appear in our Annual Report in 15 years' time. It makes you think about the future without being hampered by knowledge of today. Many 5-year plans are an extrapolation of the latest management accounts (making sure that sales go up faster than costs).

My long-term Chairman's forecast is always fun to do. I enjoy writing, and, over the last 20 years, it has become a favourite pastime. I first got the writing bug in 1997. I was complaining to my advisor, Michael McAvoy, that we didn't get enough credit for the innovative way we ran our business when he suggested that we should get someone to write a book about it. I decided that I would write the book myself.

That is how I came to write my first book, 'Dear James', which led to more books including this one, and got me a column in the monthly magazine 'Real Business'. After a few years, they asked me to write a business agony column, which was eventually transferred to the Daily Telegraph. My Telegraph column, which has been running for over 10 years, is probably the nearest we get to advertising; every week, readers come into our shops to talk about my latest piece in the paper.

The books and the column led to regular speaking requests, mainly business conferences, where I, and later James, talk about our culture, recruiting from prison, giving colleagues their birthdays off and looking after looked-after children. After I had been on the speaking circuit for about five years, Alex, on hearing that I was going away to do another, said, "Haven't they all heard it before?"

Alex had a point; some had heard it and I needed to change the script before I got tired of repeating myself. That is why I get more plea-sure out of the quirky speaking engagement – The Bishop of St Asaph's AGM, Jockey Club Dinner, Worshipful Company of Distillers' Banquet, Lent Talk in Liverpool and a dinner of the Parliamentary Governance Group at Westminster. Among the more interesting business groups I have spoken to are 'The National Association of Garage Doors' and 'The Worshipful Company of Environmental Cleaners'.

These talks did a bit to spread the Timpson story, but radio and tele-vision can do much more. It takes courage to turn up at a studio (most nerve-jangling so far – 'Question Time' and 'University Challenge'). We also did two documentaries. The first was embarrassingly titled 'Millionaires', in which a nice man, Phillip Tibbenham, interviewed Alex and me at home and in Las Vegas, to find out why we fostered so many children. The second was a fairly wooden half-hour during which Peter Jones from Dragon's Den failed to grasp the finer, and indeed, the widest point of Upside-Down Management.

When, in the middle of 2014, Alex was diagnosed with biliary cancer, I started spending much of my time at home. I couldn't visit so many shops or give many talks but I could write another book (this one was about horse racing – 'Under Orders – the diary of a racehorse owner's husband') and Alex could help with the Telegraph column; I often gave her credit.

When Alex died in January 2016, I wondered how I could tactfully give the sad news to my readers because she was so regularly mentioned in my column. The chance came with a question about Mr Selfridge:

Question – Would a TV series called Mr Timpson be as dramatic as the series Mr Selfridge?

I started; 'We certainly witnessed some political drama but if you are looking for a sub-plot with socialising and sexual indiscretion, you are bound to be disappointed.' I finished by saying 'A new chapter was written at the beginning of January when Alex, the Mrs Timpson behind Mr Timpson, died peacefully after a 19-month battle against her cancer. As many readers know, Alex often helped me find the right answer to your questions. She will still play that role because, whenever stuck for an answer, I will simply ask myself, "What would Alex have said?"

Less than a fortnight after Alex died, I was asked whether I would go on 'Desert Island Discs'. It was an easy question and I was right to say yes. Being able to talk about Alex made it by far and away the most pleasing programme I have ever done.

CHAPTER EIGHTY-THREE

THE PANDEMIC

JAMES DECIDED THAT 2020 was going to be a quiet year. At the beginning of January, we had a record figure of over £22m in the bank. With no acquisitions in prospect and only about 60 supermarket pods left to open, we were forecasting a bank balance of over £35m by the end of the year – a very comfortable position.

In a fairly tough retail environment, our sales were just ahead of last year. The only weak spot was the photo side of the business due to a dramatic drop in passport photos caused by Brexit and the imminent change from EU to British passports. In 2016, the sale of our pubs, The White Eagle and The Oystercatcher, to 16 Hospitality wasn't working out as well as we hoped, so, to protect our freehold properties and the 30% stake we had in the day-to-day business, we decided to take back control. This unexpected acquisition would require no more than £1m cash and was unlikely to make a big difference to our ambition to build a significant cash pile.

James planned to use the quiet year to improve shopkeeping standards and concentrate on our training. To communicate the message, he set out in September 2019 on a Road Show, giving 83 presentations in 50 venues over a period of 6 months. The final show was due to be in Southampton on March 19th, but it never took place.

In January, while on holiday on Mustique, I followed the news from China of an influenza-type epidemic in Wuhan, Eastern China, that was first reported to the World Health Organisation on December 31st 2019. At first, the dramatic lockdown of over 10 million people sounded like an overreaction to an outbreak of 'flu, but we were grateful that the problem was in China and not nearer to home.

During the next few weeks, we discovered that the infection had broken out of China. The first report of the virus coming to the UK was on January 29th when two Chinese visitors were diagnosed with the disease in York. On February 4th, it was reported that 700 people had been infected on the cruise ship Diamond Princess and 12 had died. Two days later, a British businessman was back in Brighton when he discovered he had Covid-19, which he had picked up in Singapore. The first report of someone being infected within the British Isles was on February 28th, when a man who had not been abroad was diagnosed in Surrey.

Over the next week, the British public took the threat of coronavirus more seriously and started a spate of panic-buying, with loo rolls and anti-bacterial hand gel on the top of their shopping list.

My wake-up call was on March 11th, when I did an early interview on the Radio 4 Today programme, talking about the budget later that day. While I was waiting in the Green Room, bank rate was lowered to ¼% and the game between Manchester City and Arsenal was cancelled because, two weeks earlier, the Arsenal players had met the owner of Olympiakos, who subsequently tested positive for coronavirus. Suddenly, things were getting serious; the budget promised help for small businesses, but on nothing like the scale that Rishi Sunak was to announce a fortnight later.

I saw the panic-buying for myself on Friday, March 13th, when I spent the day visiting our shops around Southampton. The supermarkets had queues at every checkout and merchandise missing from their shelves. Our shops were quiet; sales for the day were 10% down on last year. James spent the weekend in the office with Paresh working out what to do.

James posted each day's sales on the whiteboard in his office and saw the fall against last year increase every day. By Wednesday 18th March, we were running at minus 25%; that was the day that he sent a letter to every colleague.

'I write this letter at a very critical time in our history. We are faced with a health crisis that will impact on all of us for many months and I want to let you know what the company is doing to support you and your families. There are still many unknowns, but we are all part of one big strong Timpson family. We all continue to be treated as equals, within our culture of trust and kindness. If it turns out that we need to mothball the business, everyone will still be paid in the normal way until we are allowed to reopen. When all this is over, we will still be the same company, with a strong culture and a strong future'.

It was already pretty clear that most retail shops would have to close. Earlier that week, Selfridges had shut up shop and Carphone Warehouse announced the permanent closure of all their 531 stand-alone sites. Paresh's team spent the week talking to NatWest and modelling various cash-flow forecasts from hopeful through realistic to doomsday. It was a shock to discover that our bank balance, of over £22m at the beginning of January, could turn into a £40m overdraft by the middle of June. In a very busy week for our finance team, Finance Manager Andy Pringle was also organising our pub acquisition, which was due to complete before the weekend.

Like every retailer, we were anxious to hear what help we would get from the Treasury and were pleasantly surprised. We would be able to delay the payment of VAT and other taxes and were given a 12-month rates holiday plus a grant for small shops. The cash flow looked a bit better.

The big announcement came during one of the regular 5 pm Downing Street press conferences on March 20th when the Chancellor introduced his Job Retention scheme, allowing employees to be 'furloughed', with the Treasury paying 80% of basic salary up to £2,500 a month. Within minutes, we had done the maths and our cash flow looked quite a bit better.

At the same press conference, the Prime Minister announced that all restaurants, nightclubs, gyms, pubs and bars would close at 9 pm that night. We had bought 4 pubs at 4 pm and had to close them 5 hours later.

On Saturday morning, while being interviewed on the Radio 4 Today Programme, I was asked "The Government are going to pay 80% of wages to all workers who are laid off; are you making up the 20%?". I told the interviewer that we had never considered doing anything other than guaranteeing the full basic pay. I played 9 holes of golf that morning, and, on my return, discovered that my comment was being repeated on the BBC News. When a column written by James appeared in the Sunday Times, we were suddenly being mentioned as an example of kindness that other businesses should emulate. The key bits of James's article that attracted attention were:

'We've based most decisions on gut instinct and been humbled by the support we have received from everyone in the business. Not one colleague has failed to come up to the mark, and I've read many texts and emails about random acts of kindness. Where we trade in supermarkets, some of our colleagues have been helping on the checkouts, unloading trucks and stacking shelves. At a point in history like this, job descriptions go out of the window.

Every colleague is guaranteed that their full basic pay will be paid throughout the crisis . . . for however long it takes. I've been overwhelmed by messages from colleagues saying how much they appreciate our decision. It's expensive, but it's right to support our 5,500 colleagues; it's not their fault that's this has happened'.

James was spending most of his days on conference calls, working out what to do with Paresh, Gouy and other members of his management team, then communicating the latest strategy to field managers. When John Lewis closed all their stores on Saturday evening, it was clear that a ban on non-essential retailing was about to happen. On Sunday 22nd March, James decided that we should close all our shops the following day, just before Boris Johnson announced the lockdown. I was isolated for my 77th birthday with 2,120 shops shut and the only sales coming from a skeleton staff of locksmiths and our modest online business. Three weeks earlier, we had a revenue of £6.5m a week; now it was less than £100k.

On the last day of trading, sales were less than half last year, but our branch colleagues were busy, closing down machinery and making their branch safe and secure before shutting the door without any idea when they would return. Their life changed overnight from being busy at work to being almost as busy at home – gardening, decorating, contacting friends and family on the internet and supervising children with their home learning.

The business kept in touch with weekly phone calls from the area team, a regular video update from James and WhatsApp groups of colleagues who organised virtual pub nights, bake-offs and karaoke competitions. Nearly 5,000 colleagues were furloughed but the remainder had plenty to do in protecting the company's future.

Four weeks into lockdown, we got some tragic news. Joe Shepherd, an Area Development Manager based in Middlesbrough, had died after catching Covid19. Aged 57, Joe started with us as an apprentice when he was 16. He learnt quickly and had been promoted to become a branch manager, however, when the rent of his shop doubled and we decided not to renew the lease, Joe joined Automagic but returned to Timpson 8 years later and stayed for the next 27 years. Joe had a big influence on the development of his area. He was an excellent trainer who had the ability to turn raw recruits into superstars. He was highly respected by the many colleagues who experienced Joe's patience and generosity.

Paresh made early and positive progress with the bank, but it was a psychological shock to be talking about an arrangement fee, interest rates and covenants after a decade of having money in the bank. To give long-term comfort, we discussed an overdraft facility of £50m, which we believed was much more than we needed. We could certainly see our way through the next three months but there was no knowing when the lockdown would end and how long it would take for life to reach a new normal.

We were lucky to go into the crisis with nearly £18m in the bank, but other retailers were not nearly so fortunate. Debenhams, the Arcadia Group, Accessorize and Monsoon were among many retailers that had a dangerous combination of high borrowings, poor sales and a trading loss. It was becoming pretty clear that several well-known fascias were unlikely to survive until the end of 2020. When we are allowed to trade again, there will be a lot of empty shops on the high street. Our development in conjunction with supermarkets over the past 12 years was well-timed; when the crisis started, over 65% of our business was being done out of town.

With all our shops shut, the priority was to preserve cash and plan what needed to be done for the shops to reopen. In particular, we had to find the right protective equipment for colleagues, work out the best way to keep our shops sterilized and understand how to maintain the social distance of 2 metres. James Jackson, who joined us from Johnsons the Cleaners, headed the research into health and safety.

The government prevented landlords from taking legal action against their tenants for late payment so many other retailers delayed paying the March quarter rent. However, we paid on time (James was quite clear that we had a legal obligation). But we did ask all the supermarkets – who were still trading and enjoying a mini-boom – to suspend our minimum rental agreement until we were able to reopen.

During these negotiations, Morrisons insisted that, because dry cleaning was seen as an essential service, we should be open for business.

As a consequence, James contacted The Department for Business Energy and Industrial Strategy, who confirmed that we were able to trade inside supermarkets as long as we complied with the safety measures adopted by the supermarkets themselves. Given this green light, James started to reopen branches in the week beginning April 27th.

We opened 35 shops during the week, in Morrisons, Sainsbury and Asda – Tesco needed another week to approve our health and safety measures. The new way of operating went well – signage, a one-way system for customers, sanitizing gels, face masks and sneeze screens all got the approval of colleagues and customers. But average sales were over 75% down on last year – hardly surprising with so many potential customers staying at home.

At the end of that week, we submitted our first furlough claim asking for £7.3m. Despite the lack of any meaningful turnover, we still had money in the bank, helped by the rates holiday, grants and the ability to defer big payments of VAT and PAYE. But these bills would have to be paid over the next 9 months, and, with sales likely to be well down on last year, we would need a big cost-cutting drive to keep our cash under control.

The cost-cutting had to start at Timpson House – anyone who didn't have a direct influence on our day-to-day sales was at risk. We were forecasting a drop in sales until the autumn of between 15% and 20%, so a slimmed-down overhead was essential to help our cash flow. After 25 years of growing the business, it was tough to slam on the brakes and go in reverse – we kept reminding ourselves that it wasn't our fault and lots of other people had even bigger problems. Besides, from now on, we would be judged by how well we could handle this major crisis.

Gouy Hamilton-Fisher had the unenviable job of organising the redundancies and telling a number of long-serving and loyal colleagues that they were about to lose their job. They were nice people who proudly wore a badge which declared they were members of the Timpson family for up to 40 years, but, with a business full of great colleagues, when you need to cut costs some of the most loyal members of the team have to go. James, Paresh and Gouy had to make many tough decisions that threatened to undermine the caring company culture.

Against a background of job losses and sales up to 75% down on last year, James needed to keep a positive atmosphere. He lifted spirits by opening shops ahead of other retailers, and by the end of May, all the supermarket concessions were open. Dry cleaning sales were poor, dropping more than 70% on last year, the photo business was more than 50% down, with no business coming from passport pictures, but the core Timpson business was more encouraging – some days were less than 30% below last year.

James did well to establish our right to reopen ahead of other 'non-essential' retailers. Dry cleaning was already on the essential list (although demand for the service was pitifully poor). The Government agreed that we could open inside supermarkets, and, two weeks later, added the right to open our pods. However, despite getting Government approval, James had to negotiate with stubborn supermarket executives who wanted to dictate where and when we could open. When the Government conceded that we should be classified as ironmongers, we were able to open the Timpson shops on the high street, but Max Spielmann had to wait until June 15th when all non-essential retailers were allowed to start trading again.

On June 15th, when the high street was free to open, at least half of our neighbours were still closed. Barbers, nail bars, gyms, restaurants and pubs had to stay shut, but many other shops didn't open either. Charity shops were wary of being swamped by the results of a nationwide clear out of superfluous possessions that would all need sanitizing, and some businesses, including Carphone Warehouse, were closed for good. The streets lacked buzz, but our shops did better than we expected with overall sales about 30% below last year.

Shoppers were met with a masterclass in social distancing, with retailers turning their shops into an obstacle course marked out with arrows and two-metre distancing tape. There wasn't a hint of fun or joy;

masked shoppers obeyed the rules, kept their distance and shuffled along slow-moving queues without any hint of enthusiasm.

Despite this lacklustre return to town centres, we were doing well enough to forecast that September sales would be no worse than 15% down which would produce a reasonable profit, assuming we were able to cut costs.

James and Paresh decided to make massive cuts, especially in our payroll. In two months, we were to change from an organization geared for growth to one that was slim enough to weather the doomsday possibility of a second spike of the virus and further periods of lockdown. With others following our example, unemployment rates were certain to rocket by the autumn.

In retrospect, the furlough scheme was certain to lead to redundancies. When our shops and support departments started to reopen, we brought back the strongest colleagues, ones that we rated 9 or 10 out of 10. Being so good, they were able to do all that was needed without further help, so, as a result, we became much more efficient. Inevitably, those left on furlough found their jobs were at risk; in total, we made over 1,000 colleagues redundant. Understandably, several of those who lost their jobs expressed their feelings in messages to James and through social media, but many more understood it was not our fault and realised, with falling sales, we had to cut costs to protect our future.

Through June, sales were well behind last year but beat our expectations, especially in the core Timpson business where we soon got within 15% of the previous year (photo was about 30% down and Dry Cleaning 50%). Shops in the City of London suffered worst of all, with some only reaching 10% of last year's level. City workers had stopped commuting, at least 80% were working from home, and with so few customers around, a few of our shops stayed shut until September.

By mid-August, we started to make money again. We had survived for months of lockdown without having to use the overdraft facility with NatWest. However, there was no sign that the pandemic was coming to an end. Localised lockdowns and an upturn in Covid cases around the world raised the chances of a second spike, so we remained ultra-cautious.

James and his wife, Roisin, took a close interest in reopening the pubs we had purchased on March 19th, 5 hours before they had to close. The Old Hall in Frodsham had great potential but needed a £3m refurbishment so it was mothballed for another day. However, The White Eagle and The Oyster Catcher on Anglesey, together with The Partridge near Warrington, were redecorated and opened very successfully (helped by Rishi Sunak's 'Eat Out and Save' initiative and a special hospitality cut in VAT to 5%). Our chain of 3 pubs, under the name 'Flock Inns', was overseen by one of our Timpson Area Managers, Adam Yates, who adapted his skills remarkably quickly from cobbling to hospitality.

We weren't the only retailer to be making colleagues redundant; almost every big name on the high street was laying off staff. Marks & Spencer, Boots, Debenhams and W H Smith were all closing stores and making a sizeable number of redundancies. Most blamed Covid19 and a 50% increase in online shopping. The long-running lockdown led to a dramatic, and probably permanent, shift in the future of retailing.

With the government steadily relaxing restrictions during July and August, footfall increased, sales got better, and, with the redundancy programme complete, our profits in September nearly matched 2019, on sales that were still down by 20%. However, in October, the crackdown started to reappear, with the virus showing the first signs of a second wave. We had stabilised the business and still had cash in the bank, but the future was still full of uncertainty, especially for dry cleaning, with sales still falling by 40%.

By mid-October, the severe cost-cutting was paying off. All parts of the business were profitable and our bank balance was better than last year, but with severe local regulations spreading throughout the country and Wales having a total lockdown 'icebreaker', sales started to deteriorate against 2019. Still, our long-term cash forecast looked good until Boris Johnson announced a 4-week total lockdown starting on November 5th.

Dry cleaning and the Timpson range of services were regarded as essential so those shops could stay open, but it was more difficult to make a case for photo services. We argued that Photo I/D was essential and James introduced a laundry service into Max and Snappy Snaps but we still had to shut some shops.

With the 80% government support extended for another month, about 300 colleagues were furloughed; nevertheless, we braced ourselves for some dire sales and serious losses.

The second lockdown severely affected business, with our total sales 50% down on 2019. City centres saw few shoppers because most office workers stayed at home and out of town shopping malls were particularly quiet because, being non-essential retailers, most shops were shut. When the Welsh firebreak ended, our shops were busy, but, within three weeks, Wales brought in some tougher regulations and, as we approached Christmas, our pubs couldn't sell beer and some photo shops had to close. We now realised that the borrowing facility negoti-ated as a safety measure would certainly be needed during the first half of 2021.

A new variant of the virus played havoc with our Christmas trading. Restrictions were tightened across the country with a new, higher, tier 4 across south-east England causing all non-essential retailers to close and the relaxation of family gatherings over Christmas being reduced from five days to one. With the pandemic likely to continue well into 2021, we took up £20m of the £40m government-backed borrowing facility negotiated earlier in the year, which gave us a total available credit of £34m. With £10m in the bank on New Year's Eve, we felt confident that we would survive whatever 2021 had in store.

As we entered 2021, the Government announced another lock-down, with everyone instructed to stay at home whenever possible. Max Spielmann and Snappy Snaps, as non-essential retailers, had to close, and, with high street footfall 70% below last year, we closed a number of the Johnsons and Timpson branches – by claiming the grants on offer for closed shops and using the flexible furlough scheme, many shops lost less money when they were shut.

Our hopes were pinned on the vaccine which was being distributed to 500,000 people a week. By the beginning of May 2021, with all our shops open, we were matching the profits of 2019. Dry cleaning was still dire and photo was 20% down on 2019 but the Timpson shops were doing really well, demonstrating the strength of the Timpson brand.

CHAPTER EIGHTY-FOUR

THE SIMPLE STRATEGY – A CULTURE OF KINDNESS

OVER THE LAST 25 YEARS, we have developed a distinctive way of running the business which has been at the centre of our success. The adoption of 'Upside-Down Management' has been the trigger to creating a culture that recognises individual colleagues and has shown how kindness can be good for business.

We wouldn't want to run our business in any other way; it is a management style that has increased sales, put up our profits, encouraged friendly customer service, improved our reputation and made Timpson a much better workplace.

For many years, James and I have been writing and talking about what we do. We have tried to help other leaders understand why it works so well, but have found it almost impossible to convince professional top-down managers, who use their MBAs to follow best practice, that there could be a better way to run a business. I haven't given up – this chapter explains why upside-down management works so well.

Let's start by exposing the biggest business myth. Most people think that companies are run by the people in Head Office who know more about the business than anyone else in the organisation. Chief Executives and their close advisors set and communicate the company's strategy, but, in my world, it is colleagues on the shop floor and in the front line who put strategy into practice.

A lot of damage is done by Head Office-based executives who produce policies that become processes that the front-line colleagues have to follow. These policymakers think they are the experts, but few leave their desk to discover the real pundits who do the job every day and know their area of business better than anyone else.

Policies and process can do a lot of damage. They go against the principles of upside-down management by telling colleagues how to do their job. Skilled individuals aren't allowed to use their initiative; they have to follow the laws laid down by an invisible hand sitting in Head Office. It gets worse; Head Office carries out surveys to check that colleagues are following the proper procedure, adding an unnecessary pressure to the colleagues who deliver the end result.

Policymakers believe the way to achieve an objective is to work out the theory, put in the perfect process, make sure everyone sticks to the rules and success is guaranteed. That simply doesn't work. Instead of creating a clear winning path, the process puts obstacles in the way of front-line colleagues, who, instead of using their expertise to solve day-to-day problems, just do as they are told.

It is so much easier and more successful to pick the right people, tell them what needs to be achieved and then let them get on with it.

Instead of issuing orders and devising procedures, Head Office should be a support centre which makes life as easy as possible for colleagues on the front line and clears obstacles out of their way. I will never forget my visit to Lancaster during the lockdown in 2020. Laura, in the Timpson branch, was taking between £6,000 and £7,000 a week all on her own. In our shops, it isn't just a case of putting the money in the till, Laura had to repair the shoes and watches, cut the keys, complete the bankings, tidy the shop, place the stock orders and talk to customers. I asked Laura how she managed to do so much without help. "I do get help," she replied. "From my Area Team, the Warehouse, the Office and all our Excellence Centres. They make my life easy by making sure everything works and I've got all the stock I need. If I have a problem, there is always someone at the end of a phone." That, in a nutshell, is exactly what the Central Office should do.

Another way that most companies differ from my upside-down world is in the way a boss does their job. To make sure that colleagues were free to use their initiative, we told every boss that they couldn't issue orders; they are not allowed to dictate how their team members carry out every task.

It took time for our managers to work out how to get the best results, but eventually, they worked it out. Great bosses succeed by helping the members of their team to be the best they can possibly be. They get there through training, praise, encouragement and being a mentor to help clear any obstacles that get in the way.

Our bosses don't have a set of rules, they don't manage by following procedures, they use their personality, instinct and experience to support their team. Like everyone else in the business, they are free to do their job in the way they know best – as long as they give the same freedom to every member of their team.

This only works if you employ the right people – positive personalities who are ambitious and kind to others. You need great people to create a great business so only recruit those who rate 9 or 10 out of 10. For a lot of big businesses, recruitment is turning into a process using online applications screened by artificial intelligence. Successful candidates are selected for having the perfect CV and completing a competent application form. I don't trust computers to pick the right personalities.

Early in 2021, before taking part in a podcast about our company culture, I asked the interviewer what he knew about the company and why he wanted to talk to me. "I only know about your business as a customer," he responded. "Wherever I go, I ask people I meet in business how much they enjoy their job. Over the last two years, I've been to five of your shops and everyone I met told me how much they love working for you. One colleague cut a key for my garden shed but it was an old key so he was unsure whether the copy would work so he wouldn't take any money. If it worked, I was told to pay next time I was near the shop. I had to find out how a business can create that amount of loyalty and common sense". Those comments confirmed my faith in interviewing applicants face to face and picking them on their personality.

You can't have a company full of great colleagues unless you are prepared to say goodbye to the passengers and poor performers. Big organisations, ruled by their HR Department, are particularly bad at tackling weak and disruptive colleagues. As a result, management spend over 80% of their time dealing with people who get in the way of success and irritate your star performers.

It is unfair to force excellent colleagues to work alongside people who regularly take time off, and, if they do come to work, spend much of their time complaining. Mr Dull, Mrs Grumpy and Miss Slow probably don't like their job and you should nicely, generously and quickly, help them to find their happiness elsewhere. Warning letters and Performance Management Programmes aren't the best way to help a poor performer. If possible, have a 'part as friends' conversation; it's the kindest way to say goodbye.

We gave freedom to front line colleagues to give exceptional customer service but have now discovered that 'upside-down management' makes a massive difference to the company culture.

CHAPTER EIGHTY-FIVE

ON REFLECTION

I WONDER WHAT MY GRANDFATHER would have thought. He would certainly be amazed to discover the business has over 2,000 shops but could be perplexed and somewhat surprised to find that we don't sell any shoes.

He would almost certainly show concern at the speed of our recent development, in the same way as he criticised his son, Will, for expanding the business and opening a shop in Liverpool.

Although pleased to see that there are still Timpsons in the Board Room and that they both have William as their first name, in his memory, William would have been unhappy to read those chapters in which his magnificent shoe factory in Kettering was closed and the Board Room row led to my father's dismissal and the company going out of family ownership. However, before jumping to any conclusions, he ought to look at all those other businesses founded by his contemporaries that failed to survive for over 150 years. A visit to today's high street will reveal that Olivers, Hiltons, Stead & Simpson, Trueform, Saxone, Lilley & Skinner, Manfield and many more have all disappeared.

He would certainly wonder why we needed to put batteries into wristwatches and the whole photo business would be a complete mystery, especially when the pictures appear by magic out of a mobile phone (which is something else we are repairing).

I expect he would want to know why I felt I had to sell the shoe shops and I can already feel myself sinking with unease as I admit that he and his son Will did a much better job than I did. Yet, if the Timpson retail business had survived, we probably would not have built the service business of today.

No doubt, he would pose a question that I'm often asked; "What are your biggest mistakes?" And I will readily admit that I often bought too many of the wrong shoes or too few of the bestsellers, but all buyers do that. I will also tell him that there were a few poorly performing managers who I should have encouraged to find their happiness elsewhere and I definitely should have put our shoe shops on the market a year earlier than we did.

Like all entrepreneurs, there were times when a touch of arrogance creeps in and you think, just because your existing company is successful, that you can run any other business in the world. We weren't qualified to run House Nameplate, a good, profitable house sign manufacturer, nor was our experience suited to the hospitality company, 'Out There Events', which I acquired mainly to give our youngest son Henry a route to developing his career.

We quickly discovered that an attempt to develop an upmarket watch repair service was unwise. Despite bringing in some superb expertise, the specialist £1m workshop team didn't believe in Upside-down Management. By forcing our shop colleagues to follow their rules, their expert service produced a 5% drop in sales. In 2016, we pursued plans to open a Timpson franchise in China. It wasn't long before we discovered the width of the culture gap between Timpson and China in general, and our master franchisee in particular.

All these attempts at diversification are no longer part of Timpson. House Nameplate and Out There Events are both thriving under experienced local management. We have withdrawn from China, and, with the specialist watch centre closed, watch repair sales have returned to the former growth path.

None of these excursions did any real damage to our cash flow but, no doubt, my great-grandfather would say, "I hope you have learnt your lessons – only a fool makes the same mistake twice".

Nor would my great-grandfather be fooled by our rosy-looking profit figures. Comparing performance over a century of a company's existence is almost as tricky as trying to compare Joe Root with Len Hutton or Andy Murray with Ken Rosewall, but inflation tables give the opportunity to make comparisons. At today's prices, the original Timpson business made a profit of over £20m in 1949, a figure that was next beaten (only just) in 1960 and was only passed by the current Timpson in 2014.

Although William Timpson might not be very impressed by the profit performance, he must surely acknowledge that the nearly seven-fold growth, from £4m in 2002 to £30m in 2019, during a period of low inflation and tricky trading, is quite impressive.

Some other features should put a smile on his face:

Our aim to maintain a bank balance of over £10m
Our habit of each visiting at least 750 shops a year
The programme to employ ex-offenders
Our work with children's charities
The way we look after our colleagues
The emphasis we put on training
Our culture of kindness

The way we survived through the pandemic

And, most of all, that Timpson is 100% a family business and two of the original Mr Timpson's great-great-great-grandsons have already been seen behind the counter.

ABOUT THE AUTHOR

JOHN TIMPSON is the 4th generation leader of a family business founded in the 1860s. His life and his career have been strongly influenced by his late wife Alex, who, after nearly 48 years of marriage, died in January 2016. The couple had three children – Victoria, James and Edward – before adopting Oliver and Henry. John and Alex were also foster carers to 90 children over a period of 31 years.

In 1960, John started work as a Timpson shoe shop assistant in Altrincham. After graduating from Nottingham University, John was a shoe buyer before becoming a Timpson Director just in time to witness a boardroom bust-up that took the company out of family hands for the next 10 years. Appointed Managing Director in 1975, John was known as the maverick who set new customer service standards in footwear retailing.

Since 1995, John has been associated with his unique style of Upside-Down Management, which made him a popular speaker at business conferences and is the central theme of his business books. He has been writing a weekly column in The Telegraph for 15 years.

Beyond the business, John was a Director of Barclays UK, an active school governor of both state and public schools and leads a campaign to encourage schools to understand attachment problems and the special needs of looked-after children. Previously a Trustee of ChildLine, John, now on the Board of Frontline, is passionate about improving the efficiency of children's social services.

John plays tennis, real tennis and golf, is a Manchester City season ticket-holder and supported Alex in her love of horse racing, which he describes in his book 'Under Orders', the diary of a racehorse owner's husband.

In 2005, he was awarded a CBE and in 2017, received his knighthood for services to business and fostering.